BEING PRESENT

A Practical Guide for Transforming the Employee Experience of Your Frontline Workforce

KRONOS

First printed October 2019

The paper used in this book meets the minimum requirements of the American National Standard for Information Services ANSI Z39.48-1984 (Permanence of Paper for Printed Library Materials).

Cover design by Kronos Incorporated.
Interior design by Diana Davis, Upright Arts, Inc.

ISBN 978-0-9723300-5-3 (print version)
ISBN 978-0-9723300-6-0 (e-version)
Printed and bound in the United States of America.

Kronos Incorporated
900 Chelmsford Street
Lowell, MA 01851
Phone: (978) 250-9800
Fax: (978) 367-5900

"Most of us have jobs that are too small for our spirits."

– Studs Terkel

Working: People Talk About What They Do All Day and How They Feel About What They Do, 1974

TABLE OF CONTENTS

SECTION THREE: WORK INSPIRED

Your people are the heart of your organization. Build a culture that empowers employees to reach their full potential, work their way, and work smarter. You'll unleash exceptional results for your organization and all of its stakeholders.

FOREWORD

Christopher (Chris) Todd, JD
President, Kronos Incorporated

When I was growing up in Marion, Ohio, a sprawling rural town northwest of Columbus and home to just under 35,000 people, it was a hotbed of industrial activity: Whirlpool, Eaton, Quaker Oats, and Marion Power Shovel were just a few of the companies with plants in the town. Marion's claim to fame was equal parts being the birthplace of President Warren G. Harding and headquarters to Wyandot Snacks, which was the world's largest exporter of popcorn at the time, earning the city the title of "Popcorn Capital of the World." The annual three-day Popcorn Festival was one of the highlights of every fall.

From a young age, I saw the incredible value of the work performed by frontline workers. Like many of my classmates, I worked in one of these factories after high school. Marion was built on line jobs and I felt an inherent sense of pride in the products I helped to make and the support they provided to the community. While the work was hard, it taught me to work as a team to build something I couldn't do by myself.

I was lucky enough to witness, through my dad, the impact work has on a community. He was the executive director of the local Marion YMCA, a nonprofit funded largely by the local United Way. This role was, and still is, one of the biggest jobs in our tightknit community, up there with the mayor, the high school principal, the athletic director, and the chief of police. He served as both a member of and a provider to the community because of his unique position to help people obtain meaningful work right at the YMCA, in addition to the programs the organization provided.

I watched as my dad personally employed people who, because of status, disabilities, or other arbitrary reasons, might have been considered "unemployable." From assistant basketball coaches and administrative professionals to janitors and custodians, he gave them jobs and he did it because it was the right thing to do.

Through the seemingly simple act of employment, there was a really amazing butterfly effect that followed: Those "unemployable" people, by finding and keeping a daily job, gained a sense of self-worth and confidence that they didn't have before, which then manifested into new relationships between them and the community members visiting the YMCA. Pride in their job became pride in the community, in customers, and in themselves.

My dad realized that, as a leader in the community, if he didn't provide these people with jobs, they might be getting into trouble in Marion or find themselves without a place to go. They'd be without structure or meaning. Instead, his employees became fixtures in the community for all the right reasons, and he showed the YMCA visitors, adults and kids alike—who might one day become managers and leaders themselves—that everyone is deserving of meaningful work that brings purpose to their lives and in turn positively impacts their entire community.

About 15 years ago, at my father's retirement party—held not coincidentally in the YMCA gymnasium—I got to see something remarkable. There was a small collection of people who showed up who, for years, had been calling my dad "dad." This group of people in my hometown saw him as their own father figure because of the purpose and respect that he gave them. I realized that having a dad that so many others think of as their own dad is a very special thing. In replacing "boss" with "dad," these employees were growing personal roots in their lives that took hold and would stand strong for many years to come.

More recently, when I've visited my hometown, I've seen that Marion mirrors many other small, rural cities through the country. The headlines about rural America are true: Line jobs—jobs that once bolstered these small cities—are going out of fashion and communities are growing increasingly desolate. Lost jobs are just the tip of the iceberg. Crises like the opioid epidemic, which thrive on isolation, ignite quickly and easily.

The majority of working people worldwide are frontline workers—meaning they must be present to do their jobs. Yet most management advice about issues like work-life balance or employee experience assume the answer lives in telework and other laptop-enabled solutions. We do frontline workers a massive disservice by assuming that giving them a great place to work looks exactly the same as making white-collar, laptop-toting, remote-flexible workers happy. If organizations want to retain their nurses, manufacturers, teachers, and government workers, they need to crack the code on both physical and cultural engagement through a unique combination of ingenuity, creativity, and technology. If business owners and community contributors across the globe think about their obligation to create and provide opportunities for all kinds of work, I truly believe that we can change the world.

Work is more than a means to a paycheck; it gives meaning to people's lives on a deeply personal level. Work is one of the enablers to allowing people climb the full pyramid of Maslow's hierarchy of needs; it allows them to meet the base needs of food, water, and warmth, all the way up to self-actualization and achieving their full potential. When you have a job that gives you purpose, you feel better about yourself, show respect for others, can be more present with your family, and build immediate connections in the surrounding community.

Meaningful work creates harmony in society. In fact, I believe that a lot of the challenges we're facing around the world are a result of a lack of meaningful work. When people don't have work to do that gives them purpose, they feel disconnected. It can be harder to gain shelter and food. They're more likely to feel dispossessed. And as skilled workers struggle to keep jobs or find new ones, this feeling is passing from generation to generation.

But if we address the issue of work, and do so successfully, the benefits are enormous: Work is so deeply personal to how people feel about themselves. Many organizations across the world of all shapes and sizes realize this and are thinking deeply about how to create an environment where employees view their jobs as more than an income: as a place of belonging. It's about the manager, the engagement, the work, and the culture. It's about having a place to go and feeling like you're a part of something bigger. Being inspired at work has a direct impact on the broader global economy and the future of work.

Even the highest-performing organizations, those with impressive retention and engagement (like Kronos), are striving to stay ahead of the curve. Our new era of digitization can make this challenging, especially for those in industries that are being automated at this very moment. These high-performing organizations are thinking ahead, working on future-proofing their business strategy and their culture in tandem with one another. This is exactly what led Kronos CEO Aron Ain to publish his book, *WorkInspired: How to Build an Organization Where Everyone Loves to Work*, which revolves around the importance of the employee experience.

Meanwhile, a large group of organizations, which are dependent on their frontline jobs, aren't thinking about out how they can retain their employees for the next decade or year—they're literally trying to get them to come to work *tomorrow*. There is a new trend of younger workers "ghosting" job offers; yet in many of these organizations, ghosting *shifts* is a daily battle. They're focused simply on engaging employees enough to fill schedules and meet staffing requirements.

In my conversations with Kronos customers, I've come to realize that all organizations, regardless of size or situation, share one thing in common: They know that getting the future of work right matters. Whether it's investing in employee-friendly technology, focusing on cultivating their culture, or driving employee retention and engagement—and, many times, all three—it's more important than ever for organizations to enter the future of work with their people top of mind.

Being a great place to work is no longer simply a cultural addendum for organizations; it's a dramatic differentiator for prospective employees and drives better performance, effort, and innovation. It's also important for the community and for society.

Kronos is proof positive: Nearly a decade ago, we undertook our own cultural transformation and began to see our name on best place to work lists. Since then, the number of resumes we receive annually has more than tripled, meaning we've benefitted from three times the incredible recruiting pool as we had before and three times the opportunity to onboard talent that, over time and through sky-high levels of employee engagement, create better business results for us and for our customers. Arguably more impressively, only 20% of our new hires come from outside applicants. The vast majority are from employee referrals, followed closely by internal transfers and direct-sourced candidates. While the increase in external applicants is a testament to the brand recognition from being named a best place to work, actually *being* a best place to work has led to our own workforce taking the initiative to grow the community we've created.

This is why we believe and invest in a truly inspiring culture at Kronos, and why we work hard to support other organizations in their endeavors to inspire their own people every single day. It's important to remember that being present has more than one definition. In addition to being physically present in the space of work, it's the positive outcome of employee engagement on the world. People are present when they find meaning in the moment of work and carry it with them throughout the day and into their community. People are present when they see their manager as a trusted coach, ally, or maybe even a parental figure—like my dad was to so many—rather than just a boss.

This book provides a lot of great ideas that you can use in your organization to transform the employee experience for the frontline workforce. Create a place where your folks love to come to work, and you'll see that it's not just good for business—it's good for the world.

INTRODUCTION

Joyce O'Donnell Maroney, MBA
Executive Director, The Workforce Institute at Kronos Incorporated

So, what does the title of this book mean, anyway? Is this another one of those mindfulness books? Well, not exactly. When we talk about "being present," we're referring to those jobs where employees must be present — every day, in the flesh — to do their jobs. Think of that barista at the coffee shop where you go every morning who always gets your order just right, the airline ticket agent who somehow got you on that last minute flight so you wouldn't miss your best friend's wedding, the preschool teacher who took your crying 3-year-old's hand on that first morning and somehow knew to take her directly to the block area where she immediately settled down to happy building, or the home healthcare worker who enabled your grandmother to keep living independently in her beloved home.

Throughout this book, we'll refer to these types of jobs where presence is required as "frontline" jobs. Frontline workers make up most of the workforce around the globe, yet their jobs are often not considered in discussions about work-life balance, career growth, employee experience, creative benefits, etc. Nurses, firefighters, truck drivers, and mechanics are just a few examples of workers who must be present in a specific place, at a specific time to perform their jobs. However, much of the common wisdom intended to boost employee experience at work assumes jobs that can be done remotely via a laptop. In this book, we'll share insights that can work for those whose jobs require presence as well as those with "laptop" jobs that can be done virtually anywhere.

Why this book now? We spend a significant portion of our waking time at work. If that time is spent in a workplace culture where employees feel respected and valued, they are more productive and satisfied at work. They benefit, their families benefit, and society benefits. Conversely, if people spend their days at work feeling disrespected and unsupported, that poor experience can fuel a downward spiral of burnout, depression, and poor health. They suffer, their family and friends are affected, and the larger society around them is somewhat worse off.

This book is a collection of chapters that can be read in sequence, or according to your specific interests. Our authors all share a commitment to improving people's lives at work, while coming at this challenge from many different perspectives. They are business leaders, consultants, HR practitioners, authors, teachers, and futurists.

We have organized the chapters according to three major themes.

Section One—Work Your Way

As this book is being published, unemployment is at record low levels in the United States, and many employers are struggling to find and keep critical workers. In this supply side labor market, workers are being lured away not only by better wages and benefits, but also by cultural factors that encourage employee autonomy, well-being, and work life balance. The Millennial and Gen Z workers who make up the majority of the workforce expect their employers to support them in achieving that balance and will avoid those who don't.

"Working your way" doesn't mean not working, but it does mean having more control over when—and if possible where—one works. Having control over one's schedule is one critical driver of worker satisfaction irrespective of job type, and one that strategic leaders will seek to provide. A 2018 study by the National Bureau of Economic Research revealed that people would give up a 9% wage increase in favor of having the ability to set their own schedule versus working a schedule set by their manager. In 2019 research we conducted among Gen Z respondents worldwide,[2] 35% were unlikely to tolerate being forced to work when they don't want to. These and many other sources of data underscore the strong preference workers have for employers who'll support their need for flexibility by investing in processes and technology that boost their mobility and self-service options.

In this first section of the book, our authors describe techniques leaders can leverage to understand what matters most to frontline workers when it comes to improving their experience. They remind us that those Millennial and Gen Z workers have different expectations for their work lives than the generations that came before. And they share practical advice on how to balance frontline workers' desire for flexibility with the need all organizations have to meet the needs of their stakeholders by having the right people, in the right place, at the right time.

Section Two—Work Smarter

This section of the book focuses on how data analytics, artificial intelligence, and other advanced technologies are fundamentally changing the workplace by helping us work smarter. By "working smarter," we mean leveraging available technology to alleviate the amount of repetitive and transactional work done by people so that they can spend their brainpower on work that machines can't do as well, such as creativity and relationship building.

Realizing that vision requires leaders to understand both the technical and human impacts of these tools, our authors talk about effective ways to design and deploy new technology without losing sight of how to care for your people while doing so—through training, performance management, and recognition.

This section will also explore ways to prevent technology from backfiring in the workplace. Many workers are already feeling the adverse effects of being "always on." The same mobile phones that deliver tremendous convenience can also lead workers to feel like they never have a chance to rest and recover from the stresses of work. Legislative examples are cropping up around the world that attempt to help people switch off by prohibiting employer demands on people's time "outside of work." But what does "outside of work" mean when it's always possible to engage?

Section Three—Work Inspired

This brings us to the final section of the book in which we focus on workplace culture. Without a healthy culture, centered on values that matter to employees, there is no way to have employees who "work inspired." This is an expression we use at Kronos to capture the essence of our employment brand promise: that everyone has the right to have a great boss, in a great workplace, that helps them deliver great results. The authors in this chapter share that belief and will provide ideas and examples on how to make this promise a reality.

We devote a significant part of this section to development strategies for frontline employees and their leaders. Younger workers are beginning to question the value of a four year degree and are turning to alternative means of acquiring the skills they need to make a living. Employers need to be similarly innovative and flexible when it comes to evaluating potential candidates and developing them on the job.

Throughout this part of the book, we emphasize the investments that should be made in leadership development. Without great leaders, employees will flounder at best and desert you at worst. We believe that in most cases, leadership skills can be developed and measured. And we discuss how leaders can be held accountable for those measurable skills, just as they are for other critical business results.

Focus On The Frontline

We've provided five "Focus on the Frontline" takeaways for every chapter in this book. As I wrote at the beginning, we want to make sure that the reader can connect the advice provided to practical applications for frontline workers. We hope that these summaries will help you do so.

As you read through this book, I hope you will keep in mind those folks I talked about upfront—the barista, airline ticket agent, teacher, and home healthcare worker who may have had an impact on your life and the lives of those you love. Think about all the people whose lives touch yours every day, most of whom show up at work ready to do their best if their leaders let them. May they all have jobs that are big enough for their spirits.

Finally, enjoy this book and share it with your friends and colleagues. It's been our pleasure to share it with you.

ENDNOTES

[1] Nicole Maestas, Kathleen J. Mullen, David Powell, Till von Wachter, Jeffrey B. Wenger, "The Value of Working Conditions in the United States and Implications for Structure of Wages," *The National Bureau of Economic Research*, Working Paper No. 25204 (October 2018). https://www.nber.org/papers/w25204

[2] The Workforce Institute at Kronos, "Meet Gen Z: The next generation is here: Hopeful, anxious, hardworking, and searching for inspiration," *The Workforce Institute at Kronos and Future Workplace Report* (June, 2019). https://workforceinstitute.org/wp-content/uploads/2019/05/Meet-Gen-Z-Hopeful-Anxious-Hardworking-and-Searching-for-Inspiration.pdf

SECTION ONE

WORK YOUR WAY

Your employees desire more mobility, self-service, and flexibility. Employers need to think about how their current expectations, processes and technology help or hinder employee experience. Make changes and investments to empower and engage today's multi-generational workforce with the experience they expect.

Neil E. Reichenberg is Executive Director of the International Public Management Association for Human Resources (IPMA-HR), where he has worked since December 1980, initially as the Director of Government Affairs. Prior to IPMA-HR, Mr. Reichenberg worked for a law firm specializing in labor and employment law. A highly regarded speaker and writer on human resources and employment issues, he has given numerous talks at leading conferences and organizations throughout the world, including in North America, Europe, Africa, Asia, Central America, and the Middle East. He has also been asked to speak at United Nations meetings, as well as to testify before the United States Congress. A graduate of the University of Maryland and New York Law School, Mr. Reichenberg has been admitted to the Bar in the District of Columbia and New York. He is a member of the American Society of Association Executives, which awarded him the designation of Certified Association Executive.

CHAPTER ONE

Providing Flexibility When Presence Is Required

Neil E. Reichenberg, JD
Executive Director, International Public Management Association for Human Resources

Technology has changed the way work is performed, reducing the need for physical presence at work for a wide range of jobs. Employers are focusing on how to improve the employee experience and to make themselves employers of choice. Traditional employment relationships have changed with the increased use of independent contractors and outsourcing. With increasing numbers of people wanting to maintain a positive work-life balance, flexible working arrangements are a potentially key contributing factor. There is a business case that can be made for flexible working arrangements. But there are those jobs for which a physical presence is required, and this chapter will discuss what employers can do to motivate and engage employees in those positions. The chapter concludes with a discussion of whether implementing reduced workweeks without a reduction in pay can be successfully implemented.

Improving The Employee Experience

Having the right people is the key for the success of all organizations. Beyond recruiting and selecting, there is a need to develop, retain, and promote employees. In an era in which applicants and employees approach work with a consumer mindset, wanting a say in where, when, and how they work as well as desiring to perform meaningful, purposeful work, improving the employee experience becomes critical for organizations that want to hire and retain the top talent necessary to succeed. Employee experience has become a key priority for organizations. The *Gartner 2019 Future of HR Survey* of 843 HR leaders found that 51% cited employee experience as a top priority, with companies now appointing heads of employee experience. In the book, *The CMO of People: Manage Employees Like Customers with an Immersive Predictable Experience that Drives Productivity and Performance*, authors Peter Navin and David Creelman contend that the Chief Human Resources Officer in an organization should become the Chief Marketing Officer (CMO) of People. While the CMO seeks to create a great customer experience, the authors contend that HR should be seen "through the same lens: drawing in talent, getting the most value from talent, and doing so on the basis of a great employee experience."

One of the biggest challenges identified in *Deloitte's 2019 Human Capital Trends Survey* is the need to improve the employee experience, with 84% of respondents rating this issue as important, and 28% saying it is one of the three most urgent issues facing their organizations this year. Research by the Massachusetts Institute of Technology (MIT) was cited in the report showing that enterprises with a top quartile employee experience achieve twice the innovation, double the customer satisfaction, and 25% higher profits than organizations in lower quartiles. However, only 9% reported they were very ready to address this issue, making it a large priority for organizations globally.

The Deloitte survey found that many employers are focusing on the well-being of their employees. Studies have shown that more than 40% of workers face high levels of stress in their jobs that negatively affects their productivity, health, and family stability. *Gallup's 2019 Global Emotions Report* found that more Americans were stressed, worried, and angry in 2018 than had been at most points during the past decade. This is not just an American phenomenon according to Gallup, with several other countries reporting similar levels of stress.

Hourly workers complain about a lack of scheduling flexibility, while salaried workers complain about the difficulty in disconnecting from their jobs. Individuals are working more and taking fewer vacations. The Deloitte research found that there remains a gap between what employees value and what organizations offer their employees in a variety of areas, including flexible schedules and telecommuting as detailed below:

- Flexible schedules—86% of employees value it, only 50% of organizations offer it
- Telecommuting—70% of employees value it, only 27% offer it

The Workforce Institute at Kronos *Working Your Way Survey*, which polled nearly 3,000 employees from eight countries, found that employers negatively impact the experience of their employees due to outdated beliefs about time off, productivity, and workload. Survey findings included:

- Almost half of employees have had time-off requests rejected by their employers. Nearly half blame their manager when a time-off request is rejected thus potentially damaging a key organizational relationship that can negatively impact both engagement and retention.
- Less than half of employees globally believe preventing employee burnout is a top priority of their organization.

The Business Case For Flexible Working Arrangements

The Chartered Institute for Personnel and Development (CIPD) in Great Britain issued a Mega Trends report on Flexible Working that includes the business case for working arrangements that allow employees "to vary the amount, timing, or location of their work, usually to the mutual benefit of the individual and organization." The report notes that flexible working arrangements can impact:

- **Attraction of talent**—Advertising jobs as offering flexibility can result in access to a larger talent pool, since according to a report, 87% of people want to work flexibly. Additionally, it could help to develop a future talent pipeline, citing a British government study that found 92% of young people want to work flexibly.
- **Improved engagement, job satisfaction, and loyalty**—Flexible workers have a higher level of job satisfaction and commitment. They will also increase their discretionary effort as compared to those who do not work flexibly.
- **Reduced absenteeism and improved well-being**—Flexible working arrangements can reduce absence rates and better allow workers to manage health conditions and care giving responsibilities resulting in increased well-being.
- **Employee retention and progression**—Flexible working arrangements result in employees at all career stages being satisfied with their work and staying with their employer. The report cited a study in the US where retailer Best Buy ran a trial giving employees flexibility over working time. They measured productivity and found that voluntary turnover rates were reduced by 90% and productivity increased by 41%. For employees who are parents, flexible working arrangements allow them to continue to work and better balance work and family responsibilities.
- **Productivity**—Flexible working arrangements increase individual performance with a study showing that 90% of employees consider

flexible working to be a key motivator in their productivity, even greater than financial incentives.

- **Agility and responsiveness to market change**—The report cites the CBI Employment Trends survey finding that 99% of all businesses surveyed believed a flexible workforce is important to competitiveness.

Telecommuting can have a positive impact on the environment by reducing the number of people who are commuting to work. Flexible working arrangements also can show the commitment of employers to the wellness of their employees. *The Mercer 2018 Global Talent Trends Survey* found that half of employees would like to see a greater focus on well-being at their companies. Employers should strive to create a culture of wellness at their organizations by offering mental health days, flexible working arrangements, as well as wellness programs that include health screening, educational sessions, standing desks, meditation programs, and onsite/offsite gyms.

Flexible/Adaptive Schedules

To truly enjoy their jobs, employees must feel that their employers respect them and will provide them with what they need to be successful in both their professional and personal lives. *The 2018 Mercer Global Talent Trends Study* collected input from 800 business executives and 1,800 HR leaders, as well as 5,000-plus employees across 21 industries and 44 countries around the world. Mercer used this data to analyze how both employers and employees are reimagining the future of work. Among the findings, Mercer identified three factors that employees and job candidates are looking for in a company including permanent workplace flexibility, a commitment to health and well-being, and working with a purpose.

The strict nine-to-five workday is becoming increasingly outdated—and it won't help employers attract or maintain today's top talent. *The 2018 Mercer Global Talent Trends Study* found that 51% of employees wish their company offered more flexible work options. No matter the industry, flexibility is incredibly important to employees and job seekers. Companies that offer employees flexible work options in the form of telecommuting, flexible schedules, and unlimited paid time off (PTO) help employees maintain a positive work-life balance. Flexibility has also been shown to reduce workplace stress, boost mental well-being, and encourage productivity. Similarly, a 2016 survey by FlexJobs found that working parents ranked workplace flexibility ahead of salary. An overwhelming 84% of working parents said work flexibility is the number one most important factor in a job, with work-life balance ranking a close second at 80%.

While flexible hours and schedules are an important aspect of a flexible workplace, the 2018 Mercer study also noted that flexibility comes in more forms than just work arrangements. Flexibility also involves rethinking what work is done, how it is done, and by whom. The trouble with these types of flexibility is that many employers still require employees to ask permission to act on these flexible benefits. Mercer claims that companies need to adopt a more permanent arrangement to workplace flexibility. To do this, employers need to reinvent their flexibility policies and address the barriers surrounding flexible working. For workplace flexibility to become a permanent solution, employees need to know that they are encouraged to act upon all flexible benefits. Mercer suggests that employers work on developing a culture of trust, as well as support remote working by providing the technology that remote workers need to get their job done.

The *2019 Mercer Global Talent Trends Report* titled "Connectivity in the Human Age" found that one thing that nearly all workforce segments agree on is the growing importance of adaptive schedules. The report noted that 54% of employees said that managing their work-life balance is one of the top five things their company can do to help them thrive at work. This is up from 40% in 2018 and 26% in 2017. 82% of employees overall said they would be willing to consider working on a freelance basis in order to achieve greater work-life balance. This percentage is even higher in some countries: Mexico (94%), China (93%), and the Middle East (92%). "The ability to manage my work-life balance" was cited globally as the top factor that would help employees to thrive at work. By country, this was ranked #1 in the US, Italy, China, Hong Kong, Singapore, and Australia.

The pharmaceutical company Sanofi was cited in the report for making adaptive working a key component of its strategy to attract top talent. The company identified its policies as well as the mindsets of managers as barriers. They established guidelines for flexibility at work such as compressed workweeks, adapted hours, remote working, and flexing away from work (i.e., parental leave, study sabbaticals). One key element was eliminating managerial approval for flexible arrangements, thus placing more responsibility on employees to make it work. In the year since its implementation, Sanofi has seen a boost in productivity.

Raytheon is another company that has implemented flexible work schedules as part of its corporate culture. The company offers a variety of flexible work arrangements that include compressed work weeks, flextime, job sharing, reduced hours, and telecommuting. The options depend on the type of work performed and the work location. The program can consist of:

- Every other Friday off by working 80 hours over nine days resulting in Fridays off in the second week of the schedule.
- Every Friday afternoon off by working nine hours Monday through Thursday and four hours on Friday morning.
- Modified work week by working either more or less than eight hours in any day of a pay period provided the balance of hours worked at the end of the pay period is 80 hours.

In Great Britain, a Flexible Working Taskforce was established in 2018 to increase the use of flexible working. The taskforce includes government, business groups, trade unions, and charities. Employers are encouraged to advertise their jobs as being flexible by using the tagline "Happy to Talk Flexible Working" in their job advertisements regardless of level or pay grade. It was noted that the number of employees using formal flexible working arrangements such as part-time working, term-time working, compressed hours, and job sharing has not increased since 2010 despite the right to request flexible working being extended to all employees in 2014. Similarly, the US Bureau of Labor Statistics in its annual time use survey found that working from home for either all or part of their work has remained between 22% – 24% of the workforce during the past several years.

The reasons for encouraging flexible working arrangements include:

- Allowing more control over work-life balance.
- Reducing commuting time.
- Allowing more time for leisure and study.
- Providing time to care for children and other dependents.
- Improving the environment.

By contrast, there have been several large companies such as Yahoo, Bank of America, Aetna, and IBM that have reduced or eliminated their telecommuting programs. Increasing collaboration, teamwork, and innovation were among the reasons cited. Other research conducted by Global Workplace Analytics found that telecommuting in the United States grew by 140% during the past 10 years. Of those who telecommute, 31% do so full-time. It is important to remember that telecommuting is just one component of flexible working arrangements.

The ROI Institute conducted a study with an insurance company which allowed two job groups to work from home—claims processers and claims examiners. The employees volunteered to work from home under several prescribed conditions. The work from home program was seen as a win for the insurance company which realized an ROI of 299% based on improved productivity, office expense reduction, turnover reduction, and a reduction in unplanned absences. It was a win for the employees since they were much more satisfied, experienced less stress, reported improved work-life balance, and saved on commuting costs.

The biggest barrier to remote employment can be managers who believe that employee presence is needed to ensure that employees are working. Managers need to be trained on how to manage teams remotely.

Working from home does require discipline and organizational skills. People with a need for high levels of social contact may not like teleworking. Some also are concerned about career progression if they work from home.

Providing Flexibility In Jobs That Require Physical Presence

Even in occupations such as law enforcement and emergency dispatch where there is a need for employees to be present most of the time to perform their jobs, it is possible to provide employees with flexibility. For example, in Great Britain, police officers can request alternative work schedules that meet the needs of both the employees and the police force. Examples of flexible work arrangements can include:

- Part-time work.
- Job sharing where a full-time job is divided between two or more workers.
- Term time work in which pre-determined periods of time off is provided such as during school holidays.
- Compressed hours, including a shorter week of longer days.
- Variable shift arrangements that allow for shifts to be worked that are longer or shorter than the normal eight hours.
- Zero hour contracts in which an employer does not guarantee the worker a fixed number of hours per week. The worker agrees to be on-call for designated periods but does not receive pay unless they work.

- Flexibility to work from home on an occasional basis, for example to write reports.

Motivating/Engaging Employees In High Stress Positions Requiring Physical Presence

Some positions in organizations such as public safety and emergency communications are very stressful, yet workers in these positions are required to be present. The challenge for employers is finding a way to reduce burnout and high turnover, while ensuring high morale, engagement, and improved employee health. It is a continual struggle to staff emergency communications centers because the jobs are so stressful and provide limited opportunities for flexibility. Here are examples of some initiatives that have been implemented:

Charleston County, South Carolina

In Charleston County, significant investments were made in developing wellness facilities for law enforcement and providing leadership training above and beyond law enforcement training. Many officers expressed interest in other occupations outside of law enforcement and corrections work, especially if they had served sufficient years to retire but wanted to continue to work for the County. Engaging law enforcement in focus groups, committees, projects, and other work assignments outside of their law enforcement work has been very effective, breaking down many silos and opening their understanding about other services essential to operating a County. Other steps implemented include:

- Supplemental retirement allowances.
- Lump sum bonuses.
- Separate police and fire pay plans.
- Incremental stipends or certification increases for added skills/ knowledge for 911 center employees, exercise facility, and a therapy dog to support stressed staff.
- For emergency medical services effective electronic timekeeping tools were essential to improving tracking time and ease of use for employees.

New York City, New York

New York City opened a new 911 communications center that includes additional amenities such as a new locker room that gives dispatchers greater space, and quiet areas where they can rest and gather their thoughts after a difficult call. The new center also includes entire rooms for dispatchers to use for exercise and a cafeteria.

Billings, Montana

Billings, Montana has a new 911 communications center with a workout facility, sleeping rooms for staff who have to work additional hours during emergencies or storms, a kitchen and break room, and other amenities. The sleep rooms also allow a place for dispatchers to go after difficult calls. The workstations rise and lower to allow both sitting and standing on the job. The dispatchers can take time away from their workstations and use available exercise equipment.

Hancock County, Indiana

Hancock County recognized that 911 dispatchers cannot leave their desks for most of their workdays and have taken steps to improve their physical health and emotional well-being by purchasing workstation bikes for their use while on duty. The bikes fit under desks and allow exercise to be undertaken while handling calls. The County also has added workstations with desks that automatically adjust to a person's height to allow dispatchers to stand if they prefer. A moveable treadmill also was purchased to allow dispatchers to turn any workstation into a walking desk.

Other initiatives being implemented by organizations include:

- Making structural changes in the areas of recognition, pay, providing supervisors with overtime due to the demands of the job, and longer shifts with additional days off, which were based on the results of an employee engagement survey.
- Establishing part-time dispatcher positions to provide more work-life balance.
- Reducing the use of seniority as a basis for determining vacations and weekends off in unionized environments. One organization cited that it can take five years to get weekends off and qualify for summer vacations.
- Moving dispatchers to nicer facilities.
- Giving pay increases, using 4/10 schedules, and providing 10 hours of pay for holidays.
- Using per diem dispatchers who are retirees.

- Redesigning emergency dispatcher shifts to provide more days off rather than working more overtime.

Can We Reduce The Length Of Workweeks?

A 2017 British study by Vouchercloud of nearly 2,000 full-time office workers found the average time spent working is two hours and 53 minutes each day, with workers also spending time on social media and websites, personal calls and texts, talking to co-workers about non-work related matters, searching for new jobs, and taking smoke breaks. A predicted boom in flexible working could contribute $10.04 trillion to the global economy by 2030 based on an analysis commissioned by Regus and conducted by independent economists who studied 16 countries. Given this, can we reduce the workweek, providing employees additional time off with no loss of productivity? Here are two examples that will show that there is not a definitive answer to this question.

Perpetual Guardian, a New Zealand company, embarked on an eight-week-trial in 2018 for its 240 employees that changed the work model to give everyone a paid day off each week. All other employment conditions, including pay remained unchanged so the staff worked 30 hours per week but were paid for 37.5 hours, and were asked only to deliver the same amount of output as in a standard week. Perpetual Guardian engaged academic partners, The University of Auckland and Auckland University of Technology, to measure the outcomes of the employee engagement and publish the results. What was unique about this trial is that it reduced work hours while maintaining full-time pay.

The results of the trial were positive with team engagement levels increasing, output remaining the same, work-life balance improving significantly from 54% at the start of the trial to 78%, and stress levels being reduced from 45% at the start of the trial to 38%. The analysis concluded that the trial "showed employees were ready to embrace change—empowering teams to be actively involved in the set-up and review of the trial and trusting employees to consider the possible impacts upon customer service and others around them. A key to success is empowering staff to come up with solutions under the guidance and coaching of leaders."

In February 2015, the City Council in Gothenburg, Sweden voted to have an 18-month pilot program at an elder care home in which the staff would move from working an 8-hour day to 6 hours per day, without taking a pay cut. The study was designed to see if reducing the number of hours per shift would lead to improved patient care. The results were positive with interaction with patients improving and the staff being more engaged. The number of sick leave days taken also was reduced significantly. The pilot will not be made permanent due to concerns about the cost, since the elder care home had to hire 17 additional staff. One successful example of the use of six hour working days, is Toyota's Swedish service center. A number of years ago, shifts were cut resulting in a boost to productivity and increased profits. The company has kept the shorter shifts ever since.

Perpetual Guardian's trial was successful, since employees were able to accomplish in four days of work what they were previously accomplishing in five days. Employees were motivated to work more efficiently in order to get an extra day off per week while not suffering any reduction in pay. By contrast, the Gothenburg, Sweden pilot resulted in extra costs due to the need to hire additional staff in a facility that requires 24-hour staffing. Being more efficient during reduced hours of work did not change the fact that there needed to be round the clock staffing in the elder care home. Therefore, the nature of the work may dictate whether a reduced workweek will be financially sustainable.

Conclusion

The use of technology and artificial intelligence will continue to expand and change the way work is performed resulting in the creation of new jobs and the elimination of others. The boundaries between work and life are blurred. Having a motivated, engaged, and committed workforce will remain crucial to organizational success. Improving the employee experience will be emphasized by those employers that want to hire and retain the skilled workforce that they need. Employees will want meaningful work that provides flexible working arrangements that contribute to healthy work-life balances. Those organizations that want to be successful will need to make flexibility part of their culture with a commitment from senior leadership and the development of policies supporting flexibility. Managers will need to be trained on how to manage remote workers in order to ensure high levels of performance and accountability.

FOCUS ON THE FRONTLINE

1. Remember to focus on the "employee experience" of all your employees, regardless of how high or low they rank in the company.
2. 86% of employees say they value flexible work arrangements—so it's safe to assume that your employees do too, even if they haven't felt comfortable asking for them.
3. Don't immediately assume that an employee can't work flexibly because he or she has a role that requires presence—remember that flexibility also involves rethinking what work is done, how it is done, and by whom.
4. Compressed work weeks, flextime, job sharing, and reduced hours are all flexible work arrangements that can be deployed in roles that require presence.
5. A key part of making flexibility a part of your culture is training managers on how to manage it—don't ignore that important change management work.

REFERENCES

Gartner. (2019). *Gartner 2019 Future of HR Survey*. https://www.gartner.com/smarterwithgartner/top-3-priorities-for-hr-in-2019/

Navin, Peter, and David Creelman. *The CMO of People: Manage Employees Like Customers with an Immersive Predictable Experience that Drives Productivity and Performance.* Boston/Berlin: Walter de Gruyter Inc., 2018. https://www.amazon.com/CMO-People-Predictable-Productivity-Performance-ebook/dp/B07NDD2891

Deloitte. (2019). *Deloitte's 2019 Human Capital Trends Survey*. https://www2.deloitte.com/insights/us/en/focus/human-capital-trends/2019/leading-social-enterprise.html

Gallup. (2019). *Global Emotions Report*. https://www.gallup.com/analytics/248906/gallup-global-emotions-report-2019.aspx

The Workforce Institute at Kronos Incorporated. (2018). *Working Your Way Global Survey.* https://www.kronos.com/about-us/newsroom/organizations-often-undermine-their-own-employee-experience-finds-workforce-institute-kronos-survey

The Chartered Institute for Personnel and Development. (2019). *Mega Trends Report on Flexible Working.* https://bit.ly/2sI2F6b

Mercer. (2018). *The Mercer 2018 Global Talent Trends Study.* https://www.mercer.com/our-thinking/career/voice-on-talent/people-first-mercers-2018-global-talent-trends-study.html

FlexJobs (2016). *Survey of Working Parents*. https://www.flexjobs.com/blog/post/survey-parents-rank-work-flexibility-ahead-salary/

Mercer. (2019). *The Mercer 2019 Global Talent Trends Report*. https://www.mercer.com/our-thinking/career/global-talent-hr-trends.html

US Bureau of Labor Statistics. *Annual Time Use Survey.* https://www.bls.gov/tus/

Global Workplace Analytics. *Telecommuting Trend Data*. https://globalworkplaceanalytics.com/telecommuting-statistics

Vouchercloud. (2017). *British Study Into the Online Habits and Productivity of Workers Across the Nation*. https://www.vouchercloud.com/resources/office-worker-productivity

Perpetual Guardian. (2018). *Eight Week Trail that Changed the Work Model*. https://www.theguardian.com/world/2018/jul/19/work-less-get-more-new-zealand-firms-four-day-week-an-unmitigated-success

City Council of Gothenburg, Sweden. (2015). *18-month Experiment at Svartedalen Elderly Care Home*. https://www.equaltimes.org/swedish-researchers-examined#.XV3B2ZNKjUJ

Bob Clements is President of Axsium Group Ltd., a leading workforce management consulting firm. He is considered one of today's brightest and most influential human capital management thought leaders, and is often asked by the press to comment on different trends and topics impacting the workforce. In addition, he gives presentations at many workforce management industry events. Mr. Clements led the National Retail Foundation's (NRF) Association for Retail Technology Standard (ARTS) committee to establish standards for workforce management integration. He also helped developed ARTS' Standard Request for Proposal for WFM which is widely used by retailers. Prior to joining Axsium Group Ltd., Mr. Clements directed product strategy for leading workforce management solutions including Infor Global Solutions, Workbrain, 360Commerce, and Simplified Workforce Solutions. He has held senior management positions at Orbit Commerce, Platinum Technology, and Browning & Clements. He holds a BA from Colorado State University.

CHAPTER TWO

Building A Digital Relationship With Your Frontline Workforce

Bob Clements
President, Axsium Group Ltd.

Where Is Your Phone?

That question likely stimulated an almost-Pavlovian response to reach into your pocket or your purse to affirm that your smartphone is where you left it and chances are that it is not too far away. Don't worry—you are not alone. Our mobile devices have become an indispensable part of our personal lives. They are a nexus for communication and entertainment. They document our personal milestones, both meaningful and trivial, through images and video. They provide access to virtually unlimited information. They have become our wallet and a gateway to commerce. And, they connect us to each other in ways that were unimaginable a generation ago. Behavioral studies have shown[1] we have developed an interpersonal attachment to our smartphones and experience separation anxiety when we have left our phone at home or, God forbid, when it runs out of battery!

We Are Living In A Mobile World

Today, virtually everyone has a mobile device. This is not hyperbole. Globally, nine out of ten people have access to a mobile phone while eight out of ten have a smartphone.[2] Pew Research Center says that 95% of Americans own some kind of cellphone. Age, country of residence, and income have little bearing on whether or not someone has a mobile device. In fact, Pew has found that younger, non-white, and lower income adults are more likely to be reliant on their smartphone for internet access.[3]

White-collar workers have long used mobile phones for work. First with voice, then with email through devices like the Blackberry by Research in Motion, and for the last decade with data accessed by the modern smartphone, mobile devices have become part of the professional workforce's toolkit. But, the hourly worker has been left out of this revolution—until now. Now, given near universal adoption, your frontline workers want to get in on the game and use their mobile devices to manage their work life.

So, what do your frontline workers want to do with their phones at work? In a word, they want convenience. They want to replace activities that have traditionally required verbal or written communication with more efficient electronic communication. For example, they want to be able to access their schedule on their mobile device wherever they are instead of having to go into work to view a printed copy hanging in the break room. They want to view vacation balances, request time-off, set their availability, swap shifts with co-workers, and pick-up extra hours.

The desire of your hourly workforce to use their smartphones also creates opportunities for you, the employer, to connect with these workers in new ways. It gives an organization the opportunity to improve communication with its workforce. It opens a new avenue for recognizing and rewarding your people. It offers a new channel to deliver learning and develop new skills. And, it provides a platform to empower your workers as brand ambassadors.

Understanding The Digital Employee Relationship

Allowing your frontline workers to use their mobile devices to connect with their work lives changes the relationship that you as an employer have with them. It opens a new door to create a digital relationship with them. This digital relationship has the potential to extend, strengthen, and amplify your existing employer-employee relationship and can be a critical part of the employee experience. If the employee experience is the sum of all interactions that an employee has with his or her employer, the digital experience is the subset of those interactions that are technology-driven. This shift from analog or physical to digital has profound implications, and to understand those implications let's talk about how organizations are designing employee experiences.

Most employee experiences are structured as set-piece initiatives around key milestones in the hire-to-retire employee lifecycle. These milestones are typically events like performance reviews, training, and promotions. A popular milestone to design an experience around is on-boarding. After all, many organizations want to make a new employee's first experience with the company as good as possible. Deloitte, for example, has invested US$300 million in Deloitte University,[4] which is designed to provide an immersive and memorable experiences for new employees as well as those receiving promotions.

As a worker reaches a milestone, an experience is constructed through a combination of tangible and intangible elements that, hopefully, produce a positive perception of the organization and his or her relationship with it. The challenge is deciding what tangible and intangible elements affect the experience, and the experts do not agree on exactly what these soft factors are. Futurist Jacob Morgan describes the employee experience as being a culmination of physical workspace, technology and tools, and an organization's culture. Gallup, on the other hand, suggests aligning the employee experience with an organization's purpose, brand, and culture while remembering the importance of the manager-employee relationship, ensuring workers' role are clear, making them a valuable part of their team, the space in which they work, and the impact their work has on their well-being. Ultimately, organizations need to decide what factors are important to produce an experience in their work environment.

There is a lot of whitespace in this traditional approach to designing employee experiences. Given the tenure of a typical employee, how much of their time with you as an employer is spent having an experience in each stage? A few hours? A few days? Maybe even a few weeks? This is a very small percentage of the time that a worker stays at an organization, and an employee will have a lot of unplanned experiences in between these planned, milestone-based interactions.

With a digital relationship, the whitespace starts to be filled with guided, partially-guided, and self-guided digital experiences. Because the technology is always-on, frontline workers create their own experiences when they are ready to start or continue a journey. Some of these digital interactions may replace traditional milestone-based experiences like on-boarding, training, or performance reviews. Such replacement experiences provide convenience for both the employee and employer.

However, the real opportunity is to create small, transactional experiences which were not possible without technology. Such experiences will streamline and strengthen the employer-employee relationship. Consider how hard it is for a frontline worker to pick-up an extra shift today. Sure, an employee can ask his or her manager if there are any open shifts, or ask colleagues if they want to give up hours, but, the pool of people is relatively small because the worker only has access to the location he or she works, and it takes a bit of luck to find someone that can or wants to give up a few hours of work. On top of that, the entire process of tracking people down and asking them if they have a shift to give up is time consuming. Now, imagine reinventing this clunky, manual process with a digital one. Managers could post open shifts and workers post unwanted shifts to an online shift marketplace where employees can readily find extra shifts to work. Picking up an extra shift is simply a matter of signing into an app and tapping a shift listed in the marketplace. This digital experience could even knock down traditional physical barriers by allowing frontline workers to find shifts at other locations either nearby or to supplement their income while traveling. And of course, the technology would ensure that workers can only pick up shifts they are eligible to work and prevent employees from picking up too many hours that they need to be paid overtime.

So, what's the risk of not developing a digital relationship with your frontline workers? The reality is that in your absence your employees will use technology to create their own digital relationship with each other. The vast majority of large organizations that I have spoken with have discovered frontline workers using Facebook, WhatsApp, and even free, specialized shift management and messaging apps to make their work lives better on their own. This phenomenon is referred to as Shadow IT.

Shadow IT is the use of information technology within an organization without the organization's express permission. While your frontline workforce can be complimented for showing initiative, Shadow IT puts your company data outside of your visibility and control. It creates undocumented and unauthorized data flows which makes complying with regulations difficult. Therefore, it is critical that organizations take control of their digital workplace and proactively develop a digital relationship with their employees.

The benefits of building this electronic relationship with your frontline workforce can be great. Today, most organizations recognize that an engaged workforce delivers many benefits over an unengaged or actively disengaged one. According to Gallup[5], organizations with high employee engagement outperform those with lower engagement in several areas including employee retention, absenteeism, productivity, safety, and customer service which, in turn, drives 20% higher sales and 21% higher profits.

Employee engagement is a result of several factors but one of the most important is the relationship that employees have with peers, their managers, and the organization. Strengthening these relationships requires higher quality, more frequent interactions and communication between all parties. And, that mobile device that we talked about earlier—the one that all your frontline workers have and now want to use to manage their work life—provides an ideal channel to develop and improve their relationship with you.

The First Five Steps To A Strong Digital Employee Relationship

The digital employee relationship is a new concept, especially as it relates to frontline workers. Those organizations that I have worked with that have embraced digital as part of their employee experience and successfully grown their digital relationships with their employees have done five things early in their program. While these five things are only the beginning of the journey, they will get your organization off on the right foot as you embrace the digital future.

1. Start At The Top: Assign An Owner

Who owns your digital customer experience? These days most organizations have someone who is responsible for coordinating their digital customer relationship across a variety of platforms from mobile devices to chatbots to online advertising. The role may vary from an analyst to someone in the C-suite depending upon the breadth with which customers engage with an organization, but there is likely an owner.

Who owns your employees' digital experience in your organization? Chances are the answer is "nobody" and you are not alone. Because the concept of a digital relationship is so new, few organizations have someone whose job description is "to develop and manage the digital relationship with our employees." This is one of the first things that must change as you begin to shape your digital employee relationship.

Where that person sits in the organization will vary from one company to the next. For some, the digital employee experience owner will be part of human resources. For others, it may be part of IT or a broader digital transformation team. I have even seen the role report directly to the CEO when the CEO is the initiative's sponsor. Similarly, the title analyst, manager, director, or vice president—will be driven by the size of the workforce and the importance your organization places on its digital employee relationship. Nevertheless, you will need one person to spearhead this program. The ideal candidate is someone who is passionate about the digital employee experience, carries credibility with your frontline workforce, and can coordinate cross-functional workstreams and measure the results the program.

2. Assemble A Cross-Functional Team

If your organization is like many that I have worked with, there are budding initiatives in virtually every department that plan to deliver mobile solutions to your frontline workers either through company-owned devices provided in the workplace or employees' personal devices. While each department has the best intentions, fragmented initiatives are inefficient and expensive with multiple groups working to solve similar technology challenges even though the actual functionality that they want to deliver is different. It also puts the organization at financial and legal risk because they are operating in a silo without oversight (more on this in item 5 below). On top of that, as these initiatives get deployed, frontline workers will be faced with a kaleidoscope of apps and technologies, creating a confusing and disjointed user experience. As a result, employees will not know what to do with all the different technologies, adoption will be low, any planned benefit will not be achieved, and worst of all, this unconnected user experience will translate into a bad employee experience which hurts rather than helps your digital relationship.

To overcome this challenge, the digital employee experience owner needs to pull together the leaders from these disparate, departmental initiatives into a cross-functional team that can coordinate activities, prioritize projects, and capitalize on shared technology. The goal of this cross-functional team should be to create an exceptional digital employee experience which strengthens the digital relationship being developed with employees. Ownership of the initiatives does not necessarily need to be taken away from the departments and centralized. In fact, it may make more sense to let the departments continue to drive their initiatives because they are subject-matter experts and may be the best group to determine what functionality the frontline workers should access. This frees up the digital employee experience owner to focus on elements that are shared across departments such as communication and the user interface along with the rest of his or her job.

While the team should include any group that wants to deliver a digital experience to your frontline workers, it should also include others that have a vested interest in the digital employee relationship. That likely includes human resources and information technology, if they are not involved already. It should also include legal and finance to help overcome potential project roadblocks.

3. Let Frontline Workers Be Your Guide From The Start

It is important that your frontline workers' voices are heard as you develop your digital employee experience strategy and roll out technology to support it. After all, you are trying to build a digital relationship with them, and digital relationships, just like real-world relationships, are two-way streets. Unilaterally deciding the course of your digital relationship with your employees is a sure-fire way to fail. Inevitably, what you deliver will not resonate with the other party and cause your credibility as the employer to suffer. While failure is not insurmountable, it takes a lot of effort to recover lost credibility, and once you do, you still have to build the relationship you set out to establish in the first place. The best way to avoid this situation is to establish an advisory committee of frontline workers to help define the elements of a strong digital relationship with them.

The committee should be formed at the start of your digital employee experience initiative, before too many decisions are made. The voice of the frontline worker will provide insight, guidance, course correction, and validation throughout the program's lifetime. Early on, this group will help you gauge which frontline workers are most interested in developing a digital relationship with you, which ones are indifferent, and which ones are not interested. Later, the committee will help you prioritize experiences and guide the design of the interactions. It should be involved in the testing of any digital experiences to ensure that the solution hits the mark and meets the needs of your frontline workers. Finally, its members will also provide credibility to your initiative and become your biggest champions as digital experiences are delivered to their peers.

An advisory committee should be made up of members who represent a cross section of the frontline workforce. This involves segmenting your workforce much like you would segment your customers. Beyond customer-like demographics such as age, gender, income (or wage), and geographic location, you should also consider their employment status (full- versus part-time), title, seniority, and if possible, reason for working. Each segment will have different expectations with regard to their relationship with you as their employer. Understanding each frontline-worker segments' wants and designing digital experiences to fill their needs will put you on a path to building a strong digital relationship with them. Do not get too hung up on the size of your committee. It is more important to have representatives from each segment rather than to keep the group small. With that in mind, larger groups will be more challenging to manage. In such cases, you may want to form a subcommittee of particularly large or influential segments or macro segments (i.e., all part-time workers with a particular job, in a particular age group, or with access—or lack thereof—to a particular technology). The other segments (those not involved in the subcommittee) may be involved in focus groups or workshops that are relevant to them rather than broader discussions around the digital employee experience strategy.

4. Set Your Vision, Prioritize, And Be Prepared To Go Fast

You have identified a digital experience owner. You have created a cross-functional team, and formed a representative advisory committee of your frontline workers by performing segmentation analysis. Now, the real work begins. It is time to form a vision about what you want your digital relationship with your frontline workforce to be and establish a strategy to achieve it. Most importantly, it is time to prioritize the various experiences that you want to deliver to your employees. For many organizations, this is the hardest thing to do. Each department believes their project is the most important or has the greatest return on investment.

I have seen organizations that struggle to prioritize and try to boil the ocean to deliver a comprehensive set of digital experiences, all at once. This is a mistake for two reasons. First, it slows you down and time is your enemy. Your frontline workers want to use their mobile devices with their work life now, if they are not doing it already. The more you put into the first delivery, the longer it takes to start building your digital relationship and the more likely that Shadow IT will creep in.

Second, it is easy to make mistakes early in your digital journey. The paradigm from physical or even web-based interactions changes as you move to a digital employee experience based on a mobile platform. Such mistakes can be more readily managed when it affects one or two digital experiences rather than all of them.

The good news is that many of the technologies used to create digital employee experiences can be deployed quickly and new functionality can be layered on top in the future. It is not unusual for organizations to deliver their first digital employee experiences four to eight weeks after the initiatives have been prioritized. On top of that, experiences as consumers have prepared our employees to absorb iterative and incremental improvements to mobile technology if it is designed well. Have you seen the Facebook user manual? Of course not. Consumer-grade technology does not need a user manual because it is so intuitive to use, and this is what you should be striving for with your digital employee experience technology.

Ultimately, it is much better to prioritize and take a test-and-learn approach to deploying mobile technology to your workforce. Start small—with both functionality and a pilot group of workers—to make sure you get it right and then expand the functionality and user population over time. Start with things that make the experiences sticky to keep workers coming back to your technology again and again. Depending upon your frontline workers, this may be access to their schedule, access to wages outside of the normal pay cycle (often called daily or same-day pay), the ability to request time-off, communicate with managers and colleagues, or something else entirely. These sticky things may not have the largest return on investment, but they will ensure that the technology is adopted which ultimately paves the way to maximizing the ROI of those more financially attractive experiences that get delivered down the road.

5. Prepare To Overcome Roadblocks

Every initiative runs into bumps in the road and success depends upon the team's ability to avoid or safely navigate them without the wheels coming off. Your digital relationship with your frontline workforce is no different. The good news is that many organizations run into the same roadblocks and preparing for them before you run into them helps you to overcome them without derailing your project. Most roadblocks stem from concerns about legal, financial, and security concerns about letting hourly workers or non-exempt salaried workers use their personal mobile devices for work-related matters.

The first concern that is usually raised is "when an employee engages with technology offered by the employer, is that time considered work?" This is an important question, because if it is considered work then it is compensable time which means you need to pay that worker for the time spent engaged with the technology. Most organizations I have worked with say that using work-related technology is not compensable time if the activity is (a) not required and (b) is performed for the convenience and benefit of the employee rather than the employer. For example, checking his schedule or viewing a paystub online is not considered work by most organizations whereas taking an e-learning course or completing a performance review would be. A rule of thumb is that if a task was non-compensatory without technology, replacing it with a technology-enabled task should not make it compensatory.

The second concern is "if an employee is using her mobile device, do we need to pay for her device, phone charges, or data plan?" This one gets tricky, especially in the United States, because some jurisdictions have passed laws that mandate reimbursement for necessary expenses. Generally, it is a good idea to make use of mobile technology optional. For example, if an employee wants to check her schedule, she should be able to look it up on her phone, call her manager, or view a printed copy on the bulletin board in the breakroom. Let those who want a digital relationship engage digitally and let those who want a traditional relationship engage using traditional methods.

The third concern is "what happens to our data if the employee loses his or her mobile device or leaves the organization?" Some organizations invest in mobile data management (often abbreviated as "MDM") to retain control of data; however, these solutions are expensive when deployed to a large population, like your frontline workforce. And, some employees view them as overreaching and breaching their privacy. For many, a better solution is to have the app control access and data. When it does, data is typically not stored on the device and credentials are checked with every login to ensure that the person trying to access the data is allowed to access it.

Ultimately, you need to work with your legal, finance, and security teams to ensure that they understand and support your approach. It is easier for them to say "no" than "yes" because "no" is an easy answer to many of the questions. In their minds, "no" eliminates risk; however, it does not change the equation that your frontline workers want this convenience.

Your organization, like many, is at a crossroads. Although the idea of creating a digital relationship with your frontline workers may be new and for some it may be scary, the seeds of that relationship were planted several years ago. Beyond corporate systems which have become part of your employees' daily jobs, electronic pay stubs, online benefit enrollment, and e-learning have begun to sow a digital relationship with your workforce by connecting their work lives and personal lives through technology. Now, the mobile devices that these workers own provide a fertile ground to cultivate that relationship and let it flourish. Organizations that embrace this relationship will reap countless benefits and attract workers from those employers that don't. Which path will your organization follow?

FOCUS ON THE FRONTLINE

1. Talk with your frontline employees to see if they are craving more mobile technology options.
2. Include your frontline employees in any mobile technology initiative from the very beginning—their input will ensure you design something that employees will use.
3. Make sure the priorities of the frontline workforce are front-and-center, don't let their wishes fall to the bottom of the priority list or you'll risk alienating them before you even get started.
4. You will face roadblocks from within your organization. Educate these folks on the critical importance of your frontline workforce and the need to have a good digital relationship with them.
5. Don't let perfection be the enemy of done—pick something small that you know frontline workers really want and try to deliver it quickly. This will start things off right.

ENDNOTES

[1] Veronika Konok, Dóra Gigler, Boróka Mária Berecky, and Adám Miklósi, "Humans' Attachment to Their Mobile Phones and Its Relationship with Interpersonal Attachment Style," *Computers in Human Behavior,* 61, (2016) 537-547. Crossref. Web. https://www.tib.eu/en/search/id/BLSE%3Avdc_100037822352.0x000001/Humans-attachment-to-their-mobile-phones-and-its/

[2] Deloitte's Global Mobile Consumer Trends Survey. Global Mobile Consumer Trends 2017/2018, Deloitte. https://www2.deloitte.com/il/en/pages/technology-media-and-telecommunications/articles/global-mobile-consumer-survey.html and https://www2.deloitte.com/content/dam/Deloitte/us/Documents/technology-media-telecommunications/us-tmt-global-mobile-consumer-survey-exec-summary-2018.pdf

[3] Mobile Fact Sheet, Pew Research Center. https://www.pewinternet.org/fact-sheet/mobile/

[4] Dan Gigiss, "How Deloitte's $300 Million Investment In Employee Experience Is Paying Off," *Forbes* (April 30, 2019). https://www.forbes.com/sites/dangingiss/2019/04/30/how-deloittes-300-million-investment-in-employee-experience-is-paying-off/#4a1ea3f9ecc1

[5] Gallup State of the American Workplace: "The Right Culture: Not Just About Satisfaction," *Gallup Workplace Business Journal*. https://www.gallup.com/workplace/231602/right-culture-not-employee-satisfaction.aspx

Steffi Burkhart is a human capital evangelist, author, and visiting lecturer at two German universities: FOM University for Economics & Management and SteinbeisTransfer-Institute GEDANKENtanken. She aims to shape the world of work with a "millennial's mindset" and is a frequent guest speaker at conferences and events promoting this topic as well as specific workplace generational differences. Her areas of expertise are economic psychology, talent management, human resources management, and change management. Her first book, published in 2016 titled *They are Crazy, These Youngsters! An Instruction Manual for Generation Y* gives human resources departments and managers guidance on how to develop new strategies for better engaging and managing the younger generations. Prior to her career as an author and speaker, she worked in both large, corporate environments as well as at a start-up company. A top athlete, she holds a PhD from German Sport University Cologne.

CHAPTER THREE

Wake-Up Call From The Millennials

Steffi Burkhart, PhD
Speaker, Author, Visiting Lecturer

By 2030, most of the G20 countries will be in the middle of a deep labor crisis. Germany alone will lack between 8 and 10 million people in the workforce—that is about one fifth of the overall German workforce required. In other words: We will experience a period of full employment. Contrary to what some politicians might proclaim, this is not happening because of any specific political measures; it's much more a result of an aging and shrinking population.

While full employment is a great thing in many ways, it is not without its problems. Boston Consulting Group estimates that if we wanted to achieve a similar growth of our German GDP (gross domestic product) in 2030 to what we have today (approximately 3%), we will need a workforce of about 46 million people. However, by that time, there will only be a workforce of roughly 37 million available—that's what I call a huge discrepancy! In almost all G20 countries, except for the US, the figures look similarly alarming.[1]

How Do You Prepare For A Global Workforce Crisis?

Bringing skilled workers to Germany, for example, will not be that easy: People, very contrary to goods and services, are much more immobile than you might think. By 2030, we will all face the same problem anyway: Countries such as France, Great Britain, Spain, Italy, and Japan, who will still be in "good shape" (and officially have a labor surplus) in 2020, will face a workforce deficit by 2030. Then companies will no longer "just" be competing for Millennials—Generation Y (born between 1980 and 1995) and Generation Z (born between 1995 and 2010)—in the same industry sector or within the same region or country. It's going to be a worldwide competition—a global war for talent that could trigger a global economic crisis even worse than the financial crisis of 2008 and 2009. And while you are reading this chapter, Google, Microsoft, Amazon, and other tech giants are making sure they recruit the available talent in the market by offering tremendous salaries and benefit packages to ensure they retain their leading market positions and stay ahead of the curve in the world's largest growth market—the technology sector. This is already putting German global players such as SAP, Bayer, and Continental under pressure. But the German small and medium sized businesses—the real backbone of the German economy—will be the ones hit hardest.

It's A Lot Easier To Live With Your Eyes Closed

In the past the availability of capital, technology, and resources such as oil and gas were the most important drivers for growth, but in the future the lack of human resources will be the greatest obstacle to sustainable growth of companies and even entire nations. Next to information, data, and knowledge gained in real time, human resources will be the scarcest resource of the future. The consequences can already be felt today: a lack of young talent is slowing down organizations in terms of performance, sales, and growth. There is a shortage of young talent not only in traditional sectors, but also in new areas such as biotechnology, nanotechnology, photonics, microsystems technology, and in key technology areas such as blockchain and artificial intelligence. The entire high-tech sector is severely affected by a lack of talent.

Cultural Change Now!—Please Talk To Us Instead Of About Us

Although the problem is not new, very little change has happened thus far—which is not very surprising when managers are only allowed to think in terms of quarterly reports and annual financial statements. But even the public discussion seems to have stopped entirely. The reason is that we Millennials have no lobby internationally to support our interests, and because we are still a minority compared to the older generations.[2] This is why I think we urgently need more representation of the younger generation in politics and business—right up to the top echelons. In addition, governments at the federal, state, and local level must finally start a real dialogue with us. Millennials want a real open exchange and dialogue—a dialogue that needs to happen on equal terms, independent from political lobbies or outdated political parties. To me, that would create valuable understanding.

Digital Change—New Requirements, New Jobs

In addition to the demographic change, we are experiencing another massive disruption: digitization. The CEO of Google, Sundar Pichai, presented their artificial intelligence "Google Duplex" earlier this year.[3] This robot can make appointments with hairdressers or make reservations by telephone and acts very much like a real human being. It can handle human interactions and phrases such as "mmm-hmm" and adapts to the voice pattern and the speed of the person talking on the other end of the line. Fully automated logistics centers, such as the one belonging to Chinese online retailer Alibaba, reduce the manpower required by up to 70%. Over the next 10 years, banks around the world will cut around one million full-time positions and simultaneously create 250,000 new jobs in the digital sector.[4] The merger between the older banks in Germany (Deutsche Bank and Commerzbank) has been abandoned,[5] whereby Wirecard, a pure Internet bank without any retail branches, has become the most valuable bank in Germany with the help of Softbank, and is now listed on the German Stock Exchange (DAX).[6]

Three years ago, I had an interesting discussion with a large drugstore chain about whether it's possible for shelves to replenish themselves in the future without the use of personnel—or whether the classic shelf system still has any future at all. Convenience stores like 7/11 will die: Delivery services like Amazon already deliver food to the door today. The British online supermarket Ocado[7] does this with small self-propelled electric cars, so-called Cargopods. Amazon Key even delivers the goods into your home.[8] Smart home technology makes all this possible. Let us think one step further. Because shelves in supermarkets need a lot of space and the delivery of food to a home is more environmentally friendly than if we all go to the supermarket by car, a policy could be implemented to reduce VAT on food items delivered to your home by 2%—a simple measure with an immediate effect.

To make a long story short, we are at the beginning of the second stage of digitization, in which it is no longer just about digitizing marketing or sales, but about increasing the digital footprint by implementing and developing profitable digital business models and technologies such as artificial intelligence, robotics, automation, the Internet of Things, Big Data, or 3D printing.

Skills Mismatch—Heating Up Global Talent Shortage

The speed of change in technology is already causing jobs to disappear. However, this does not imply that we can simply fill the gap caused by changes in demographics with robots. Artificial intelligence or robotics will help us, but digital change requires something much more sophisticated: It requires more human intelligence and more creativity. Job profiles change and completely new jobs are created.[9] Most of tomorrow's tasks don't even exist today. For example, would you have thought 10 years ago that we'd need something like a social media manager or chief digital officer in today's world of work?

Another issue of note: Although Millennials are digital natives, most of the generation belong to the group of digital users. Even though we can operate our smartphone, tablet and laptop; set up a WordPress website; or digitize marketing—that's about all we can do. What we need now, during the second stage of digitization, are digital experts who are really familiar with the new technologies and who are involved in changing the infrastructure of the Internet. There are people with these skills—but they are scarce. Supply and demand are out of balance and this is only going to get worse. We don't only see our global pool of labor shrinking, but the proportion of the *right* talent is decreasing.

Employment Change—The Freelance Economy

As if that wasn't challenging enough, organizations today are faced with yet another phenomenon: According to some forecasts, up to 30% of the Millennials in Europe will be working for companies as freelance or gig workers by 2030 instead of being employed.[10] This is called the Freelance Economy. Millennials live in a zigzag movement between full-time employment, self-employment, part-time employment, sabbaticals, stays abroad and industry changes.[11] Which is why, currently, the most unpredictable part in the working world is talented people—even the coolest tech companies in Silicon Valley are facing problems hanging on to their talent. Self-employment is particularly popular amongst the highly qualified, which makes it even more difficult to attract and retain young talent. Of note, many companies are currently facing this issue.

So—What's The Solution?

In order to face the war for talent, there are a few actions to take: In Germany, politicians must stop wasting taxpayers' money on redistributions just to win elections. Instead, we must invest massively in digital infrastructure, SME growth, cutting-edge research, start-ups, and education. All over the world, more women need to be integrated into the labor market as full-time workers and with equal pay. We need to re-architect the way we work and drastically improve our organizational structures.

We need to empower young people to work with and alongside machines that will be increasingly intelligent and increasingly connected, instead of competing against them. We need to create new professorships, or even better—create new universities that really prepare our young generation for the working world of tomorrow. Just think, Jack Ma, Founder of Alibaba, left his position as CEO of his wildly successful company to work in education—what a wake-up call for other leaders!

To Put It Briefly—Talent Is The Resource Of The Future

Staff shortages, digitization, and the freelance economy are leading us straight into the "War for Talent." By the way, McKinsey already warned us about this issue more than 20 years ago. At that time, McKinsey described the driving forces that would determine the success or failure of a company as "attracting, developing and retaining highly motivated and talented employees."[12] It's not oil or money—but talent—that is the scarce resource in the today's and tomorrow's world of work. We urgently need to prepare young generations for tomorrow. In addition, organizations need to focus on better staffing their Human Resources departments and on developing a more intelligent and proactive Human Resource Management strategy.

Millennials—Who Are They Anyway?

In contrast to many of our parents, Millennials do not live a classic three-phase biography of school, work, and retirement. Instead we live our life in a variety of ways: Moving between full-time employment, self-employment, part-time employment, sabbaticals, stays abroad, and industry changes. We are the first generation that will probably change jobs at least six to eight times, according to the World Economic Forum. We tend to live in zigzag movements and want to develop horizontally rather than work our way up the vertical career ladder over the years. If we feel the need to find a better working environment elsewhere or to develop ourselves or to have more impact, then we are quickly gone.

Why Millennials Are Crucial For Tomorrow's World Of Work

Today we live in a VUCA reality. The acronym "VUCA" was created in the 1990s by the US Army War College and stands for the four terms Volatility, Uncertainty, Complexity and Ambivalence. These four phenomena are shaping our world—digitization can be added as a catalyst to the mix. They form a new world that cannot be explained by old textbook theories nor by any experiences that influenced the way people acted previously. Take climate change as an example: The increasing frequency and extent of extreme weather events associated with climate change will increase the frequency and degree to which we lose harvests around the world. The effects of the 2010 heat wave in Russia resulted in a loss of 40% of the grain and corn harvests, forcing the Russian authorities to impose embargos on grain exports. This caused chaos in commodity markets and a massive rise in food prices, leading to food riots and violent unrest in Asia and Africa—which we called "The Arab Spring." Many still believe that this was a purely politically motivated movement. People also demonstrated in places like Tahir Square in Cairo because food prices rose at an exorbitant rate and left them hungry and close to starvation. One event, two explanations—political science and natural science. This is what we call "Ambivalence."

Coping with the global mass migration caused by climate change will actually be our most pressing issue in the coming 30 years and is going to be an even bigger one than the labor crisis.

The use of intelligent technology, in particular the information and data collection as well as its processing in real time, will enable us to defeat disease, decode the human genome within minutes for the price of a cheeseburger, prompt people to make smarter decisions, change complex weather patterns, and revolutionize agriculture through the use of robotics. The most important innovations will probably take place in the area of energy production and reduction using turbines in rivers and oceans, innovative solar panels, or the construction of nuclear fusion reactors for power generation. Dubai, for example, has just built the largest solar field in the world.

All of these technologies must be researched, developed, programmed, and controlled, and nobody is more adept to do so than those who grew up in a VUCA reality. These folks have a mindset that is shaped by the digital world and is collaborative, thinks in networks, and has the capability to interpret the most important mass technology of our time—the Internet. Who are these folks? They are the Digital Natives. "Pay attention to those who are 30 years old. They are the Internet generation. They are the builders of the world," says Jack Ma, the previously mentioned former CEO of the Alibaba Group, and one of the richest men in Asia.

A lot of iconic new brands were actually based on the thinking and skills of Millennials. After all, Facebook, Google, Instagram, AirBnB, and countless others were either founded by Millennials or the vast majority of their employees belong to this generation. It is noteworthy that the value of these "young" companies is already much higher than the valuation of many "old economy" companies. We need more of these new business models and this new way of thinking.

New Thinking

AirBnB is a prime example of "new thinking" in comparison to the "old economy." One of the largest hotel chains in the world is the Hilton Group. It has been in existence almost 100 years, has almost one million beds, and a company value of around $25 billion US dollars. On the other hand, the company value of AirBnB—a community platform founded in 2008 without a single hotel room of its own—is already at $35 billion US dollars, with an IPO coming this year. AirBnB founders have achieved something astonishing by taking the old principle of "staying overnight out of town," revamping it—and in just 10 years have overtaken an established, century-old company.

New Values

The Millennial way of thinking is not only directed towards the outside world, but also looks at the inside—the corporate culture. The representatives of our generation live by completely new values. A 2014 survey conducted by the Boston Consulting Group of 200,000 job seekers in 189 countries found that the three most important points for young applicants are (a) appreciation of their work, (b) good relationships with colleagues, and (c) a good work-life balance. Salary ranked eighth in this survey, which stresses the importance of corporate culture. It also raises issues around salary transparency, equal pay, and rethinking or even abolishing hierarchies.

The Experience Model—Worth Nothing In An All New World

When the rules of our world change, we need a new way of thinking and a new way of acting. Thinking and acting in hierarchies is getting outdated, the future is all about building networks not just in organizations and countries, but also internationally: the technologies are already available. They just need to get used intelligently to transform companies into agile organizations that react quickly to new market challenges.

If only it were that simple. You see, in order to become smarter as an organization, cultural change is needed on three levels: technology (digital transformation), structure (organizational design and workflow architecture), and people (employee empowerment, leadership culture, customer centricity). Once the disruptions caused by hierarchies have been eliminated, collective intelligence can develop in organizations. By the way, behavioral economic experiments have shown that both mixed-gender and interdisciplinary teams perform better with regards to collective intelligence than purely homogeneous teams. Without Millennials—without our ideas and our collaborative and experimental mindset—the urgently needed cultural change will hardly be possible. Millenials are the closest to the world of tomorrow.

Behavioral Plan For More Diversity

As an influencer of the German-speaking business world, I speak to over 10,000 people at more than 100 events each year. Whether I have 10, 100 or 1,000 "Old Economy" executives sitting in front of me in Germany, Austria, or Switzerland I always encounter the same phenomenon—80%–95% of them are male.

It's quite a similar set-up in the (tech) startup industry as well: While $58 billion US dollars in venture capital investments went to male founders in 2016 worldwide, only 3% of the startups founded by women were financed with an amount of only $1.5 billion US dollars. This draws quite a sad picture. If there were more women at senior levels of private equity and venture capital companies, the probability of female tech companies being financed would increase directly by a factor of two—this statement comes from Melinda Gates directly. She has now implemented clear measures: Over the next 18 months, she wants to support ideas that are clearly committed to gender equality.[13]

Need For A New Behavioral Model

Overall, women in business have come a long way. We can be proud of what we have achieved so far but the truth of the matter is, we probably even have a longer way in front of us until we see real gender diversity throughout the business world. Because stereotypes and old-fashioned ways of thinking are deeply engrained in our brains and subconsciously guide our decision-making processes. I would not even dare to take any bets on the time when women will become a positive stereotype in everyone's mind for strong and positive leadership in the business world.

So, are equal opportunities and cultural changes through diversity just a dream then? One approach gives us hope: An absolute gamechanger on the subject of gender equality in business, politics, science, and the arts is the relatively new science of behavioral economics. If our brains are making decision based on stereotypes and are therefore "brainwashed," we need other ways and means to finally make equal opportunities a reality.

A few have already understood it and changed their rules. An important tool here is real time data analysis. Google gives us an example: data analysis illustrated that young mothers left the company twice as often as the average of all employees. Shortly afterwards, Laszlo Bock, head of the human resources department at the time, changed the rules of the game for parental leave. The immediate effect: 50% fewer young mothers have left the company since then.

This is an impressive example that a correct behavioral model begins with data.

Where To Begin?

Understanding how Millennials differ from prior generations helps all organizations make smarter decisions about attracting and retaining them. Rooting these decisions in data leads to more effective, less biased talent decisions. In a world with increasing talent supply shortfalls, we can't afford to leave anyone behind.

FOCUS ON THE FRONTLINE

1. Your organization must undoubtedly start thinking about how it will attract workers when we reach full employment in the not-too-distant future—start thinking about your strategy now, don't wait until the last minute.
2. Many frontline employees *are* Millennials—make sure you are aware of the major differences amongst this generation from those previous as you communicate and work with them.
3. Millennials are motivated differently than other generations; meaningful work and work-life balance are often of more importance than salary—keep this in mind as you look to hire and retain them.
4. Diversity is key in your frontline workforce—we live in a multi-cultural world and your frontline workforce should reflect that. Look to hire more women and people from different cultural backgrounds to make your frontline workforce the best it can be.
5. Using data analytics to understand your workforce will lead to decisions that are less biased and more effective.

ENDNOTES

1 Rainer Strack, Jens Baier, Matthew Marchingo, and Shailesh Sharda, "The Global Workforce Crisis—$10 Trillion at Risk," The Boston Consulting Group, 2014. https://www.bcg.com/Images/The_Global_Workforce_Crisis_Jun_2014_tcm108-84781.pdf

2 Zahlen Demographie, https://docs.google.com/spreadsheets/d/1gvPi0mxBd1dGimwzwiZnwn952yL92qtSOzoNw0DgP68/

3 Google Duplex: A.I. Assistant Calls Local Businesses To Make Appointments, (May 8, 2018). https://www.youtube.com/watch?v=D5VN56jQMWM

4 Inside Alibaba's Smart Warehouse Staffed by Robots, (September 20, 2017). https://www.youtube.com/watch?v=FBl4Y55V2Z4

5 Handelsblatt: Bessere Chancen ohne Fusion? Sewings riskante Wette, https://bit.ly/2MxWWvY

6 Handelsblatt: Wirecard ist erstmals mehr wert als die Deutsche Bank, https://www.handelsblatt.com/finanzen/maerkte/aktien/finanzbranche-wirecard-ist-erstmals-mehr-wert-als-die-deutsche-bank/22911468.html

7 Online-Supermarkt liefert Einkäufe autonom, (June 30, 2017). https://www.n-tv.de/wirtschaft/Online-Supermarkt-liefert-Einkaeufe-autonom-article19912631.html

8 Amazon Key, (October 25, 2017). https://www.youtube.com/watch?v=wn7DBdaUNLA

9 Carl Benedikt Frey and Michael Osborne, "The Future of Employment: How Susceptible are Jobs to Computerisation?" *Oxford Martin Programme on Technology and Employment* (September, 2013). https://www.oxfordmartin.ox.ac.uk/publications/view/1314

10 US Department of Labor/Bureau of Labor Statistics, 2018. www.bls.gov/news.release/pdf/tenure.pdf

11 Lynda Gratton and Andrew Scott, "The Corporate Implications of Longer Lives," *MITSloan Management Review* (Spring, 2017). https://sloanreview.mit.edu/article/the-corporate-implications-of-longer-lives/

12 Ed Michaels, Helen Handfield-Jones, and Beth Axelrod, *The War for Talent* (Boston: Harvard Business School Publishing, 2001). https://www.amazon.com/War-Talent-Ed-Michaels/dp/1578514592

13 Melinda Gates and Her Hope for Women & Girls—YouTube, (September 27, 2017). https://www.youtube.com/watch?v=VLAN-TXXYQI

SECTION TWO

WORK SMARTER

To keep up with shifting consumer demands, evolving labor laws, and an increasingly competitive landscape, streamline and automate workforce processes to free your people to contribute more strategically. Provide them with actionable data and insights that will amplify their capabilities, and you'll enable them to deliver better outcomes.

David Creelman is Chief Executive Officer of Creelman Research. An HR analytics expert, author, speaker, and global thought leader, Mr. Creelman helps HR leaders and CFOs identify, understand, measure, report, and address critical issues in human capital management. His client base includes think tanks, consultants, academics, and organizations worldwide. He was Chief of Content and Research for HR.com, and a management consultant in Canada and Malaysia, most notably with the Hay Group. He has taught in the Executive Education MBA program at the University of Malaya, and earlier in his career worked for Gulf Canada and Wood Gundy Inc. Mr. Creelman authored with John Boudreau, PhD and Ragvin Jesuthasan, MBA the book *Lead the Work: Navigating a World Beyond Employment*. He has served on several thought leadership panels at the Human Capital Institute. Mr. Creelman holds an MBA from the University of Western Ontario and a Combined Honours B.Sc. from McMaster University.

CHAPTER FOUR

Reckoning With Rideau Recognition: Empowering Your Frontline Workforce To Be A Source of Innovation

David Creelman, MBA
Chief Executive Officer, Creelman Research
Speaker, Educator, Author, Thought Leader

Have you ever worked at a great company? Have you been in one where the atmosphere was discouraging and the quality of work mediocre? We can learn some of the secrets of building a great workplace by delving into companies that do it well. One such workplace is a family-run company in the north end of Montreal: Rideau Recognition.

Rideau Recognition is—and this will come as no surprise—in the recognition business. This means they do everything from manufacturing the prestigious Alberta Order of Excellence and L'Order National Du Québec to delivering an analytics-based technology that advises individual managers on how to use recognition to improve their team's performance.

Rideau is a long-surviving business and it has achieved this by being adaptive enough to shift with changing times. It was founded just before World War I to make military insignia and emblematic jewelry. Later, they started manufacturing incentives for Avon and then made the jewelry Avon sold door to door. Eventually they shifted their focus to products for employee recognition, and have won awards for their recognition technology. While the artisanal side remains a core and stable part of Rideau's identity, much about the business has changed.

This isn't going to be a story about a company like Google which dominates the world or one like Zappos which promotes new theories of management. This is the story of a company that does well, endures, and creates a great workplace. If you follow the research of Jeffrey Pfeffer, PhD, Stanford University professor and author of books including *The Human Equation: Building Profits by Putting People First*, you'll recognize Rideau as the embodiment of a high-involvement workplace.

As Cindy Bray, a Senior Manufacturing Associate in Quality Control says, "It's nothing like the other dozen places I've worked at." Let's figure out why that is.

How Does The Culture Show Up?

Sometimes the culture of Rideau shows up in dramatic human stories. In one case, a Rideau employee became aware that one of their client's employees was due for a significant recognition award—but was lying in hospital. The Rideau employee, on their own initiative, went down to the factory, found the award being processed through the system, pulled it out, and drove to the hospital to hand-deliver it. This sort of special effort shows up more often than you might think; this story is impressive but not unusual.

On a day to day basis, the culture shows up in Rideau employees doing a bit extra. In one case, a motivated employee realized there was a better way to run the conveyor system and sketched out the solution for management. Another worker stepped out of her comfort zone to take on a challenging quality control role when asked. Then there was the stone setter who noticed the color of one stone in a ring was too dark to bring out the ideal balance and ensured that got fixed.

It's a culture where workers care about quality because they care about the customer. Once they had a problem with getting certificates placed properly between two planes of glass. An employee noticed and cared enough to figure out a solution. Management listened and the idea worked perfectly. The surprising thing was that this wasn't even someone in production, it was someone in customer service.

Isabelle Lavigne, Chief Human Resources Officer says, "It's definitely not one thing and there's definitely not a magical recipe." It's everyday quality, everyday effort, and everyday process improvement that creates success.

What's It Like To Work There?

Alex Kazarossian, the stone setter I mentioned earlier, explains "People are very open to each other. We enjoy each other's company. If there is something that I'm unsure about I can go to my boss. I'm comfortable asking questions and the management listens to my suggestions."

Shannon Bell, a Client Program and Relationship Manager, says, "Here, if I don't think something is going to work, I don't just let it pass, I'll say something.

Here the managers pay attention to what I'm saying. Then they'll say, 'let's figure out how we can fix it'."

Meanwhile, Cindy Bray, mentioned earlier from Quality Control, has a reputation for "being everywhere" because she pitches in to help wherever it's needed. In return, she says, "I get tremendous support from my managers and teammates." Workers also enjoy the social activities such as the frequent summer barbeques and other events. Cindy Bray also says, "It's just not like this at other companies. The moment I walked in, I felt comfortable. They always ask 'How it's going? Is everything okay?' They make sure you have what you need."

In terms of Rideau's physical layout, production processes, and organizational structure—there is nothing unusual. Yet it's a place that workers say has a spirit that's different from other places they've been employed.

Nurturing A Culture Of Appreciation

Rideau has a culture where employees solve problems, pitch in as a team, and drive continuous improvement. How do they create the culture? Jonathan Hart, Director of Product Development and Cost, says, "It starts with caring."

Shannon Bell experienced this caring when she was relatively new and saw another job within the company that appealed to her. She hesitantly mentioned this to her manager. Within the hour, her manager had walked over to speak to the head of the other department and secured her transfer. She says, "The biggest thing for me here is the opportunity I've had to grow as a person, and professional."

It's not just the workers who feel this way, Lance Bannister, Vice President of Operations, says the culture makes for a great professional experience for managers as well and has made him a better person. That both Shannon Bell and Lance Bannister mention the professional and personal in the same sentence is not a coincidence. Everyone says that Rideau "feels like a family."

Like Shannon Bell, Cindy Bray deeply appreciates Rideau's willingness to help her grow. She started as a temp and was soon offered a permanent job in distribution, was moved to quality control, and then onto another department to learn epoxy.

In terms of management theory, Rideau has what Peter Navin (Chief Human Resources Officer at a California tech firm) calls "an immersive, predictable employee experience that drives productivity and performance." It's not one big thing, it's everyday little things that are consistent. For example, Alex Kazarossian talks proudly about the company's work of raising money for cancer research and the hiring of refugees who escaped the war in Syria. The company cares about him, he cares about others, everyone cares about the customer. It's a consistent spirit.

Alex Kazarossian reminds us that, simple as these everyday little things are, they are missing in many organizations. He says that at a previous organization, managers would come by to talk to a supervisor but walk right by the workers. "They'd never greet you; they'd never even look at you." At Alex's Kazarossian's previous company, employees went through a period of long, late shifts to meet an urgent order. In the ensuing town hall, the CEO showed gratitude to the managers for achieving those targets, without mentioning the workers once. It's never like that at a town hall at Rideau; Chief Executive Officer Peter Hart expresses his appreciation for employees at every meeting. Alex Kazarossian says, "Here there is encouragement. Other places there is not."

Improving The Operations

The operations team at Rideau has been trained in the practices of Kaizen, Six Sigma, and MAMO. The latter is a French acronym for *"Mouvements Automatic Main-Oeuvre"* (Automatic Movement of People). It's an approach to moving staff around so when work starts building up in one area another team member comes over to help. All of these methodologies draw on the active participation of employees. This is where the human and operational systems intersect. The family feeling at Rideau is not just an admirable value or means of retaining employees; it's also a way to get workers to contribute to continuous improvement.

For continuous improvement to work, employees have to be willing to make suggestions. At Rideau workers make suggestions because they know from experience that their ideas will be listened to. More generally, by investing effort in building a comfortable relationship between workers and management, and between one worker and another, it makes it easier to speak up.

Another cultural trait that is useful in operations is the feeling that you are on a team with a common goal. Shannon Bell faced challenges in global fulfillment but didn't feel she needed to solve them on her own; the people involved met weekly so they could all get the full picture, and then find ways to improve the process. The naturalness of the people working as a team flows in part from the family-oriented culture.

A technique Rideau uses—which is quite common in manufacturing, but perhaps looks a bit different in light of how workers feel about the company—is the display of the common goals and progress towards them. In the context of the culture, this serves to reinforce the ongoing common sense of purpose while motivating action in the moment to ensure goals are achieved.

Another aspect of teamwork worth remembering is that if you want people to work effectively as a team, it helps if they understand what each other is doing. Cindy Bray notes that one way they address this is through awards ceremonies. The ceremonies are not only used to celebrate achievement, they are used to provide employees insights into what other people do. The manager's comments about an employee's achievement are shared (in French and in English) while they celebrate employees talking about what they do. Additionally, town hall meetings show workers how the company is doing and what is wanted by clients.

Finally, Rideau creates a mutual understanding between parts of the operation and between the office and operations as a side effect of transferring people throughout the company. For example, Shannon Bell has made many moves within the company. A nice bonus for the company is that she found the methodology of continuous improvement she learned in manufacturing was useful in improving office processes.

The operations methodologies and the culture are mutually reinforcing. To replicate what we see at Rideau, leaders need to convince themselves to consistently deliver on these programs and practices day after day, despite all the pressures of management, so that the full benefits can emerge.

Talent Management Practices

Let's imagine you like the way continuous improvement methodologies can fit hand in glove with an appreciative culture. What are the specific talent management practices that Rideau uses to support this approach?

This first is creating a foundation with high retention; their turnover is less than 10% most years. It is easier to sustain the culture if you are not constantly bringing in new people. The workers are around long enough to learn their job, get a sense of the broader operations and, in some way, each become a carrier of the culture. The appreciative culture helps retain people and long tenured workers in turn help reinforce the culture.

It probably goes without saying that Rideau practices promotion from within. Promoting from within takes a certain amount of courage and patience. If you move people into unfamiliar jobs, then there is a risk it won't work for them immediately and it may take patience from the organization and co-workers while they learn the ropes at a new level. Yet it is easy to see why courage and patience are worth it when you see how these fit into the broader people and operations strategy.

Shannon Bell is a great example of promotion from within. She started as a cleaner, was promoted to the role of shipper after a few months, then was moved to call center as a customer service agent. She did so well at that she was promoted to account coordinator, then into continuous improvement and training, and now to her current job as a client program and relationship manager. Isabelle Lavigne says, "When people have potential, we not only notice it but most importantly, we sustain their career development by offering extensive coaching and training. Whether you are working in the front office or in the back there is no difference. We treat everyone the same way we want them to treat our customers. This is our golden rule."

When they can't hire from within, Rideau takes great care in who they hire from outside. They try to hire people they know something about by using an employee referral program. It's not enough for an employee to pass on a name, HR will ask how they know that person and why they think they are a good fit. If the person has the necessary minimum skill set, has values that align with Rideau's, and has a personality that fits the department, then they get hired. Given that they hope to keep the person a long time, and that person may move to different jobs over the years, emphasizing the soft skills and values makes sense.

The everyday culture of appreciation is supported by an extensive suite of recognition programs. (All the employees I spoke with mentioned these programs.) There is recognition for one, three, five and fifteen years of service, as well as for birthdays. Beyond the formal processes, there is a consistent recognition culture. Alex Kazarossian says, "You get respect, day after day, from your teammates, from your managers, and from the CEO."

Another useful talent management practice is offering real flex work instead of a flex work policy that exists only on paper. Shannon Bell says that if you have something going on in your personal life, Rideau managers will do everything possible to accommodate it. For example, when an in-law passed away unexpectedly she could take a week off. This may sound unexceptional, yet at a previous company when she needed to take some time off her manager said, "No, it's not a good time." In truth it's never a good time—but at Rideau flexibility is real, and concern about the worker trumps any resulting inconvenience.

Rideau also practices something that goes beyond an open-door policy. As part of the onboarding process the Chief Executive Officer meets with every new employee in their first week—they call it an "entry interview." He wants to know who you are, what you like, learn about your family, and last but not least, understand your career aspiration. This informal meeting lasts 15 to 30 minutes. There is also a very similar meeting conducted by the head of each department, so the new hires know who are Rideau's executive members.

The Chief Executive Officer also does a follow up at three months for new employees in a group of six people for three hours—it's called the "Platinum Tour." In this session, he talks about how the company evolved over the years and what each department is doing. The new employee is, in essence, being invited to become part of that history and see their work not as their task in their department but as part of the whole. How is this part of an open-door policy? It sets the stage for a policy where employees really do feel comfortable walking through that open-door. Cindy Bray says, "When I was at another company, I might talk to the boss five times a year, here, the door is always open, you can talk to whomever you need to."

There is something subtle, but I think important, about the Platinum Tour. It's exactly the same tour given to customers. Part of the talent management philosophy—their golden rule—is to treat employees like customers, and they live that value on the tour.

The Chief Human Resources Officer at Rideau reinforces the process to ensure the onboarding process is working effectively, with her own one-on-one meetings. It's a chance to build a relationship with new employees and identify anything they need in order to become successful in their jobs. Feedback is then shared with respective managers.

When we look down the list of talent management practices, other companies might say they do the same things. The question to ask is do they execute on those practices so that they really deliver on what they are meant to achieve?

Serving The Customers

The focus of this study was primarily on the methods used to manage talent and culture, yet employees kept mentioning the customer. A guiding principle at Rideau is that the customer comes first, and employees live up to that principle. They say they like the clarity of having customers as their priority. The primacy of customers seems to fit smoothly with the family-oriented culture; the employees take care of each other and it's only natural that extends to taking care of customers with the same sincerity.

Is This About Servant Leadership?

Robert Greenleaf wrote a popular book called *Servant Leadership: A Journey into the Nature of Legitimate Power and Greatness*. You can probably imagine what that's about just from the title. Should we see the leadership team at Rideau as "servant leaders"? The idea of servant leadership is that a leader's role is to help employees get whatever they need to perform well. It's not always the right model. When you hire someone to help you move furniture, you are probably not going to be a servant leader—you're the boss; their role is to serve you.

Things cross a threshold when you have dozens of people working together in some kind of operation. At that point, it's not about the leader having subordinates around to help; the leader is one person who is part of a larger operational whole. A servant leader isn't a servant to their employees, they are a servant to the operation. For effective operations, the leader must ensure every employee is appreciated, trained, and supported—that's the leadership model we see at Rideau.

We can break out things like motivation, training, support, and other talent management factors into separate concepts and programs. However, in a given interaction between manager and employee, all these things are mixed together. A leader should be asking "What can I do to help this employee get their work done? Am I showing them how much I appreciate their work?" It's these simple questions that help guide leaders in their day-to-day work.

Understanding Their Secret

Workers often say they've worked at other places and Rideau is different—what's the secret?

The first secret was leaked earlier in this chapter by Jonathan Hart: it starts with caring. All the talent and culture programs flow naturally, and work effectively, because of caring. It may be a corporate value, but it works because it's a personal one.

Jonathan Hart shares a second secret: it doesn't take 10 or 15 minutes to show you care, it takes two minutes. You don't have to have an in-depth conversation every time you walk by an employee. You ask how their weekend was; if their kid got on to the hockey team, or if the new machine is working the way it's supposed to work.

A third secret is that even if you don't care at first, taking those two minutes to ask people how they are doing at home or at work is the path to caring. Once you learn that someone has a disabled child training to play sledge hockey or is behind schedule because they have to keep realigning the new machine every hour then you'll start caring about them as an individual not just a cog in the operations.

The reason the things I'm calling "secrets" are secret is that they are so simple they are easy to overlook. It's worth revisiting Alex Kazarossian's comment that it's a company where you are respected. There isn't a company in the world that has a policy of disrespecting workers, yet in the experience of actual workers it's surprisingly rare to feel regularly respected at work. It's not the idea of respect that is important, it's believing it deeply enough to execute in the face of distracting pressures and priorities.

It's also interesting to note that Chief Executive Officer Peter Hart typically doesn't talk about *motivating* people, he talks about *appreciating* them. If we talk about motivating people, it's too easy to see people as simply a means to an end. You can see a recognition program as a way to reward performance or you can see it as a means of showing your appreciation for performance. Peter Hart leans towards the latter. It's a small distinction that's easy to overlook—perhaps this should be listed as a secret too.

The latest ideas about production techniques, analytics, and human resource tactics are important. However, those ideas are more likely to have an impact in the context of an organization where workers and management are closely aligned as a team. That alignment needs to rest on a basis more solid than a system of cascading goals. It needs to rest on honestly caring about one another. That's the foundation Rideau constantly seeks to reinforce.

FOCUS ON THE FRONTLINE

1. Empower your employees—regardless of their rank or salary—to do more. Think about that Rideau employee who became aware that one of their client's employees was due for a significant recognition award, but was in the hospital—and so hand-delivered the award to the employee in the hospital. Empower your people, and they will often exceed expectations.
2. Care about your employees—people at all levels do well and thrive when they feel their company cares about them as individuals. Encourage employees to deal with each other with compassion and a spirit of family, and make sure your managers are doing the same.
3. Appreciate employees at all levels—remember that it's not just the managers who deserve credit for great results—it's each and every contributing employee all the way down to the entry-level newbie who just started. When you are thanking people, thank everyone!
4. Challenge your employees—just because someone is a frontline or entry-level employee doesn't mean you shouldn't challenge them. Rideau applies complex management theories like Kaizen, Six Sigma, and MAMO to all employees. This gives everyone a stake in the business and encourages continuous improvement at all levels.
5. Focus on retention—it's easier to sustain a great culture if you are not constantly bringing in new people. The workers are around long enough to learn their job, get a sense of the broader operations and, in some way, each become a carrier of the culture. The appreciative culture helps retain people and long tenured workers in turn help reinforce the culture.

REFERENCES

Rideau Recognition. https://rideau.com/

Alberta Order of Excellence. https://www.lieutenantgovernor.ab.ca/Aoe/index.html

L'Order National Du Québec. http://www.ordre-national.gouv.qc.ca/

Pfeffer, Jeffrey. *The Human Equation: Building Profits by Putting People First*. Boston: Harvard Business School Press, 1998. https://www.amazon.com/Human-Equation-Building-Profits-Putting/dp/0875848419

Kaizen Methodology. https://www.sixsigmadaily.com/defining-kaizen-the-methodology-and-applications/

Six Sigma Methodology. http://www.6sigmastudy.com/Six-Sigma-Methodologies.asp

Greenleaf, Robert. *Servant Leadership: A Journey into the Nature of Legitimate Power and Greatness 25th Anniversary Edition*. New York/Mahwah, NJ: Paulist Press, 2002. https://www.amazon.com/Servant-Leadership-Legitimate-Greatness-Anniversary/dp/0809105543

Dan Schawbel is a *New York Times* best-selling author, Partner and Research Director at Future Workplace, and the Founder of both Millennial Branding and *WorkplaceTrends.com*. His three best-selling career books are titled: *Back to Human, Promote Yourself* and *Me 2.0*. Through his companies, he's conducted dozens of research studies and worked with major brands including American Express, GE, Microsoft, Virgin, IBM, Coca Cola, and Oracle. He is the host of "5 Questions with Dan Schawbel," a podcast where he interviews a variety of world-class humans by asking them 5 questions in less than 15 minutes. In addition, he has written countless articles for *Forbes, Fortune, TIME, The Economist, Quartz, The World Economic Forum, Harvard Business Review, The Guardian,* and others that have combined generated over 15 million views. He has been recognized on several lists including *Inc. Magazine's* "30 Under 30," *Forbes'* "30 Under 30," *Business Insider's* "40 Under 40," *BusinessWeek's* "20 Entrepreneurs You Should Follow," and as one of *Workforce Magazine's* "Game Changers." Mr. Schawbel holds a BS from Bentley University.

CHAPTER FIVE

Humans, Robots, And AI Collide On The Frontline

Dan Schawbel
Partner and Research Director, Future Workplace
Founder, Millennial Branding, LLC and *WorkplaceTrends.com*
Author, Speaker, Thought Leader

Artificial Intelligence?

A lot of people think that artificial intelligence (AI) is synonymous with machines, robots, and even technology as a whole, but it's not. AI is a computer system that processes information and makes decisions using human intelligence principles, thus AI requires us to help it make better decisions using data that we provide. The goal of AI is for a machine to be able to perform the same tasks that normally require human intelligence such as decision-making and speech recognition. AI is intended to make our lives easier, yet over the past several years there has been much concern that it could do damage as well.

AI's Impact On Jobs

There's been a large debate in the media, based on research and insights from experts, economists, and institutions, of how AI will impact jobs. The two most cited studies on this topic come from the World Economic Forum (WEF) and the University of Oxford. According to the Future of Jobs Report from the WEF, AI will displace 75 million jobs, while 133 million will be created, which is a net 58 million jobs. On the other hand, Oxford estimates that 57% of jobs are at high risk of automation. There are countless more studies that project either a net positive, neutral, or negative outcome for jobs in the age of AI. What's important to note is that as AI becomes more a part of our workplace, especially in HR, the demand for uniquely human skills will grow relative to the automation of routine tasks. The ManpowerGroup has conducted a few important studies on the skills gap and impact of AI. They found that tasks will be automated—not full jobs—and that

87% of employers plan to increase or maintain their headcount because of automation. HR professionals need to assess their own talent needs as their workforce shifts due to their organizations' need for AI.

Humans And AI Working Together

While there's been a portrait painted in the media of AI taking over our jobs and our world, it's simply not true. We have to recognize that humans and AI will need to work side-by-side in the future for humans to stay relevant and for our companies to compete. An example that proves that AI cannot exist without humans is Japan's Strange Hotel, which is the world's first robot hotel. At first, people were excited to stay at the hotel because there's nothing else like it and they were curious about the experience. Then, the hotel decided to lay-off its own robots because they created more work than reducing it. Many of the robots were broken, couldn't answer guest questions, and couldn't handle tasks like carrying luggage to customer rooms. As a result, the hotel has hired human staff to cope with the additional workload and take over many of the tasks of the former robots. HR has to assess where AI is most appropriate and where it's not, and help workers make sense of what that relationship looks like.

AI is only as effective as the humans who program it. Amazon programmed and used AI as a recruiting tool in an effort to eliminate unconscious bias, but it backfired. The same bias that recruiters translated into the AI's bias, discriminated against women because it tried to find candidates who resembled its current workforce population, which is primarily men.

We can't depend on technology to solve all of HR's problem, but we can use it to make their jobs easier, more efficient, and free up time for them to put the "human" back in HR.

IBM wanted to see if robots were smarter than humans but came up short. Their six-year-old AI debating system called "Miss Debater" went head to head with 31-year-old Harish Natarjan, a decorated practitioner. Harish beat Miss Debater in a 25-minute exchange about pre-school studies. While Miss Debater lost, a future more advanced version will probably beat the human. AI machines are able to learn just like us.

In an interview with tech journalist Kara Swisher, Tesla CEO and tech luminary Elon Musk said, "As AI gets probably much smarter than humans, the relative intelligence ratio is probably similar to that between a person and a cat, maybe bigger. I do think we need to be very careful about the advancement of AI."

AI In HR—The Research

In 2018, my firm Future Workplace partnered with Oracle on a study where we interviewed 1,320 U.S. HR leaders and employees on the topic of AI in HR. We discovered that while 29% of HR leaders recognize the potential benefits of AI to HR, only 6% are actively deploying it in the workplace. While many haven't implemented it, they do see the benefits of doing so. The top ways they believe they will benefit from AI are a significant cost savings, a better customer experience, and an improved employee experience.

AI is now a C-suite issue, so HR is under more pressure to experiment with it, get the right skills, and start to implement. One third of companies don't have the right AI skills to be able to implement it in their organization. The top skills that they are looking to hire the most of right now are software engineers, machine learning, data science, big data development, and algorithm engineering. While AI can be intimidating and overwhelming for HR, they realize that there are big consequences if they fail to adopt it not just for them, but for their workforces. They say if they fail to adopt AI, they will be less productive, have fewer relevant skills, and that employees could even lose their jobs.

In order to better understand how to implement AI and promote it throughout their organizations, we asked HR leaders how it's currently being used in the employee lifecycle. They said recruiting, development and performance management. Now, we will examine how HR is currently implementing AI in these key areas with real case studies from top companies.

AI In The Employee Lifecycle—Recruiting

The biggest and most successful use cases for AI in HR are in recruiting. AI is a tool to help recruiters streamline the hiring process to make a recruiter's job easier, without replacing the human element.

Pitney Bowes, a global technology company most known for its postage meters and other mailing equipment and services, had to increase its workforce dramatically after opening up a new fulfillment center. They turned to AI to solve their hiring needs. When candidates go to the Pitney Bowes career website, they see a Chatbot (an AI robot that conducts conversations through chat) that shows them open positions, and then walks them through a pre-selection process. Some of the questions asked included, "Are you able to lift 50 pounds?" and "Do you prefer working a day shift or are you flexible?" With the right answers, the Chatbot schedules an interview by sending an email with an invitation. They realized that the power of AI was to be able to address their high-volume recruiting challenge by cutting down the candidate pool and eliminating the routine and stressful, task of setting up interviews. Pitney Bowes measured the effectiveness of their Chatbot and found that it helped reduce the time to fill positions by 10%.

Another example of how AI can help make a recruiter's job more effective and efficient is Hilton's Ally Chatbot. Much like in the Pitney Bowes example, Ally helps candidates determine their fit for a role through a series of screening questions. Sarah Smart, the Vice President of Global Recruiting for Hilton, measured the results of their use of AI as part of the candidate experience. She found that they have increased their speed-to-hire by 85%, increased the diversity of their talent pool, and enabled their recruiters to identify top talent faster than before. When asked about the future of how Hilton would use AI, Susan Smart said they intend for it to improve new hire onboarding and provide internal talent mobility for their employees. Instead of eliminating the role of recruiters, her goal is to upskill recruiters so they can stay relevant, while eliminating the tedious tasks that don't provide as much value and can be streamlined through AI. People will continue to make the final hiring decision.

Last year, Unilever used AI to hire all of their entry-level employees. Instead of the use of a Chatbot, like Pitney Bowes and Hilton, they had candidates play a neuroscience-based game to measure traits and abilities, which were recorded and analyzed by AI. The games tested their aptitude, logic, reasoning, and how they handle risk. Then, the AI algorithms used data from successful employees to compare against the applicants to assess their suitability for the role they were applying for. The algorithm collected data by examining videos of candidates answering questions to determine fit. Overall, Unilever cut the time invested in screening and hiring candidates by 70,000 person-hours. After the candidate screening, the rest of the candidate experience becomes human. A total of 3,500 candidates spend a day with leaders and recruiters. Then 800 people are given job offers, while the rest receive feedback on why they didn't make the cut.

In our research, we found that a bad candidate experience, without feedback, makes candidates never want to apply to the company again, post negative reviews online, and even shop at competitor companies. The results of the program have been impressive. Unilever hired its most diverse entry-level class to date, increasing their pool of non-white applicants from 840 to 2,600. Applications to jobs doubled within the first ninety days of their posting over the previous year from 15,000 to 30,000, and the time recruiters spend reviewing applicants declined by 75%.

AI In The Employee Lifecycle—Onboarding

rLoop, a decentralized engineering organization, is one of the few companies that has implemented AI as part of their onboarding. Their goal was to improve the efficiency and effectiveness of their new hire onboarding by using a Chatbot that would help employees find answers to basic questions. For instance, some of the questions those employees could text to the Chatbot included, "What is the company dress code?" and "What holidays do we have off?" HR used to need to respond to these common questions but now the Chatbot handles them, while they can answer the more emotional or advanced questions.

AI In The Employee Lifecycle—Employee Development

Some companies are using AI to engage, develop, and help manage the careers of their employees. TIAA, one of our clients, had overwhelming and complex learning content that they wanted to have individualized for their employees. Their solution was adaptive learning using AI algorithms. They were able to achieve 100% effectiveness through their content and a reduction of seat time by more than 50%. When we asked them what lessons they learned, they said to make a strong business case for AI, you must get your team in the right mindset to use it, have instructional designers to meet these objectives, and have a business sponsor to ensure the right level of investment and support.

Another great example is from our client GE, who created BrilliantYOU, their social learning platform. BrilliantYOU has become a model for the consumerization of learning and development for GE employees—including the hugely popular GE Crotonville podcast *Brilliance Leadership Learning*. GE recognized a number of key insights through the development, testing, and implementation of the platform, including the need to clearly connect performance management and learning. They also discovered the importance of making learning more personal and social so it can be relevant for each user. The outcome of their efforts was that AI shaped learning behavior and learners demonstrated significantly greater engagement in their own development.

One of the biggest workforce needs in recent years is coaching. Citizens Bank NA, a subsidiary of Citizens Financial Group, launched an AI-powered career coach for over 1,000 of their employees. They named it Myca, which is short for "my career." The AI coach is programmed to suggest new jobs, training, and videos that employees can watch based on individual career interests. While the beta test was for 1,500 employees, it will eventually reach 18,000 in the next year. Citizens views AI as a game changer, as it allows them to scale their coaching to their workforce.

All of these examples of how companies are implementing AI as part of the employee lifecycles can be a source of inspiration and help HR sell AI to decision makers. Note that there's a process for identifying, testing, and implementing AI in your organization. In the future, every organization will be using AI for HR, but we are still at the beginning of the larger movement. It's better for you to get ahead of this AI revolution so you don't get left behind and can take advantage of all that it has to offer.

How To Get Your HR Team On Board With AI

Before you can get your HR team on board with AI, you need to understand their concerns and any barriers that get in the way of adoption. These include the following: change management, communication and understanding of AI, leadership buy-in, cost, lack of alignment with current tools, fear that technology will replace them instead of become a competitive advantage, and lack of skills. Once you know what you're up against, then you need to focus on the following key initiatives to get your team on board:

1. **Identify the business problem you want to solve using AI.** I recommend that you start with one aspect of the employee lifecycle. (The one that is most proven is hiring.) Show your team case studies or bring in a company that has used AI successfully to prove the value.
2. **Do an analysis with data you already have.** Collect data on the current state of the problem, such as the time to hire a candidate or the number

of candidate or employee complaints about your recruiting or onboarding system. Without data, it will be harder to build a business case to get senior leadership to take it seriously.

3. **Educate key stakeholders.** A great way to get AI adopted within your company is to form a cross-functional team, with leadership, made up of those who would be most impacted by it. These can also include members from your IT or marketing department.
4. **Develop learning opportunities for specific roles.** Make sure you have specific groups involved in learning about the application of AI in their roles. These could include members from recruiting, new hire onboarding, and corporate learning.
5. **Identify AI skills and map them to new roles.** Figure out what skills employees need to learn in order to help implement AI in the workplace. If AI will eliminate certain tasks, think about what new tasks will be required. Training team members using internal expertise or external consultants will help them get up to speed. If this isn't possible, you may need to hire for the right talent that has the AI skills required.
6. **Align performance management to skill development.** Make sure that you measure the effectiveness of HR professionals who are acquiring AI skills and are implementing AI. Employee skills should be measured and rewarded as they learn how to use AI across the employee life cycle.
7. **Ongoing development.** As you continue to improve your AI capabilities, you will continue to have to upskill and retrain employees on new tools and applications.

AI may seem intimidating at first, but as you learn and continue to educate yourself, you'll be excited to implement it. AI makes our jobs easier and frees up precious time so we can be more efficient and focus on higher impact tasks. Instead of fearing AI, embrace it, and be an AI evangelist so you can help prepare everyone for the current and future workplace.

FOCUS ON THE FRONTLINE

1. Educate your frontline workforce about AI—help them see AI is not a threat to their employment, but a way to help them be more effective.
2. One of the best ways to get started with AI is to use it in your recruiting process for your entry-level (often frontline) workforce—see Unilever example on page 60.
3. Make AI fun! Work with HR to develop trainings for your frontline workforce that use gamification to make mundane processes more engaging.
4. Enlist your frontline workforce—and their firsthand experience with your daily business—to help determine the areas where AI might make the biggest impact.
5. Make sure you always include a representative from the frontline in any stakeholder group—these folks offer a unique perspective that you don't want to leave out.

REFERENCES

World Economic Forum. (2016). The Future of Jobs. http://www3.weforum.org/docs/WEF_Future_of_Jobs.pdf

World Economic Forum. (2018). The Future of Jobs. https://www.weforum.org/reports/the-future-of-jobs-report-2018

University of Oxford. (2019). The Future of Employment Report. https://laedc.org/2019/03/06/quickweb4/

Manpower Group. (2017). 2016/2017 Talent Shortage Survey. Milwaukee, WI: Manpower Group. https://www.manpower.us/Website-File-Pile/Whitepapers/Manpower/2016-Talent-Shortage-Whitepaper.pdf

Briefing on Artificial Intelligence. (2019). IBM's AI 'Miss Debater' Lost Man-Vs-Machine Challenge. https://fortune.com/2019/02/12/man-versus-machine-ai-artificial-intelligence-ibm-project-debater/

Oracle AI at Work Report. (2018). AI at Work: It's Time to Embrace AI. http://www.oracle.com/us/products/applications/oracle-ai-at-work-report-5037501.pdf

Ongig Blog. (October 16, 2018). 5 Uses of Chatbots in Recruiting. https://blog.ongig.com/ai-recruitment/5-uses-of-chatbots-in-recruiting

LinkedIn. (March 2, 2018). AllyO and Hilton Presents:"Future of Recruiting with A.I." https://www.linkedin.com/pulse/allyo-hilton-presents-future-recruiting-ai-sahil-sahni/

HR Tech Outlook. (2018). How Hilton Rendered "Hospitality" into Recruiting Process. https://talent-management-software.hrtechoutlook.com/cxoinsights/how-hilton-rendered-hospitality-in-to-recruitment-processes-nid-608.html?utm_source=google&utm_campaign=hrtechoutlook_topslider

HR People + Strategy Blog. (August 16, 2018). Start Using AI For HR: Identify Your Business Problem. https://blog.hrps.org/blogpost/Start-Using-AI-For-HR-Identify-Your-Business-Problem

Marr, Bernard. "The Amazing Ways How Unilever Uses Artificial Intelligence To Recruit & Train Thousands of Employees." *Forbes*, December 14, 2018. https://www.forbes.com/sites/bernardmarr/2018/12/14/the-amazing-ways-how-unilever-uses-artificial-intelligence-to-recruit-train-thousands-of-employees/#32966cfa6274

BrilliantYOU, GE Social Learning Platform. (May 17, 2017). https://www.youtube.com/watch?v=wz4TFWpHLQM

Recode Daily. (November 2, 2018). Kara Swisher interviews Elon Musk. https://www.vox.com/2018/11/2/18054328/elon-musk-kara-swisher-interview-tesla-spacex-vox-google-walkout-apple-spotify-profit-petty-thrones

Citizens Bank. (February 13, 2019). How Citizens Bank is Transforming Its Talent. https://1.dam.s81c.com/m/5278bb5107d2814b/original/2780-pdf.pdf

John Frehse is Senior Managing Director at Ankura where he co-leads its Labor Strategy area. A well-known expert in hiring and retaining employees, Mr. Frehse's professional specialties include union negotiation strategies, employee engagement methodologies, change management in shift work environments, productivity, and morale improvements. He has been credited with developing and implementing strategies for companies spanning a wide range of industries, always delivering innovative labor solutions that incorporate solutions to employee needs. A sought after speaker on best practices in the labor management field, he has also written numerous white papers and articles. Before joining Ankura Consulting Group, Mr. Frehse was a founding partner of Core Practice LLC, an international labor strategies firm. He was also head of Global Strategic Services Sales for Blue Pumpkin Software, now known as Verint. Mr. Frehse is a member of the advisory board for HR.com's Workforce Management practice. He holds a BA from Wake Forest University.

CHAPTER SIX

The Transformative Power Of Access To Information

John Frehse
Senior Managing Director, Ankura
Co-Head, Labor Strategy
Author, Speaker, Thought Leader

People today have access to information all the time. We can use Google, Yelp, Uber, and countless other services to find what we are looking for anytime, anywhere, and usually within seconds. This means better products at a lower cost, better service, a more productive and efficient lifestyle, and less waste (whether it is time or money). Innovative companies are using large amounts of data, and most importantly data from a wide range of sources, to help people live a better life. This digital revolution is still in its infancy, but shockingly powerful already.

In contrast, in many instances when employees are at work, they are starved for information and left to hunt down the data they need manually, transform it into useful information, and attempt to make timely decisions. The rise of instantaneous access to information in our personal lives has laid bare the inefficiency that exists in our professional lives. In a world where an employee can plan a family vacation using the Internet faster than they can approve time off requests, something is clearly wrong. If you are not working to give your employees consumer-grade experiences with access at work, they will use sites like Indeed.com (another great multi-dataset company) to find a company that will give them this desperately needed access.

There are many companies harnessing the power of data to do amazing things. They each have a different approach and impact on the communities they serve.

The Google Effect

Google doesn't want us to have to work too hard to find an answer to a question. Whether it is through Google Search, Gmail, YouTube, or any other platform they own, Google consistently does the same thing—they provide access to information in a useful format. This allows us to make better decisions faster. It's that simple. Google Search polls massive amounts of individual data sources and prioritizes the results of their efforts based on an algorithm that measures relevancy. Each product in the portfolio does the same thing, just in a different way. Google Maps does it with geography to help people figure out how to get places. YouTube does it through video to give people access to information and entertainment. Almost all of Google transactions are based on a search and a result. This access allows us to pick the results we find most relevant from an already culled list to search for answers in a more focused way. Google Maps may give us multiple routes based on tolls, traffic, and total distance and we can choose the one best for us. However, the vast majority of Google transactions are based on a search and a result.

The Google model is supported with advertising. The customer is everyone who has a computer or phone and needs to find something.

This service is a dramatic departure from going to an encyclopedia—which was never up to date. Searching the phone book (remember those?) for a phone number or address was a long and painful process. Picking restaurants was always a struggle as well. You might read about something in the newspaper or find a special offer in a circular, but these decisions were mostly word of mouth and often limiting. Now, we can search by cuisine, by distance, by customer reviews, and other key variables. Everyone has access to this kind of information all the time.

The problem is that your employees have grown accustomed to having this information. They can get answers to anything. If they need to fix something, they can watch a tutorial on YouTube. If they want to know how many kilometers are in a mile, they can Google it for the answer (1.6 is the answer, fyi). Conversely, when they show up to work each day chances are they find themselves in the dark with little access to the relevant information necessary to enable success.

Does your company provide employees with access to information in a useful format? The answer is probably "no." Whether an employee is hourly or salaried, everyone wants to win. At the end of each day, it is not the money alone that drives satisfaction, but one's ability to have an impact, make a difference, and drive results. Without access to information in a useful format, employees struggle to be effective, have visibility into results, and to feel genuine satisfaction. Even when they do make a positive impact on the business, they may never know about it.

Instead of Googling information, massive data requests arrive days late, and then hours are spent using pivot tables and other processes to find the answer. By the time results are tabulated, the information is old and worth very little. Compare that to Google's response time. Whenever and wherever you search, they not only tell you how many results were retrieved, but how long it took to get them, and it is always less than one second. I Googled "analytics" and got 683,000,000 results in .79 seconds! That is a lot of results—but algorithms make sure that the most relevant results are on the first page. Thank you, Google.

The Uber Effect

Although completely different from the Google model, Uber learned a few things from the search giant about the power of data. Where Google mastered the search, Uber has taken it one step further. Not only does Uber search for large amounts of data, they also combine the results of the search using a wide range of financial and geographical calculations, mostly related to supply and demand, to create an efficient marketplace. Uber saw an inefficient market and knew digital transformation could completely transform the way the taxicab (remember those?) model operates.

The traditional taxicab concept was effective in densely populated areas, but even then, the supply of cabs was often in the wrong place at the wrong time and both drivers and customers were not getting what they wanted. Fares were fixed based on mileage or zones and all the cabs were the same size with the same amenities (none). In a place like New York City, this was okay. It got the job done most of the time and when it failed, there were always alternatives like the bus, subway, or limousine services to come to the rescue. In less densely populated areas, the concept of a dispatch was used. Employees were staffed 24 hours a day, seven days a week, to answer ride requests and dispatch vehicles to locations. Drivers spent most of their time waiting for a call both because demand for these services was low, and it was hard to determine the right number of drivers needed. The amount of effort it took to find a company, make the call via a payphone (remember those?) and wait for the driver, was too much effort and often potential customers would drive themselves to avoid the hassles. This costly and inefficient model was ripe for disruption.

Uber set out to perfect the process. The first thing they did was figure out how many data sets would be needed to eliminate waste and create an efficient marketplace. Location services were critical. By using GPS to make sure they knew the location of all drivers as well as the location of all customers, paired with an application that sat on a mobile phone, customers could hire drivers, and the need for dispatch was eliminated. By doing this, they also solved several other key problems. Customers could see how long it would take to get picked up because both locations were known. Adding traffic datasets also allowed them to know how long it would take to arrive at their destination. UberX, Uber-Black and UberXL also give customers more choices. Customers can select the level of vehicle luxury they want and also the size of the vehicle based on the number of passengers traveling or the amount of luggage being transported. Using supply and demand, Uber created a marketplace which included things like surge pricing based on periods of higher levels of demand. Customers are willing to pay more, and the drivers are paid more because of this. If you are not in a rush, UberPool allows drivers to pick up multiple passengers and everyone gets a better deal, including the driver who gets more customers and a higher rate of pay overall.

To fill lower periods of demand and to provide additional services to customers Uber added UberEats to their portfolio. Now drivers can also be a delivery service and make additional money during their workdays. In some cities, customers can rent electric scooters through the Uber application as well. Location based data allows all of this to work seamlessly and efficiently.

Uber has created a marketplace and solved several consumer problems along the way. This efficient marketplace is all based on large and numerous data sources. The driver, the customer, mapping services, traffic services, payment processing, customer and driver rating systems, and others.

The *Kayak.com* Effect

Before *Kayak.com* and other travel aggregator sites like Travelocity and Orbitz, booking a trip required multiple steps and multiple websites. The travel website aggregators have helped pioneer the great digital transformation era as much as Uber. Travel aggregator sites poll all the potential deals to get you the best options based on price, departure time, total travel time, and preferred airline. To get this same valuable information, one would need to visit every individual airline website and run this same query. *Kayak.com* does the work for you and includes all the results, or just the results from the airlines you prefer, after one search. This "aggregator" of data creates a better user experience where customers find the lowest price and most convenient options.

Moving beyond just airline data, travel aggregator sites have also added hotel and rental car options into the equation. By buying a bundled offering, customers get a better price and *Kayak.com* is able to be a larger dealmaker, driving their revenue higher. This captive customer selling model where we know the customer is traveling and so we want to meet ALL of their needs, is not lost on the individual companies in the travel space. United Airlines will try to sell you a Hertz rental car after booking—and may also suggest a hotel. This is the same for Delta and other major carriers.

None of these travel solutions would be possible without digital transformation and data aggregation. They are also striving to be decision-making tools for customers who are not sure about what they want to buy. If a family of four is looking for a vacation at the beach, many of these sites can make recommendations. Historical weather forecasts, political stability, exchange rates, level of luxury, and distance from home can all be added on many of the sites to indicate the experience desired. The websites can then make suggestions based on how each of the variables is weighted. The basic premise is we shouldn't have to search too much to find what we are looking: "I want to go to the beach with my family of four, for seven days, leaving March 15th, and it can't cost more than $4,000." (And as if this process hadn't been simplified enough already, someday soon we'll be asking Siri or Alexa to take care of the whole thing for us!)

The *Indeed.com* And *Glassdoor.com* Effect

Indeed.com and *Glassdoor.com* started as sites where employees could review their employers. They grew to be sites where employees could disclose their compensation, job openings could be posted, and leadership teams could be ranked (including your CEO!). By pulling different types of data, these sites can now rank companies based on their competitive offerings for employees (including culture) and give potential hires a decision-making tool.

This ability to see into a company's culture is a dramatic departure from the not-too-distant past, when job fairs and advertisements on college campuses were the best ways to find top recruits. Taking a recruiter's "word for it" when they talked about culture was the best a prospect could do. A company's reputation was often based on great advertising campaigns, but little needed to be based on fact because, other than working there, employees had no other source of information about culture.

Although this level of radical transparency may seem daunting and unfair to corporations, it has, in many ways, actually been a blessing, especially to those who walk the walk and just don't talk the talk. Corporations with great company cultures are being rewarded based on great online reviews. The best prospects are drawn to these places and little-known brands are becoming hotbeds of great hires due to newfound visibility through these websites.

Essentially, newly hired employees have clear expectations based on information available online. And ensuring a great new hire experience has become even more important for employers because uneven employee experiences can translate into highly publicized criticism online.

The Impact Of A Data-Rich Society On The Workplace

We've established that we now live our lives each and every day in an incredibly data-rich society where massive amounts of simplified data are at our disposal 24-7. But what's the impact of this on the workplace? Well, the human experience has fundamentally changed and so have our expectations. And here is where most workplaces are falling short. When employees need large datasets to make better decisions, to meet their goals, make an impact, and often to get bonuses, promotions, and raises, and are unable to get that access, frustration runs rampant. Lack of access to useful information in the workplace drives low morale, poor performance, and higher turnover. It also can destroy company culture.

What Happens If You Don't Fill The Workplace With Actionable, Reliable Data?

An environment where access to information is limited typically has a dysfunctional culture where trust is lacking, and performance is mitigated. Where data is in short supply, employees often fill the void with perceived truths and rumor. Their perception of the truth is often wrong and damaging to others in the organization. The vacuum created by a lack of access to information in a useful format will at best leave your employees lacking the tools they need to help you win, and at worst will be what destroys your culture completely.

The suggestion is not that confidential human resources information or financial information is suited for a general audience. The information must have certain characteristics relevant to the employee. This data should:

1. Allow them to understand how their job makes an impact locally in their area as well as across the broader enterprise.
2. Give them decision rights. When employees are asked, "are decisions made higher up than they need to be" on a Leichter scale employees respond on average with a 4.2 out of 5. Not only have we starved them of information, we have removed their ability to make decisions.
3. Provide employees information they need, so they can make better decisions in their local area of impact. Allowing them to do so will drive performance and engagement.
4. Demonstrate how rules are applied equally across the enterprise so they know they are treated equally.

The Rise Of Fair Versus Equal

Employees are often concerned about favoritism and whether they are being treated equally in the organization. Sometimes they use the word "fairly" and that is a dangerous word. Although feverishly debated whenever I raise this topic, there is a clear difference between something that is "fair" and something that is "equal." Without clearly defined work rule parameters and transparent decision making, employees may see decisions as favoritism when really the rules are being applied equally. This can destroy culture and can be avoided through access to information. Digital transformation can give us the transparency needed to end the argument about equality—or identify where these problems exist and fix them.

Fair is a subjective term and, even if we all agree something is fair, it may not be equal. Equal is completely objective. There is no judgement applied to things that are equal—they either are or are not. This differentiation is important when looking at access to information, how work schedules are assigned, labor strategies are derived, etc.

What is a fair work schedule? It depends on who you ask. Is the location unionized? Does seniority matter? Is it performance based, skills based, done based on favoritism?

Rotating shifts create an environment where employees work every shift, whether it means covering a weekend or a night or an afternoon shift, over the course of a multi-week cycle. Everyone works an equal number of these often less-desirable shifts and many companies use these schedules today. Some do it based on skill balance, and it has nothing to do with fair or equal treatment. Nuclear power plants, as an example, cannot afford to have weaker or less experienced skills at any point in time. Therefore, they rotate the shift schedules and as new employees are hired and trained they are evenly distributed throughout the organization. Would you really want all the new people at a nuclear power plant on night shift together, left alone to "figure it out?" Major accidents, including Chernobyl, Three Mile Island, and Bhopal occurred during night shifts and are clear lessons about the value of skill balance. One may not think it is fair, but objectively it is equal. The application of "equality" needs to be transparent, especially with something as emotionally charged as shift schedules, because without the facts, employees are left to guess how decisions are made.

The Next (Nerve Racking) Step—Working The Way They Want

Employees want more flexibility at work. Although not every organization can provide unlimited flexibility, those that can, and do so, are seeing results. Before the start of digital transformation, single data sets like labor requirements or skill requirements determined how a company would staff an area. Earlier, we discussed the taxi business historically as well as its transformation through Uber. The conversation was about data, supply and demand, and creating an efficient marketplace. The old taxi business model would require the review of historical volumes by day and by time of day to determine the number of cars required. Drivers would get called for pickups or in some cities, like New York, they could be hailed on the side of the road. This system was fraught with inefficiencies. What if the forecast was wrong? What if the passenger was visiting that location and didn't know the company? How much would the ride cost? How long would the ride take?

We spent a little time discussing the "Working Your Way" impact of this digital transformation. Drivers can work when they want and for as long as they want. Uber is the market maker, the dispatch, the customer service, and even the optimization equation that advises drivers where to be to get the most fares (based on historical behavior and customer density). But Uber is not the boss. They are not forcing drivers to work but allowing market forces to incent driver participation. With this advice, drivers can work during the busiest periods and in the most on-demand locations, giving them a higher rate of pay-per-hour, and enabling them to work fewer hours overall.

Digital Transformation In Traditional Industries

Other industries, like manufacturing, are taking note. Using workforce management solutions, factories are instantaneously serving up actionable information in real time to employees so that they understand where available overtime shifts exist and, based on skills, whether they qualify to accept these additional hours. Manufacturers are also looking at multiple data sets to talk about performance, and not just productivity. By pulling time and attendance data, production data, and quality statistics, manufacturers are looking at Overall Labor Effectiveness (OLE). OLE marries productivity, capacity, and quality to get a more powerful picture of success. It is a term originally coined by Gregg Gordon, a thought leader at Kronos Incorporated, in his book *Lean Labor*. Gordon writes that OLE is a replacement of Overall Equipment Effectiveness (OEE) which is heavily flawed due to the lack of consideration for labor costs (probably the number one CONTROLLABLE cost in most manufacturing environments). Pulling all of these datasets together is not easy—and for that reason they have historically not been combined automatically. Engineers have been relegated to back rooms where they spend weeks crunching data in Microsoft Excel, combining databases, and finding OLE conclusions. This manual process often means that the answers they find and the conclusions they draw, are dated and less valuable by the time they are reported.

Contact centers have a different problem. They have massive amounts of data that is constantly transformed into actionable information. This means information overload and they need to show great discipline in managing only the most powerful key performance indicators (KPIs) on a daily basis. It is always fascinating to me that the newest industries have evolved more in such a short period of time.

Yes, in the contact center everything can be measured—even the heart rate and tone of voice of the contact center agent. With all of this measurement and management, employees can have non-traditional shift schedules and even work from home with the right technology. This goes a long way to let employees "work their way." But with this freedom comes responsibility. Employees must be extremely disciplined and follow all the rules. Everything can be—and is—measured. Many contact centers have over 100 KPIs. By having so many, none of them are really seen as "key." On a daily basis, employees can traditionally only digest three KPIs. On a monthly or quarterly basis, it is okay to talk about more of them, but only in longer format meetings. Access to information is only useful if it can be digested and used. Information overload can have a negative effect.

The Way Forward

Companies like Google are training your employees to expect all kinds of services and access to information on-demand and for free. These expectations are driving discontent, turnover, and disengagement in the workplace. The solution? Turn things around and instead of wondering if Google is your enemy, make it your coach. Google does one thing very well: They provide access to information in a useful format. Fill the information void using analytical tools and enable your teams to win in the workplace again.

As the evolution of access continues, employees are going to continue to demand more from their employers and failure to provide this access will mean higher turnover, and lower performance. Access to information today is a key differentiator in fast growing organizations. It is the competitive advantage.

FOCUS ON THE FRONTLINE

1. Greater—and smarter—access to information has disrupted lots of industries for the better. Take a critical look at how your frontline employees access the data they need each day to do their jobs—is it easy, fast and intuitive or is it manual and clunky? Providing access to information in useful formats may be the key to boosting employee performance.
2. Enabling employees with access to relevant data can also allow you to provide more decision making authority at lower levels in the organization.
3. Make sure that your processes around scheduling and compensating your frontline employees are as transparent as possible. In the absence of facts, employees may get the wrong idea about how decisions are made.
4. Providing greater access to information can help address worker concerns about "Fair versus Equal" practices.
5. Investing in data analytics can empower your entire organization to work smarter and more productively.

REFERENCES

Gordon, Gregg. *Lean Labor: A Survival Guide for Companies Facing Global Competition.* Chino Valley: One World Press, 2011. https://www.amazon.com/Survival-Companies-Facing-Global-Competition/dp/0615443907

Google LLC. https://www.google.com/

Yelp. https://www.yelp.com/

Uber Technologies, Inc. https://www.uber.com/

KAYAK. https://www.kayak.com/about

Indeed. https://www.indeed.jobs/

Glassdoor. https://www.glassdoor.com/

Dennis Miller is Chief Employment Officer at Cal Poly Pomona Foundation, Inc. He is responsible for overseeing the foundation's growing human resources function and continues to evolve the foundation's human capital management strategy in talent development and acquisition, benefits, compensation, and employee engagement programs. A highly respected executive with a penchant for solving business problems through human resources initiatives, Mr. Miller has served as the Chair of the Human Resources Committee for the Auxiliary Organization Association, and has served on several of its auxiliary committees including the Executive Committee. Prior to joining Cal Poly Pomona Foundation, he was Director of Human Resources at CSU Fresno Association, Inc. Earlier in his career, Mr. Miller led the evolution of the human resources function at Systems Management Specialists (SMS) during a period of high growth at the firm. Mr. Miller holds a MS from Chapman University and earned SPHR certification from HRCI.

CHAPTER SEVEN

Using Technology To Improve Your Frontline Employee Experience

Dennis Miller, MS, SPHR
Chief Employment Officer, Cal Poly Pomona Foundation, Inc.

In my work as Chief Employment Officer at Cal Poly Pomona Foundation, Inc., I've had the opportunity to see up-close-and-personal the many challenges of overseeing and managing a large and diverse frontline workforce. One of the primary tools to do this more effectively is through the use of technology.

Overview

I've spent more than ten years as Chief Employment Officer at Cal Poly Pomona Foundation, Inc., a nonprofit organization and an auxiliary corporation to the Pomona campus of the California State University (CSU) system. The Pomona campus is one of 23 campuses that make up the CSU system and is located about 35 miles east of Los Angeles on land spanning about 1,700 acres. The Pomona campus educates approximately 26,000 students annually and the total CSU system educates nearly 500,000 students annually throughout the State of California.

The Foundation provides a wide range of services in support of the campus and its students, such as providing all of the dining options on campus (30 different venues), the bookstore, student housing, a hotel and conference center, faculty/staff housing, grant and contract administration for faculty research and development activities, and public-private-partnership operations. The Foundation employs about 2,400 employees throughout the year (including roughly 1,600 student employees) in its endeavor to deliver high quality, timely, affordable, and effective services to the campus community.

Opportunities For Improvement In HR And Payroll Processes

Although our Foundation pays about 1,100 employees each pay cycle, we process about 2,400 W-2's at yearend. As stated above, most of our employees are student workers and all work on a limited/part-time basis of no more than 20 hours per week. In fact, since our student workers are mainly here to attend college, Foundation management takes steps to actively work around class schedules to help ensure student workers keep their goal of obtaining a college degree at the forefront of their priorities. What this means is there might be two, three or four student workers each working two to four hours, to cover an eight-hour shift.

Historically, the operating environment in the human resources and payroll departments at the Foundation included the use of four different technology-based systems that interfaced with each other at varying levels—sometimes automated and other times manual, along with a range of methodologies involving paper and technology-based processes that were labor intensive and non-scalable.

One system was used only for the HR database, another was used for timekeeping purposes, another for tracking fringe time, and another used for financial accounting and reporting that included a module for processing payroll.

While having four separate systems that had some level of interfacing did allow for process outcomes that were seemingly better than using just paper processes, the operating model had serious limitations and required several workers to have multiple steps of verification, re-verification, and yet re-verification again. Often, it was nearly an impossible task of determining which system had the most current data.

One historically problematic area was the I-9 process. Prior to the time of automation, which will be discussed later in this chapter, we used only paper I-9 forms in a centralized model—meaning, all new hires would need to show-up in the HR department, complete the I-9 form, have an HR employee verify the documents, and then HR would file the completed I-9 form.

Since the overwhelming majority of our new hires are—and remain—student workers, most of those workers are not familiar with what documentation they might need to get their I-9 approved. The process would start by the employee getting hired by the hiring manager and then the hiring manager would instruct the newly hired student worker to visit the HR department to get their new hire paperwork completed.

Often, new hires would arrive at the HR department with no appointment (there was no appointment mechanism in place) to complete the new hire paperwork, such as the I-9 form, and would invariably arrive without the needed documentation—in some cases, they left the documentation at their home, which was often out-of-state.

This scenario resulted in at least two trips to the HR department for the newly hired student worker: the first trip to get the process started and to hear from HR exactly what forms of ID would be acceptable to get their I-9 certified, and a return trip to the HR department along with the required ID to ultimately complete the I-9 process. This process had to be very frustrating to these newly hired student workers and was certainly very time consuming and chaotic for our employees.

Once this I-9 process was completed, the HR department had to maintain tens of thousands of I-9 forms over a period of several years. In many cases, the HR team would take the initiative and photocopy the forms they collected, just in case they needed those forms to prove the company verified the appropriate ID forms. There were many forms reviewed and signed during the onboarding process, but none of those forms or processes were as problematic at the I-9 process and none were more important from a compliance standpoint—I-9 penalties are huge.

Another example of a serious inefficiency was our change of address process. Student workers represent about 85% of the frontline workers at the Foundation, and most of these student workers attend the University on a full-time basis to earn their college degree (their main goal in life), so working a job and dealing with employee-related tasks are not their highest priority.

As it turns out, students move their physical location frequently and with little advance notice.

The typical process to notify the appropriate parties in HR and payroll of an address change involved the following steps or tasks:

1. The individual would locate an "Address Change Form" and print it from the Foundation website.
2. The employee would complete the form and then forward it to either the Foundation HR or payroll department via the campus mail system.
3. Usually, within two to three days from the date this form was placed in the campus mail system, it would be delivered to the Foundation HR or payroll department.

Once the Foundation HR or payroll department received the Address Change Form, it would be placed into the workflow to be "processed." The exact timing of when this form was processed was directly related to the level of priority it had compared to the stack of other forms that had already been submitted and received by the HR or payroll function. Address Change Forms had a much lower priority compared to other forms, such as new hire paperwork, etc.

It was common to observe several stacks of documents in the HR department at any given time—as well as the payroll department, and it was not uncommon for the process to take multiple weeks before a particular HR or payroll form would get processed and the data would be entered into the appropriate system.

In most cases, one of two scenarios would commonly occur. If the Address Change Form was addressed and sent to the HR department, the HR system would receive the updated address first. Once HR processed the Address Change Form, it would be forwarded to the payroll department for manual entry into the payroll system, or when the Address Change Form was first sent to the payroll department it would get processed in that system first, and then get forwarded to the HR department for processing.

Although it may have taken the Address Change Form two to three days to arrive to the Foundation offices (where the HR and payroll functions are located), it would still take, on average, another 10 to 20 business days for that form to get processed by both HR and payroll departments, assuming the form did not get misrouted, mishandled, or filed accidentally.

In the meantime, while this Address Change Form was working its way through the process, a payroll cycle would have happened or was about to happen. As a result of the time it took to actually input this Address Change Form, the likelihood was all but guaranteed the payroll system would not get updated by the time payroll would have been processed, thereby ensuring the payroll check for this recently moved student worker would be sent to the wrong physical address.

This, in turn, resulted in a serious problem for the student worker since his or her paycheck would ultimately not be in the hands of the student worker in a timely manner. Even in an ideal scenario where the Postal Service was able to reroute the check and get it delivered according to Post Office standards, the paycheck would arrive three to five days late for this student worker.

Take a moment to think about a student worker, a young adult living away from home on an extended basis—often for the first time in his or her life—wanting to be independent and wanting to show their family they can stand on their own. They may be reluctant to reach out to their family for support. Now, after working for the last two weeks and coordinating their class schedule and work schedules, homework and study time, personal time, gym time, etc. all with the expectation that their small paycheck will be delivered on time and in the correct amount, they realize that their check did not arrive as planned. "Panic" is a common feeling experienced by these young people—and rightfully so.

In fact, what we observed routinely, was that once the student worker confirmed their paycheck had not arrived on the exact date they expected, the student worker would make their way to the Foundation payroll department, usually immediately and often missing a scheduled class, to explain their situation to the payroll staff with the hopes of receiving another paycheck to replace the "lost paycheck." In these cases, which happened every day throughout the day (literally), the student would often wait for their check to be processed before leaving the building.

Some may wonder why we do not use direct deposit for all employees to help reduce the impact associated with waiting for a paycheck to arrive. As a California employer with employees located only within the state, using direct deposit requires advance employee approval in all cases which means "requiring" direct deposit is not currently an option (which is not the case in many US states). Although we have a strong marketing and communication campaign including small incentives to help encourage employees to enroll in direct deposit, we still have nearly 30% of our workforce who rely on paper checks.

Fortunately for these students, our payroll department has a very caring and empathetic team with exceptional customer services skills, and the payroll team was happy to cancel a previously issued paycheck and replace it immediately to get the employee (student worker or otherwise) paid as soon as possible. Still, the constant interruption of scheduled work in the payroll function was frustrating to the payroll team members and often they were simply overwhelmed with the volume of walk-in customers.

Even in cases where a student worker was able to wait several days for their check to arrive at their new address, the student worker would still be distracted and concerned or worried about when their paycheck might arrive. This scenario, by itself, would have a negative impact on the ability of a student worker to remain focused on their coursework and learning objectives.

During high volume periods of hiring—which happened four times per year—the HR and payroll departments would hire temporary labor to help with the paper flow of work during those peak times. Once this peak hiring period ended, the temporary workers would be laid-off.

At this time in the history of the payroll function, the payroll team was deep in long-standing paperwork processes with many repetitive checks-and-balances required to help ensure all of the important tasks were completed in a timely and correct manner.

The process for handling the most basic of payroll or HR tasks—like the change of address I talked about—was completely broken. This broken process had a negative impact on the overwhelming majority of our frontline workers, and an equally negative impact on employees and our organization overall.

A Lack Of Accessibility To Time Collection Devices

Payroll and HR processes were not the only areas in need of improvement. A lack of accessibility to data collection devices for timekeeping was also a huge issue.

Frontline workers were battling a lack of access to time clocks during non-standard work hours, such as late at night or weekends when the office areas, where the time clocks were housed, were closed. Many roles in a campus environment—from resident advisors to health and wellness advisors—are needed after normal working hours, and on weekends, holidays, etc. to deliver services to students in a wide variety of areas. Since the office areas are closed during non-work hours, there was no time clock accessibility. Therefore, these particular workers would typically estimate the hours they worked during these times and then have someone enter those hours manually once the time clock became available again.

Another data collection accessibility and process problem existed where student workers would have a paid internship type of arrangement—where they would work off-campus for a client willing to pay student workers to provide some level of work for their company, while offering these same student workers a valuable learning experience related to their degree program. In some cases, the student worker might also receive course credit—a truly wonderful learning opportunity for students attending college.

When it came to paid internships, student workers were using paper timesheets to record the time they worked for payroll purposes and the employer or client would then reimburse the Foundation for the hours the students worked on their projects. There were several key steps required in this process to bring it all together:

- The student intern needed to record the hours she worked on a paper document.
- The employer/client needed to approve the hours reported by the student and make adjustments where appropriate prior to submitting that data to the Foundation for payroll purposes, which typically was forwarded via email.
- Once the hours were received by the Foundation (usually the Foundation project manager for the internship program), they were manually entered into the Foundation timekeeping system for each student worker.

All of these tasks needed to happen on a strict timeline, or the student workers would not be paid in a timely manner, thereby triggering the same types of "lost check"/panic issues mentioned previously. In some cases, changes to student worker timecards would be made by the Foundation project manager after the time worked by the students was approved by the client. Those events resulted in billing issues since the amount of time paid to student workers would be different when compared to the records held by the client related to the hours the client had originally approved to pay.

Finally, on a campus spanning nearly 1,700 acres, one can imagine the logistical difficulty of having a time clock (or anything stationary used for data collection) located at the most ideal places for a worker, such as a maintenance worker, who works in different physical locations throughout a day within the campus environment. Imagine the amount of time completely wasted traveling to or from a time clock when it was time to clock-out/in for the required lunch break. HR professionals in the State of California are (or should be) laser-focused on the penalties and negative press associated with a lack of compliance in this area, so meal period compliance is a fairly important topic for California employers and their employees. Imagine how the worker must feel knowing they must leave their worksite five to ten minutes or more in advance of their meal break to make sure they do not inadvertently trigger a missed meal penalty (and likely a scolding from their boss).

Looking For Answers

When examining all of the HR, payroll, and timekeeping processes together, it was evident that having four different technology-based systems interact with one another to handle human resources and payroll and timekeeping processes was an operational model that was no longer working for us.

In fact, the core process issues were related to a single technological defect—there were several systems interfacing with one another and each system had its own separate database.

As such, the solution toward this specific problem was not difficult or complex—it was obvious and really quite simple. What we needed was a cost-effective platform that used a single database for HR, payroll, and timekeeping.

In looking for a cost-effective platform where we would have a single database for HR, payroll, and timekeeping, we reviewed several different vendors, and reviewed our existing financial system vendor, our timekeeping provider, and our HR provider. Internally, we engaged our technology team. It seemed logical that if we could build upon our current systems, we might reduce the migration time and the learning time post migration, since there would already be some level of expertise with one or more components of the new platform.

As it turned out, there was no economical solution that would provide everything we wanted in our existing HR system or financial system. The financial system (which is the same system we used for payroll) already had payroll and we could have added HR, but they did not offer a timekeeping product. The HR system had only HR and no payroll or timekeeping, and that left the timekeeping system. As it turned out, the timekeeping system had an HR and payroll function, and they used a single database for all three functions.

Finding Solutions—And Cost Savings

Moving to a unified system was a game-changer for the Foundation. Issues that had been major problems in the past were nearly instantaneously resolved:

- All I-9's are now completed electronically through an online portal.

- Workers can use a self-service option to update their address whenever needed with the change reflected in real time in HR and payroll.
- Employees can request time off and managers can approve it using their mobile devices.
- Employees can clock-in and out wherever they are located via mobile device.
- Supervisors can easily verify exactly where and when an employee clocked-in or out using their mobile phone and google maps, if they feel the need for such verification.
- Supervisors can approve time worked for their employees using their mobile device.

Along with adopting this new technology, we also elected, after some time, to use cloud services to run and maintain it.

In-house hosting meant we had two dedicated servers for our platform, which included the production server, development server, and a part-time server for back-ups. The IT staff had to schedule and install quarterly tax updates, service packs, provide software configuration help to the HR and payroll team, address technological issues related to the hardware, maintain and tune the servers, and a long list of technology related tasks. We had a disaster recovery plan although it seemed marginal on any given day.

When we examined the options for cloud services, it became apparent that moving to the cloud would provide relief in all of these areas, which seemed too good to be true at that time. In fact, the outcome was better than we anticipated. Once we moved to the cloud the platform, the solution was maintained entirely by vendor experts.

Moving to cloud services has provided more value to our organization and to the HR and payroll function than anticipated—and, for us, this model is definitely cost effective especially when factoring in the IT team no longer needs to provide the ongoing support to the platform in-house. (This alone has given the IT team back about 500 hours annually to apply to other systems where they can continue to develop and use their talent.)

Speaking of cost, it is a fact that our operating expenses to operate the HR and payroll functions has decreased by more than 27% after making the improvements outlined above, which have occurred during the past several years. As of January 2019, our operating budget remains well below what it was five years ago.

Even more important though, is the shift in the mindset of our employees and managers on what might be possible with technology. As a rule, Foundation culture has embraced the use of technology throughout the organization—which is a good outcome—and we have leveraged technology to help all employees, all managers, and reduce the cost to the organization for operating the HR and payroll functions.

Now that we are no longer mired in the past, constantly dealing with broken processes and trying to keep pace operating four different technologies in HR and payroll, we are able to place focus on additional improvements with our delivery models and be laser-focused on strategic initiatives overall.

The future is, indeed, quite bright!

FOCUS ON THE FRONTLINE

1. Workforce management technology can eliminate a lot of frustration and busy work for your employees, providing them with a better experience at work.
2. Frontline employees will value self-service options that, ideally, they can use from their mobile devices.
3. Involving frontline employees in requirements gathering and design of new systems will yield better adoption of and satisfaction with a new system.
4. Don't underestimate the need for frequent and clear communication, delivered through multiple channels.
5. Training is critical to ensuring that your employees will get the value they should from a new solution.

REFERENCES

Cal Poly Pomona Foundation, Inc., https://foundation.cpp.edu/
Cal Poly Pomona Foundation, Inc., Employment Services. https://foundation.cpp.edu/es/

Sharlyn Lauby is President of ITM Group, Inc., a training and human resources consulting firm helping companies manage talent, and is author of *HR Bartender,* which is recognized as one of the top five blogs read by human resources professionals by SHRM. She also authored *Manager Onboarding: 5 Steps for Setting New Leaders Up for Success* and *The Recruiter's Handbook: A Complete Guide for Sourcing, Selecting, and Engaging the Best Talent.* Before starting ITM Group, Ms. Lauby was Vice President of Human Resources for Right Management Consultants. She has designed and implemented highly successful programs for employee retention, internal and external customer satisfaction, and leadership development. Publications such as *Reuters, The New York Times, ABC News,* and *The Wall Street Journal* have sought her expertise on topics related to human resources and the workplace. Ms. Lauby holds a BS from the University of Central Florida as well as SHRM-SCP certification.

CHAPTER EIGHT

Performance Management: The Art Of Giving Managers And Employees The Tools To Be Successful

Sharlyn Lauby, SHRM-SCP
President, ITM Group, Inc.
Author, *HR Bartender*

Chances are, I don't really need to explain why performance management (PM) is important. All organizations are focused on performance. But just in case you're having coffee with a contrary department manager who says, "I don't understand why we need to do these performance reviews—they're a big waste of time," here are a couple of statistics from the Association for Talent Development (ATD) 2017 State of the Industry Report[1] that might help:

- $1,273 is the average direct learning expenditure per employee
- 34.1 is the number of annual formal learning hours used per employee
- 65% of content was focused toward on-the-job learning

The last thing an organization wants to do is spend a thousand dollars and the equivalent of a work week focused on job-related training only to find out that employees aren't performing to the company standard. This is why performance management is important and companies think about performance. They make investments in training and development, so employees will perform. The process of performance management protects the company's learning investment, not to mention delivering organizational results.

The challenge for organizations is creating a performance management process that is easy to explain and understand, and is respected by the entire organization. In addition, it needs to be a process focused on aligning individual contributors with organizational strategy.

So how do we do that? Well, there's a lot of conversation about how to achieve higher levels of employee performance via individual activities such as manager one-on-one meetings, coaching sessions, and career development. But in order to truly develop and maintain an effective performance management process, we need to first understand the factors that influence employee performance.

Six Factors That Contribute To Employee Performance

During the 2018 Association for Talent Development (ATD) International Conference and Exposition, I attended a workshop on improving human performance and we talked about six factors that influence employee performance. While we went into some significant depth about this during the workshop, here's a high-level overview.

External to the Employee	Physical Resources: tools, materials, equipment, budget, supplies, etc.	Process: organizational structure, policies, procedures, mission-vision-values	Information: performance, standards, customers, data, etc.
Internal to the Employee	Knowledge: training, job aids, education, on-the-job-training (OJT), mentoring, etc.	Motives: profit sharing, recognition, bonuses, benefits, advancement opportunities, etc.	Capacity: emotional intelligence, wellbeing, energy, abilities, etc.

You might find that your organization compartmentalizes these areas a little differently. Regardless, employee performance is influenced by both the employee and the work environment, which in many cases the employee has very little control over. In terms of those areas external to the employee, there are three factors that can influence performance:

1. **Organizational processes** have a huge influence on employee performance. Not only policies, procedures, and guidelines, but organizational structure. For example, companies that have created bureaucratic cultures probably run into challenges from time to time where bureaucracy gets in the way of performance.

2. **Physical resources** such as technology, tools, equipment, etc. have an impact on employee performance. This was one of the reasons organizations started designing open office environments—to improve collaboration and employee performance. It's also one of the reasons that many organizations are reconsidering those designs.
3. **Data and information** ties into the physical resources area. If organizations are behind the curve when it comes to things like technology, they could also be limiting the amount of data and information that employees have access to, which could impact the quality of the decisions they make.

On the other side, three internal factors also influence employee performance:

1. **Individual abilities** include emotional intelligence, wellness, etc. affect performance. Organizations try to determine these qualities when they interview candidates or consider employees for promotion. Those qualities can set a candidate apart from others and help employees build a strong network of mentors.
2. **Motivation** factors play a role in employee performance—this is no surprise. The question becomes what is the motivator? Is it money, recognition, benefits, perks, fancy office—or maybe a combination of factors? The key is understanding what those factors are AND whether the organization can deliver on them (see #2 just above).
3. **Job knowledge** is an important part of employee performance. Employees want to feel that they know what to do and are being set up for success. And when they're presented with a new task, even if they're a little nervous, they want to know the company supports them.

Honestly, none of these factors are likely to be a big surprise. But it does raise the question of how much organizations are using this information when they are developing their performance management processes. And not just on an employee level. As organizations look to the future and are thinking about introducing new products and services or merging operations, do they ask themselves, "I know we're training employees but are we making sure they have all the tools to perform at a high level?"

The key is to include the factors that drive employee performance in the company's performance management process because *all the pieces of the puzzle together* create a high performing culture. It's not enough to simply think about them when it comes to employee training programs; we need to think "both/and" instead of "either/or."

The other thing this table tells us is that performance management isn't 100% about the individual employee. When we're thinking about performance management, we have to consider the employee, the department or team, and the organization as a whole. In fact, maybe in the past, we've thought about performance management from a linear standpoint. It might have looked something like this:

While this is true to an extent, it does create the perception that performance management activities can be viewed as singular events versus an ongoing process. And as such, the outcomes of an event can change regularly. Some might argue that events are not ingrained in the culture, so they might not receive the support and resources they need to be successful. For performance management to be effective, it needs to be considered more than an event. It needs to be viewed as a PROCESS and it could make sense to look at it from more of a circular point of view.

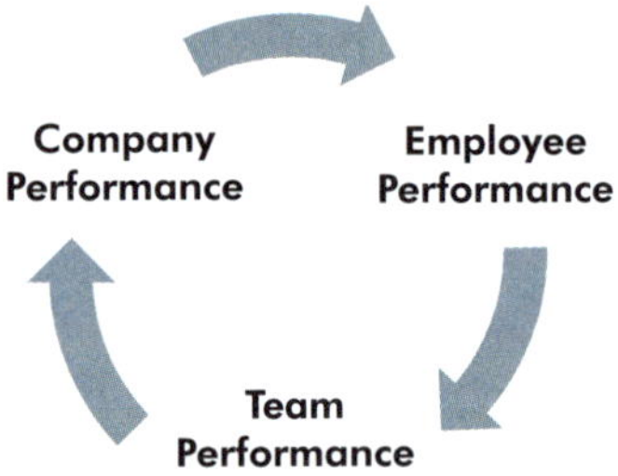

Processes have a defined consistent goal and are a regular part of the business operation. Resources are allocated to the process because they help achieve a goal.

Technology Is Changing Performance Management

The internal and external factors that influence employee performance change all the time. Some of them are controlled by the company, others are controlled by the team, and some rest with the employee. Because performance management is dynamic and happens in real-time, it makes technology an important consideration. Using automation makes the process easier to manage.

Employees today are accustomed to doing many things using technology—from depositing a check to making a doctor's appointment to learning a language. Over the past couple of decades, technology has changed the way we view and share information with others. Not surprisingly, this has found its way into the workplace. Employees can set goals and collaborate with others using software. They can leave feedback and recognition for co-workers using software. There's even coaching software out there.

It's no wonder that managers and employees are pushing back on the annual performance review form, even if the form is online. Given what we can do with technology, organizations can do a better job of connecting technology with a performance management culture. Here are a few things to consider:

Establish the goal. Whenever an individual or organization uses technology, there should be a reason. Not simply because "everyone is doing it." Companies need to think about why they're using technology. The reason companies use technology should be a part of their culture. For example, a company that has a MacGyver-esque culture will use technology to solve problems. An organization with a relentless dedication to customer service will use technology to improve customer relations.

Train employees. Once organizations establish their goals, they have to share them with employees. This will be the WIIFM (What's in it for me?) that drives training. Just because we have smartphones and tablets in our personal lives doesn't mean companies are absolved of their responsibility to train employees on the technology they will use at work. A big area of focus for companies should be to train employees on how to use technology safely and securely. Cybersecurity is much too important to ignore.

Be an effective adopter. Technologies come and go as evidenced by the demise of Friendster, Digg, and Google+, as well as the surgencies of Snapchat, Instagram, and Slack. As such, organizations have to decide when and how they're going to implement new technologies and how they are going to evaluate a new platform's effectiveness. Organizations do not have to be the first to try or switch over to a new technology. But they certainly don't want to be the last. It could make sense to create a "lab" for testing out new technologies within the organization.

Support time away from tech. As important as technology is to the business, we do have to allow for "non-tech" moments. An increasing number of studies are citing a relationship between always being on technology and employee burnout. According to a study conducted by Kronos Incorporated, employee burnout is responsible for up to half of employee turnover.[2] If we want employees to fully embrace the value of technology, we need to also allow them to step away from it. Being able to gain perspective is essential for critical thinking and performance.

Maintain technology. We've talked about the need to constantly evaluate the effectiveness of technology, in terms of performance toward goals. But there's another aspect of technology that needs monitoring—it's whether the software works. Technology is constantly being updated. It's possible that version 9.1.18 performed a task that employees loved (because it made their jobs easier) and version 10.1.0 doesn't. Again, organizations need to look at the reasons they're using technology to ensure it's still doing the job.

Technology is a key part of business today, which means it's a key part of company culture. As we talk about creating a performance culture, there needs to be a technology connection.

The "Old School" Performance Review Process

I've intentionally tried to be very careful about mentioning performance reviews because I believe the reason performance management is under so much scrutiny in today's business environment is specifically related to the "traditional" annual performance review. Of note, I wasn't around when the first performance review was created—but I'm confident that it was never designed to be a form of punishment. That being said, I must admit that performance review hasn't kept up with the times. Technology has changed the way we work, and it's changed performance. Therefore, the instrument we use to measure performance must change along with it.

It might be helpful to spend a couple of minutes reminiscing about the history of performance management. Sometimes it helps to understand where we've been in order to think about where we're going.

The story starts years ago when organizations realized the way to keep an entire organization focused on performance and goals was by measuring them. (This makes total sense.) As a result, organizations started recognizing and rewarding employees who performed at a high level and helped the company achieve their goals. They might also have had conversations with employees who weren't meeting their goals and asked them to get focused. Once this started, legal departments probably suggested that they start keeping track of all these conversations and rewards. Someone might have actually said in a meeting, "Let human resources manage it. That's what they do." (Well, maybe they didn't say it exactly like this, but you get my point.) So—HR became the owner of performance management.

For those of you who know me or read my blog *HR Bartender*, you know I'm a definitions person. When faced with a challenge, I pull out the dictionary to get clarity about a word or term in question. While some people may define performance management as some form of torture created by HR pros—let me assure you this wasn't the case when I went on my mission to find the definition of performance management. In ATD's *Talent Management Handbook*,[3] authors William A. Schiemann and Craig Dinsell suggest the primary purpose of performance management should be to "align individual contributors with organizational strategy." Using this definition—which I feel best reflects performance management and will stand the test of time—performance management becomes a collaborative process to create, monitor, review, and evaluate shared business objectives; and the performance review, a very visible component of the performance management process—provides feedback, accountability, and documentation.

As noted earlier, organizations have always been focused on performance—and although organizations, senior management, and laws have changed, the underlying purpose of performance management remains the same. It's about aligning employees with business strategy.

Performance Management: Three Components That Organizations Have Gotten Right

As an HR person, I'll be the first to admit, there are components of performance management that have become stale—but before we list those components, let's address what's good about it. Here are three things I believe are good about performance management when talking about its future:

1. **Purpose:** Organizations have to be focused on performance. It makes good business sense whether you're in a public or private organization and regardless of industry, performance

matters. People might disagree on the quality or level of performance, but not on the idea of performance itself. Stakeholders at every level expect organizational performance, so it needs to be managed.

2. **Documentation:** Most of us do not have eidetic memory (and we do live in a litigious society) so we need documentation to remind us of things, and support decisions. What we don't need is for performance management to become primarily a documentation exercise.
3. **Ownership:** While everyone in the organization plays a role in performance management, I do think HR is usually considered the "owner" of the process. Because performance management impacts many functional talent areas, HR is a logical place for performance management to reside and help maintain consistency. That being said, it doesn't absolve those outside of HR from doing their part.

Performance Management: Three Components In The Process That Have Gone Off Track

In addition to the good things mentioned about performance management, there are definite places where it has evolved into something that slows organizational momentum. We can't simply say "everything's wrong" because it's not—but performance management needs an overhaul. Here are the three pain points I hear most often:

1. **Priorities:** Somewhere along the way, performance management became more focused on administration and documentation than alignment and collaboration. We need to get our focus back on the definition and "align individual contributors with organizational strategy." Yes, administration and paperwork are necessary, but they shouldn't be primary.
2. **Empathy:** Or more specifically a lack of empathy. At some point in time, we have all been the recipient of feedback. Everyone needs to remember what others in the performance management process are experiencing. This could involve adding a training or development program where individuals receive feedback training, so they start the performance management process with the proper tools.
3. **Measurement:** Performance management is all about measuring results. If organizations haven't done a good job of defining performance standards, it becomes a challenge to identify and quantify results. In addition, if organizations haven't established the steps someone should take to improve their performance, then employees can't be coached successfully.

While there are definitely aspects of the performance review that need updating, these two aspects of the traditional performance review need immediate attention—rankings and ratings.

> **Rankings** are when employees are compared to each other.
>
> Some performance review processes do this intentionally—but it can be a form of bias. My angst with performance rankings has to do with performance standards and goals. Here's an example: Let's say the company's sales director ranks the sales team in order of best salesperson to worst. I'm the salesperson who is ranked as the worst, yet I have annual sales of $10M, and my goal was $1M. Despite the fact that I crushed my goal nine times over—I'm rated last. The problem isn't that I wasn't performing as an employee—it's that the goal and standards aren't set correctly.
>
> **Ratings** are the scales that managers use to rate performance.
>
> A common example is the "5-point Graphic Rating Scale"—where "5" represents "exceeds" expectations and "1" represents "doesn't meet" expectations. I struggle with two things about ratings. The first challenge is—what "3" represents on the scale. Typically, "3" is noted as "meets expectations" or "meets performance standards." That part I'm totally fine with—as I would like to think that most organizations have high performance standards, want to deliver an excellent product or service, and be the best in their industry. So, when an employee meets the high standards set by the company, that's a good thing. The challenge is "3" is often communicated as "average" performance—or the employee assumes his/her performance is average. The second challenge I struggle with concerning ratings is what "1" and "2" represent on the scale. If a "3" on the graphic rating scale means meeting the company standard—then wouldn't anything less simply be "not meeting the company standard?" How are there *degrees* of not meeting the standard? Either an employee does—or doesn't. I think this adds another level of vagueness to the performance review process.

The Complicated Relationship Between Compensation And Performance Management

One big reason that ratings and rankings have become a point of contention in the performance review process—and why performance management had become the target of conversation and debate—has to do with money. At some point, organizations linked performance reviews to merit increases. Since then (and I honestly don't when it first happened), employees are focused on performance reviews because they are linked to their paycheck. In addition, managers are focused on performance reviews because they can give employees pay increases (or take them away).

In my opinion, compensation and performance management are two separate processes that have been connected to the detriment of each. Unfortunately, there are managers who "game" the performance review system to reward their top performers. What results is that other managers don't know how to do this, and their employees get mad. In addition, there are managers who are reluctant to share poor performance in reviews because it will impact the pay of employees. Instead of dealing with the issue, they ignore it because they don't want to reduce an employee's pay increase (or have it taken away). Of note, should it come time to discipline an employee, there's nothing in the employee's personnel file—a frustration point for both HR and the manager.

Linking performance management and compensation has created a system where the focus isn't on performance, it's on money. There is no doubt about it—money is important, but it should be handled differently. Organizations need to find a way to separate performance management and compensation. The conversations should be different.

Staying Focused On The Definition Of Performance Management

The good news about performance management is that everyone agrees it is necessary and needed. Organizations want to measure performance because it helps them achieve their goals. Managers want employees who perform at a high level. Employees want to be recognized for their hard work. And HR wants the process to work well.

The basic definition of performance management really doesn't need to be changed. What does need to happen is that the extra components that have been thrown into performance management over the years need to find their own homes. At the core of performance management is performance, and we need to keep it that way. The performance we are talking about is employee performance.

In looking at the key components of a truly employee centric performance management model, here's a table that shows what we're talking about in terms of a shift from "old school" to today:

FOCUS THEN	FOCUS TODAY
Event	**Process**
Manager / Employee	Multi-level (individual, manager, team)
Compensation Focus	Development Focus
One-way Communication	Two-way Conversations
Performance Counseling	Performance Development
Past Problems	Future Growth and Solutions

Identifying The Need Is Easy—Implementing A Solution Is Hard

The future of performance management is about creating a process in which individuals at every level of the organization have conversations about performance, development, growth, and the future. Some of you might be saying, "I know our company needs to move the performance management process into the 21st century. I'm looking for ways to make that happen."

Let's look at a framework you can consider for your performance management process. In doing so, I want to flip one assumption. Performance management is about the employee. It's *always* been about the employee. And we need to put the employee first.

The Employee Life Cycle Is Changing

In the past, the major milestones of an employee's career have been pretty straightforward. They were hired through the talent acquisition function, trained by learning and development, coached in the performance management process, offered career development opportunities by their manager, and then transitioned out of the organization.

Today, it makes more sense to think of the employee life cycle as a continuous loop versus a linear process. So, employees are hired, onboarded, coached, developed, retained, and then transitioned to other roles within the organization. The "other roles" could be full-time, part-time, or a freelancing/consulting opportunity. Thinking of the employee life cycle as a loop shifts the focus to a more employee-centric approach, without losing any of the components. That's exactly the same shift that needs to happen with performance management. Employees and managers want and need an approach to performance management that still does what it's intended to do, but centers around the employee.

Traditionally much of performance management centers around forms and meetings. It seems to me that for employee performance management to be successful, it needs to be all about the employee in four distinct ways—job, work relationships, career, and company.

Here's one way to view these four performance areas:

MY JOB	MY WORK RELATIONSHIPS
This area is about the employee's job, and includes outcomes, goals, and Objectives and Key Results (OKRs). Activities aligned with this quadrant include: goal-setting, one-on-one meetings, and performance reviews.	This focuses on the employee's work relationships with others: their manager, peers, and possibly customers. Activities include: multi-rater reviews, reward and recognition programs, and collaboration.
MY CAREER DEVELOPMENT	**MY ORGANIZATION**
This is all about the employee and their future. Activities include: learning and development, self-learning, and career development.	This is focused on the employee's engagement with the organization. Activities in this area include: stay interviews, engagement surveys, and pulse surveys.

I divided the employee performance areas into four quadrants because the trend today is to encourage quarterly check-ins or performance meetings. For organizations already leaning in this direction, the framework provides some creative inspiration in the design of a performance management program—with each performance area having direct alignment with business goals.

The employee's job responsibilities bring value every day. Organizations create work because it brings value to the business, and therefore need employees to do a good job every day.

The employee's work relationships foster collaboration and team development. In the *Harvard Business Review* article "Collaborative Overload," the authors talk about the rise in collaborative work. We also see it in the number of open office spaces being created. Employees need to build positive working relationships. And organizations need to guide and support collaborative behaviors.

The employee's career development prepares for the future. Talent acquisition is a hot topic today because there are more job openings than candidates. This means that—in addition to their ongoing recruiting efforts—organizations are going to make developing internal talent a priority.

The employee's pride in the organization leads to retention. In a 2016 Accenture survey, college graduates were asked what's important to them when looking for an employer—92% said corporate social responsibility. Employees want an organization to which they can be proud—and companies need to understand why employees choose them.

The four performance quadrants are very flexible, which can help managers and employees take ownership of the process. While the quadrants are presented in one order, there's no reason an organization can't change it up to suit their organizational needs. Of note, if your infrastructure can support it, you could allow divisions or departments the flexibility of focusing on an employee performance area at their discretion—provided they cover all of them during a year. So, let's say your US offices use the cycle of job, work relationships, career development, and organization. Maybe your EMEA offices use the cycle of organization, work job, career development, and work relationships. HR could play the role of advisor to each business unit to discuss the best cycle for their operation. (This would be a better use of HR's time than chasing down a supervisor to see whether he or she has completed a 90-day review for a new hire.)

The other flexibility component in the framework is that organizations can use a variety of methods that managers and employees can enjoy. Repetition can lead to boredom—and the last thing we want is for conversations about performance to become boring. These employee performance areas use face-to-face, peer-to-peer, technologies, etc. to deliver feedback.

Depending on your organization's resources, you can also add or change one aspect of delivery without changing the entire process. For example, a company might start with incorporating stay interviews into manager and employee one-on-one meetings—then add electronic onboarding check-ins to the process at a later point in time. The other three performance areas don't change.

Performance Management Roles And Responsibilities

Now that we have a performance management process, let's start with what the model means for key stakeholders like HR and management. HR has been the owner of this process for a long time and to sell the company on this transformation, we need to understand our role in it.

There are three key roles in the performance management process: HR, management, and the employee. Before we talk about the role of human resources in performance management, let's take a step back and define HR, as it has a bearing on how I relate human resources and performance management. HR often has responsibility for talent acquisition—but it's certainly not the sum and substance of the role. It includes a long list of things—benefits, compensation, safety, training, employee relations, etc.

Today, when I describe what HR does, I like to say that "HR is the architect of work."[4]

Think about it. What does an architects do? An architect is responsible for creating functional, safe, aesthetically pleasing, economical structures. They get their job done by not only designing but also communicating their designs to clients, builders, and others. Human resources professionals are responsible for creating work that:

- People will want to apply for (talent acquisition)
- Pays a wage and benefits package companies can afford (compensation)
- Offers purpose to employees (employee engagement)
- Meets a business need within the organization (performance management)

Work can change—just like some buildings change over time. HR is responsible for taking a holistic approach to work, and making sure any changes align with the goals of the organization. In talking about change and alignment of goals, I'm reminded of a funny story about someone I worked with years ago. He and his wife would go out to dinner every night. One night they sketched out their dream home on a bar napkin. They took the bar napkin to an architect and said, "This is our dream home, draw us a blue print." The architect looked at the napkin and asked, "Can I make one suggestion? Put a kitchen in it." Years later, the couple built their dream home and, taking the architect's suggestion, included a kitchen. They also put a sign at the kitchen entry that said, "This kitchen is for resale purposes only." (LOL!)

My point in sharing this story is that just like the house needing a kitchen—jobs need things to do too, and the role of human resources is to be the architect of creating that work. Architects don't work in a vacuum—they design buildings with other stakeholder's needs in mind. HR doesn't work in a vacuum either—we consult with operational managers about knowledge, skills, and abilities. We coach managers on rewards and recognition.

The performance management framework I've shared allows HR to maintain its role as the architect of work. In fact, on some level, it might even bring the architect role into greater focus because HR is creating the structure but allowing managers and employees to find the functionality that works best for them. If we go back to the house example, let's say an architect designs a three-bedroom house. If once the house is built, the owners decide to convert a bedroom into a home office—the architect isn't going to storm over and tell them they can't do it. The architect created the structure, but the homeowners decide the best way to use the space. In performance management, HR—as the architect—is going to provide the performance management structure, and give managers and employees guidance on the best way to use it.

The Manager's Role As A Performance Consultant

Another key player in the performance management process is the manager. While I like to use the architect analogy for HR, managers could be considered the builder or performance consultant. Their role is to work with HR in analyzing business challenges, developing solutions to address those challenges, and implementing solutions to improve the business.

In the ATD article "What Core Competencies Do Performance Consultants Need?"[5] author Dana Robinson writes that there are two main requirements to be successful as a performance consultant: 1) capability and 2) support.[5] Both managers and human resources professionals need these skills, which means they need management skills training. It's unfair to think that everyone intuitively knows how to be a performance consultant.

Of note, when we're talking about performance consulting we're not talking about discipline. There are a lot of employees who do great work and never hear about it. Employees want and need to hear about the positive aspects of their performance.

If the only time employees hear about their performance is when something goes wrong, they will hate the process and avoid it. Not to mention that, if the only time managers talk with employees is to discipline them, managers will hate the process and avoid it. Discipline and corrective coaching are necessary, but "no news is good news" shouldn't be the cornerstone of the performance management process.

Don Levonius, Principal Consultant with Victory Performance Consulting, agrees. In an article on LinkedIn, Levonius points out that one of the most significant mistakes is "not coaching employees until or unless there is a performance problem."[6] He adds that this is detrimental because we tend to learn more from successes than mistakes.

While learning from failure is embraced more than it used to be, I agree with Levonius that employees want to hear about their successes, and they do learn from them. Which is why we need to train managers on how to coach employees. We also need to train managers on why employee coaching is important.

Giving Employees A Role In Performance Management

Performance management should be an employee-centric process. For that to happen, employees need to completely understand the process and their role in it. Not simply be a recipient of performance feedback. The way we do this is by making performance management a part of organizational culture, like ethical behavior, mutual respect, and exceptional customer service. If organizations are always focused on performance, then selling performance management on the same level as customer service should be fairly logical.

As we think about our own organizational cultures, we have to remember that building and maintaining a company culture requires hard work. Company cultures should be distinct. They should be open to change but not easily changed—meaning that company cultures need to be able to change with the needs of the business, but company cultures also shouldn't be easily swayed. It's a delicate balance but that's what makes company cultures so valuable.

When it comes to performance management, I believe that organizations want results and high performing employees. The question is, do organizations want the work and performance management process it takes to get what they want in terms of results and high performing employees?

The July 2018 issue of *TD Magazine* mentions a Dale Carnegie Survey[7] where 81% of leaders said their companies are committed to creating a high-performing culture but only 19% rated their culture as "excellent." There's obviously a gap between what organizations want and what exists. For performance management to truly become part of the company culture, there are a few things they need to do:

Build performance management into the talent acquisition process. For performance management to become a part of culture, it needs to be talked about on company career sites and discussed during interviews. Candidates should be asked interview questions about how the process works. New hires should receive training during orientation about performance management.

De-emphasize the chain of command. Including the performance management process in company culture means that conversations happen at *every* level and in *any* department. This is no longer a top-down process. This blows up the traditional chain of command. And organizations have to be very comfortable with that approach.

Give all employees coaching skills training. When organizations create performance management cultures, then PM isn't just another program. It's a program that drives what the organization does—how they make decisions, solve problems, etc. I can't imagine any program considered part of company culture not receiving training—and getting the resources to make training happen.

Demonstrate the process is just as important as the results. Performance management will not be successful if managers and employees love the results but hate the process. They'll view it as drudgery or a necessary evil. HR and senior management will have to show how the process is equally important. One way to do that is with stories about how the process is valuable.

Creating a performance review program isn't the same thing as creating a performance management culture. Don't get me wrong, creating a performance management program is a good thing and will bring tremendous value to your organization; however, creating a performance management culture is even better for all the reasons previously mentioned: candidates understand expectations before they take the job; new hires are given training to be successful; open communication happens at every level of the organization; and the entire process is valued, *not just the end result.*

If we think of the other components of our company culture, my guess is many of them follow the same criteria—but this is where having all stakeholders involved in performance management can create the high-performing organization everyone wants.

Stakeholders Need To Champion Performance Management

We know that performance management is more than the annual review. However, it could be a challenge if the organization doesn't view performance management in that light. They see it as little more than forms and performance reviews, which happen once a year. Employees get their pay increases and we're done until next year. If there's a problem, we have a training session and that's it.

Performance management can still accomplish all of the compliance-related needs of the organization while at the same time create a process that is perceived as valuable by managers and employees. There's been a lot of negative commentary about performance management, but we can't become defensive and resistant to change. It's time for us to champion the change we want to see.

How do we make performance management an ongoing process? Here are a few ideas discussed in this chapter. Of note—they all involve consistency.

Get consistent support from management. Organizations should have clear performance standards that align with the business, so managers are completely onboard. In addition, management should support the allocation of resources to make the process successful.

Create consistent performance standards. Organizations need performance standards as part of their consumer brand, product quality criteria, and customer service (just to name a few). Employee performance should be measured against the standard.

Train managers to provide consistent feedback and communication. Regardless of the performance review, effective feedback conversations still need to happen. Giving managers training and guidance benefits the employee and the company.

Build an effective process. Performance management technology solutions can reduce administrative burden, freeing up managers and human resources to focus on delivering feedback.

Changing people's opinions about performance management might not happen overnight—but if there's one thing that can make a significant change, it's viewing performance management as a process. This shift in mindset can help the organization build a performance management process that gets the support it needs in terms of technology solutions and manager training to achieve company goals.

One other reminder about performance management—it isn't just a two-person activity. It can easily involve more people than the traditional manager/employee relationship, mirroring today's more open and collaborative work environments. Performance management can include feedback, coaching, and learning. It's a process that becomes part of the everyday organizational culture.

FOCUS ON THE FRONTLINE

1. Make sure your performance management process is easy to explain and focused on aligning individual contributors—including those on the frontline—with organizational strategy.
2. Talk with employees about the external and internal factors impacting their performance and collaboratively work to optimize them.
3. Make sure your performance management process is an open, ongoing one—not a one-a-year exercise in documentation.
4. Separate the performance management process from conversations about compensation—the goals are different.
5. Empower your managers—including those on the frontline—to take an active role in performance management—it's not solely the purview of HR.

ENDNOTES

[1] Association for Talent Development. 2017 State of the Industry Report. https://www.td.org/research-reports/2017-state-of-the-industry

[2] Kronos Incorporated Survey 2016. The Employee Burnout Crisis. https://www.kronos.com/resources/employee-burnout-crisis

[3] Terry Bickham, *ATD Talent Management Handbook* (Alexandria, VA: Association for Talent Development, 2015). https://www.td.org/books/atd-talent-management-handbook

[4] Sharlyn Lauby, *HR Bartender*, May 18, 2017, "Human Resources Is the Architect of Work." https://www.hrbartender.com/2017/employee-engagement/hr-architect-work/

[5] Dana Robinson, "What Core Competencies Do Performance Consultants Need?" *Association for Talent Development* (February 21, 2018). https://www.td.org/insights/what-core-competencies-do-performance-consultants-need

[6] Don Levonius, "Want Employee Training to Stick? Teach Your Leaders to Coach," *LinkedIn* (April 23, 2017). https://www.linkedin.com/pulse/want-employee-training-stick-teach-your-leaders-coach-don-levonius/

[7] Mark Marone, "Not All Leaders Buy Into the Power of Culture," *TD Magazine* (July 2018). https://www.td.org/magazines/td-magazine/not-all-leaders-buy-into-the-power-of-culture

REFERENCES

Accenture. (2016). The Fourth Annual Accenture Strategy 2016 US College Graduate Employment Study. https://www.businesswire.com/news/home/20160512005097/en/2016-U.S.-College-Graduates-Culture-Compensation-Accenture

Cross, Rob, Reb Rebele, and Adam Grant. "Collaborative Overload." Harvard Business Review, January/February 2016. https://hbr.org/2016/01/collaborative-overload

Julia Hobsbawm is an entrepreneur, writer, and speaker who specializes in commenting on modern connectedness and its discontents, the future of work, technology, digital distraction, and how humans cope in a machine age. She speaks to corporate audiences, global institutions and symposiums—and was recently praised by James Harding, former Editor of *The Times* and BBC News Director, as "one of the UK's leading public intellectuals." An Honorary Visiting Professor in Workplace Social Health at London's Cass Business School, Ms. Hobsbawm is also Editor-at-Large for Arianna Huffington's well-being portal *Thrive Global*, columnist for *Strategy + Business Magazine*, blogger for the World Economic Forum, and podcast presenter of "The Human and Machine." Her book, *Fully Connected: Social Health in an Age of Overload,* was shortlisted for Business Book of the Year and Management Book of the Year. Her new book, *The Simplicity Principle: 6 Ways to Find Your Focus and Improve Productivity*, will be published in April 2020. Ms. Hobsbawm founded the content and connection business Editorial Intelligence in 2005, and in 2015 she was awarded the OBE (Officer of the Most Excellent Order of The British Empire) for her services to business in The Queen's Birthday Honors List.

CHAPTER NINE

The Power Of Being Human In Today's Technologically Advanced Workplace

Julia Hobsbawm, OBE
Founder, Editorial Intelligence
Author, Speaker, Honorary Visiting Professor

> "Technology is how a society copes with physical reality; how people get and keep and cook food, how they clothe themselves, what their power sources are, what they build with and what they build."[1]
>
> – Ursula K. Le Guin: A Rant About "Technology"

Today, technology has become our main co-worker. This was not always the case. The predominantly manual world of work was overturned only as recently as the Industrial Revolution a couple of centuries ago—a historical nanosecond.

The mass connected computerized technologies pervasive in society today are even more recent: Arguably the timeline runs most recently from the advent of the Personal Computer (1981); the Windows operating system (1985); the World Wide Web (1989); geolocation and GPS (1995); the Apple App Store launch (2008); Cloud Computing (1996);[2] Google (1998); the Internet of Things (1999); Facebook (2004); and on to today in which the unified communications of Artificial Intelligence (AI), Virtual Reality (VR), and Robotics are the current big tech beasts.

While offices, factories, laboratories, and all workplaces have had their share of incoming technology over the decades and centuries, until the 1980s progress was much slower. It is extraordinary to think that 90%[3] of today's US businesses use social media for marketing, when the overall business use of social networks is under a decade old.

Today's digital technologies, electronic tools, devices, and resources which store, convey, convert, and transmit digital data from parking tickets to payroll, from homework to hourly schedules, from shared workflows to, of course, email, all add significant layers of learning, time, and choice to those organizing workplaces, and to those working in them.

How does all of this change sit with us, sitting at a desk or tapping away in our "home office"? Do we feel liberated, exhilarated, or enslaved? In truth, as often in life, it is a bit of both.

Hybrid Humans

Here's an analogy: Cars. Modern cities and society have been defined by and designed for the automobile, the most pervasive personal piece of technology until the computer and the mobile phone. The 4th Industrial Revolution and the cultural earthquake in values around climate change and sustainability has recently disrupted this model. Debate has opened in politics and culture around how and why we use cars.

At the same time, cars themselves are undergoing a manufacturing, AI, and fuel revolution with hybrid models and driverless versions emerging, as we ask ourselves big questions: who do we design cities for, the human or the machine? And if we do have cars, do we want our autonomy as humans to be withdrawn? Research suggests that in terms of consumer confidence, we want a human at the wheel.[4]

A similarly radical kind of transition is taking place with human work, the workplace, and the debates about who is in the driver's seat, so to speak. "The worker" is evolving from belonging to two basic groups—Manual and Professional—into something altogether more hybrid itself. A recent study by the information technology company Unisys[5] identifies six types of digital worker: Knowledge Worker, Creative Worker, Shift Worker, Gig Worker, Field Worker, and Branch Worker. Each job demographic is divided into those who work for organizations labelled either "technology leaders" or "technology laggards." The clear implication is both that no job is untouched by technology anymore, and that successful recruitment, retention and overall organizational success hinge critically on the relationship anyone in the "worker chain" has to technology.

Today's hybrid human worker needs to be flexible in outlook, location, and skills. They need both hard and soft skills. They often need to make their own luck,

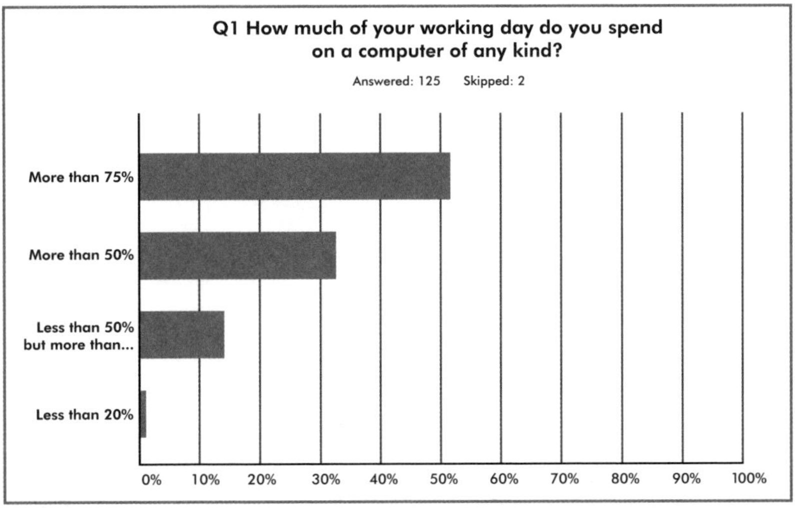

being "full time contractor" and divorced from a traditional set of hard-fought and hard-won worker rights.

While hard and soft skills are increasingly required, no one is completely sure where the priorities lie between the two (more on this from my colleague John Hollon later in this book). Employers are obsessed with reskilling, because this enables them to grow faster, to be efficient, and to develop their workforces for the future. But which particular skills, and for what purpose?

Emerging trends from LinkedIn's third annual Workplace Learning Report,[6] which surveyed more than 1,200 talent developers and over 2,000 workplace learners, are revealing: "Foundational efforts like soft skills will remain important in 2019, but will no longer take up the majority of a talent developer's time," commenting that "with the shortening shelf life of skills, creating and maintaining market leadership hinges on talent development's ability to help employees acquire and grow the right skills."

The report lists 11 "most in demand" hard skills—including "cloud computing," "artificial intelligence," and "UX design," twice as many as listed "soft skills," such as "persuasion" and "collaboration." Interestingly, "analytical reasoning" is listed as both a hard skill and a soft skill, which underscores the overlap here: The human and machine need each other, *and* one is never too far from the other.

#GenMobile

Workers may be physically far from each other in the same "place" of work. There's a hip new demographic in town: *#GenMobile*,[7] 40% of whom anticipate an increase in remote working and who want to work anywhere except an office. The desire for mobility may explain why there has been so little resistance amongst workers to the tremendous changes of our times. Unlike resistant nineteenth century Luddites destroying new machines and mills in protest of the destruction of manual jobs, twenty-first century workers embrace technology even as they know that automation may be a considerable threat to them.

Mobility and the smartphone have also ushered in far less static workplace practices. This is attracting and retaining new employees and contractors. There are actually significantly more skilled jobs than there are workers. Estimates vary, but some say the supply/demand shortages could result in as many as 85 million unfilled jobs[8] across financial and business services, technology, and media by 2030.

Take the pioneering HR work at Netflix[9] that saw trends such as unlimited holidays and reducing appraisals in favor of a more flexible, mobile system. Movement is the leitmotif of the current working era. You must be mobile, enable mobility, and embody its essence.

Two-Speed Workplace

"Move fast and break things" was the famous Mark Zuckerberg rallying cry[10] for this superfast, super broadband era. A little nagging voice at the back of my mind says that the workplace is not just speeding up, but becoming two-speed. Those with the skills in industries with skills shortages, are increasingly being loaded up with perks and incentives at a cost of a cluttered and complex landscape of onboarding, training, and reskilling. For those without skills, or with old skills, the race is on to rescue them from employment oblivion.[11]

In both cases, being a human who works has become a matter of navigating and negotiating through a forest of technology which, even when it liberates and improves productivity, creativity, and engagement also adds layers of complexity and strains mental attention. Where we work and how we work has become a perpetual dance between people and platforms.

How then, do we apply what we know as humans to how we best work with technology? Let's find out.

Ferocious Flux

> "We live in a time of ferocious flux and change ... like holding fast to a whale even as it plunges to the bottom of the sea."
>
> – Caitlin Moran: *The Times*, April 2019

The British writer Caitlin Moran coined the phrase "ferocious flux" and ascribed it to current politics and the loss of faith in the old systems "formed in different centuries, with different industries, populations, technologies, and economies."[12]

The word "flux" means change, and more specifically constant change. Unlike change that happens en route to a known and finite end point (e.g., a pregnancy or a set of exams), flux involves continuous churn for its own sake, a state of infinity. The lack of clarity in a flux state adds to a sense of uncertainty or even crisis.

The workplace is quite definitely in ferocious flux. Instability has become built-in to every aspect of every organization. While big leaps of technology affecting our lives have happened before, the so-called "4th Industrial Revolution" has ushered in what the World Economic Forum's Founder Klaus Schwab described as "in its scale, scope and complexity, unlike anything humankind has experienced before."[13]

In my own research, I have heard from countless business leaders about how everyone takes surround-sound technology completely for granted, constantly updating their installed hardware, software, platforms, and devices. One company leader described how 80% of their conference rooms are fitted with video. Another says that every one of their 25,000-strong U.K. workforce are issued iPhones upon hire with training that goes alongside regulatory and company rules about what can and cannot be looked at, downloaded, or used. Another described a ten-year transition to "re-platform" across several kinds of systems in a single department.

A workplace that constantly must update and replace its products and services is not for the faint-hearted. Flux like this can be exhausting and expensive. Investment in technology must be continuous to make it both customer and worker-friendly, as well as legally compliant.

Ferocious flux quickly turns furious when a human is not there to fix a problem that may not be caused by technology, but which cannot be solved by it either. As the social theorist Hannah Arendt put it so well in her seminal book *The Human Condition*:[14] "The whole factual world of human affairs depends for its reality and its continued existence first, upon the presence of others who have seen and heard and will remember."

Yet the fact is that today the whole world of human affairs is at risk of turning away from itself and towards its non-human colleagues. We have spent a quick 30 years learning to outsource ourselves to technology, and it is time to reclaim or at least rebalance our priorities.

The personification of non-human colleagues are of course Robots (interestingly, research shows how quickly humans invest actual human qualities in robots, giving them personal attributes and hugs[15]) despite the fact that, not only are they not actually human, but a poor imitation of them in anything resembling emotional literacy or feelings. To feel usurped in your family is a well-known emotional and psychological trauma. The workplace, facing the arrival of AI is no different: Yes, it may make life easier and faster, but it is going to require considerable new "onboarding" techniques to get it right.

No-one can agree on how many robots are coming, and how exactly they will impact jobs, but The World Economic Forum[16] predicts that 75 million jobs are to be displaced by 2022 in 20 major economies.

Although an exhaustive study of 20,000 employers in 42 countries by the workforce consultancy Manpower Group[17] shows that 86% believe automation will create jobs, the precondition is a continuous revolution in skills and training—a new workforce with new skills for new times. This is well-intentioned, but it involves constant change.

It is for this reason that words like "resilience" and "agile" have become dominant in business management theory and practice. The obvious point is this: You don't just need any old skills in the 4th industrial revolutionary workplace—you need survival skills.

Much of this is because down on the ground at work, at a granular, human level, the flux has its origin in something very fundamental: a gigantic mismatch between the scale, speed, and complexity of applications and algorithms, and their impact on the physical and neurological, cultural, and social structure of the mere mortals using them to do their daily work.

The Death Of Distance

Down on the ground at work, we are living with the so-called "death of distance,"[18] where mobile technology has reduced the space between remote server-based computers to desktops, laptops, and now mobile phones. The acronym that says it all for me is "BYOD" which stands for "Bring your Own Device,"[19] and encourages workers to connect to a corporate network and work remotely the rest of the time: To be "always on."[20]

BYOD symbolizes the collapse in boundaries between home and work. It coincides, ten years on, with "Gen Z" coming into the workforce. This is the generation that came after their older "digitally native" Millennial colleagues, and for whom, research shows, being mobile is possibly the single most important thing to them at work.[21]

The Digital Day

It is this challenge, to keep up with quantum mechanics in our normal human bodies and minds, which is the thing that should be keeping us up at night. It certainly dominates the working day.

Global research of 3,000 workers conducted by Kronos' Workforce Institute found that 79% of workers experience some kind of burnout at work, with 86% losing time on "work-specific tasks unrelated to their core job." Of note too, 40% say that an hour or more a day is lost to "administrative tasks that do not drive value for their organization."[22]

My own research[23] of 2,500 UK professionals showed that 75% of respondents use more than three devices at work, with over 75 different formats and platforms in use: From email and social media systems to shared document services, databases, and specific task-related platforms and intranets. The curse for many is email, group chats, and group messages. Of email, one person commented, "I get 3–4k emails per month. Imagine having to answer four thousand letters a month!"

As one of my interviewees put it to me:

"We're still managing an industrial 8:30am–5:30pm day, but a digital day doesn't look like fixed time slots. We're in an always-on knowledge and digital economy where people can work anywhere and at any time, and they want to, but we are still making people work the old work shift. So, the modern workplace is fatiguing people, with their expectations not balanced against reality and us not giving our workforces the tools to juggle a complex life."

That said, none of us would willingly forgo our digital enhancements. The Editorial Intelligence research shows that only 5% feel they are a "necessary evil." Could you do your job without a device of any kind, or the internet, or the cloud? Probably not. Yet you could, in many instances, not work from the office, both because this is more culturally accepted but also because in a purely physical way you no longer need to.

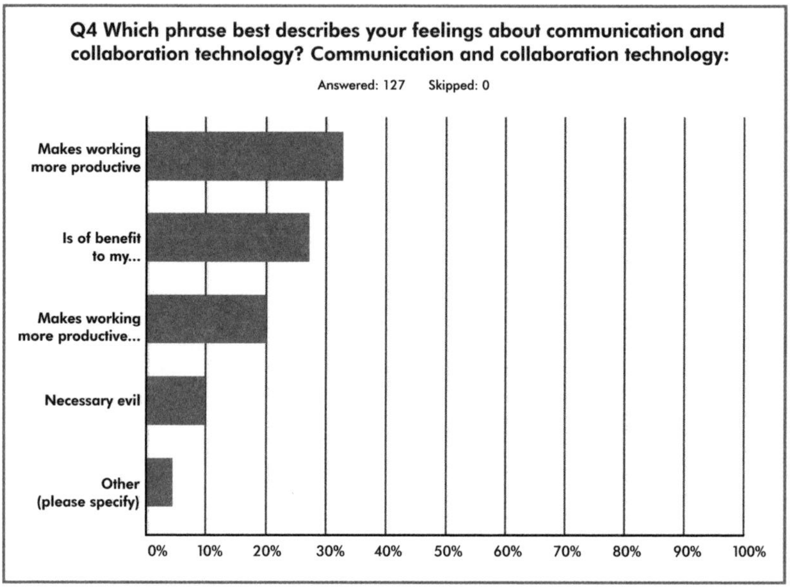

But, of course, humans are social, not mechanical. We do need people around us, and we do crave connection. The risk of a workplace that prioritizes purely technological connection over human face-to-face connections flies in the face of common sense and that of science too: empirically a face-to-face request is 34 times more successful than one delivered by email.[24]

The point about the speed and scale of change—some 2.5 billion emails flying around the world each day, computing capacity measured in trillions of gigabytes—is that it creates instability, which brings with it anxiety.

Yet if the purpose—and "purpose" is a big word in business these days[25]—of technology is to increase productivity, wealth, and wellbeing in the economy and amongst citizens, something is not quite working, as the wellbeing and productivity of workers does not seem to be improving.

Stressbusting

The common term for anxiety at work is stress, and the statistics about its prevalence in the workplace are enormous. In the U.K. where I am based, 15 million working days per year—nearly 60% of all working days—are lost to ill health attributed to stress and anxiety.[26] In the US stress-related absenteeism costs $300 billion per year.[27]

Almost every one of the leaders I have interviewed in my research raised the question of stress, at either a personal or a structural level. "People believe that unless you are working 24/7, every minute, you're not a productive or loyal employee, despite the fact that there is a ton of evidence that this is wrong. Data appears not to change people's beliefs," Catherine Lynch, Chief People Officer of the telecoms company Virgin Media, told me.

When I interviewed Professor Jeffrey Pfeffer,[28] a distinguished Stanford University academic who specializes in analyzing the toxic workplace, he was bleak in his prescription, citing more than just ferocious flux. He believes that wilful corporate neglect is at play and told me, "The issue isn't the technology: the issue is how that technology is employed. So it comes down to values. What are the values that are going to guide how we deploy the technology? What I see right now is that human health and wellbeing, equity, social connection—humanistic values—are currently peripheral to dominant values of growth. We are not inevitably and invariably doomed and there is a win-win to be attained, but I don't see a sufficient number of companies or governments working towards that."

There are cases, though, where governments are stepping in. As we are writing this book, the Court of Justice of the European Union issued a ruling that states, in part, "in order to ensure the effectiveness of the rights provided for in the Working Time Directive and the Charter, the Member States must require employers to set up an objective, reliable and accessible system enabling the duration of time worked each day by each worker to be measured." The objective of the ruling is to ensure better protection of the safety and health of workers,[31] and illustrates the shift towards a sense of Social Health amongst at least some policy makers. The challenge is on for HR and People directors to embrace this change and be on the front, not the back foot.

At this point you may be wondering where corporate wellbeing[29] comes in: This has become a firm boardroom favorite, and the rise of investment in mental health and physical health, both financially and culturally is impressive.[30] Mindfulness is an acknowledged form of wellbeing, with the global giant SAP being the first company in the world to appoint a Chief Mindfulness Officer, Peter Bostelmann, whose work is highly impressive. I hope that our understanding of mindfulness makes it an outlier for a deeper dive into social health solutions for stress at work. We certainly do have data on the way people use technology at work, and the way it makes them feel. Furthermore, we have at our disposal the neuroscience and social science around the limits of human focus, attention, and cognitive load.

We know now that the brain has rather a limited cognitive capacity and is not good at multitasking[31] (contrary to popular myth). More than this, human beings go into stress mode when faced with excessive choice and excessive stimulus.[32] I was not surprised by research showing that it takes approximately 20 minutes to refocus attention after becoming distracted.[33]

The Workforce Of The Future

As a report by McKinsey on the workforce of the future noted: "automation will create an opportunity for those in work to make use of the innate human skills that machines have the hardest time replicating: social and emotional capabilities, expertise, coaching ... creativity."[34] Human strength is to mitigate a world increasingly mediated by screen.

It is important that we keep perspective, that we don't become overly mistrustful. Yet clearly, we simply cannot rely exclusively on the robot or the chatbot (IBM says by 2020, 85% of all customer interactions will be handled without a human agent) because when we do, we fall faster and further into a distinctly inhuman place, where the very idea of untangling the technology becomes infinitely more expensive and exhausting than planning its real operational impact in the first place.

My own research[35] shows that amongst highly qualified professionals, nearly 60% feel positively that communication and collaboration technology make working life better and more productive, with 30% saying they would not limit the use of technology for their job under any circumstances.

Nevertheless, that leaves 54% of respondents who would like to "streamline" their use of technology "both when working at home and the office." One thing is clear, however: human skills and being human are what matters a great deal to a very important constituency—customers. PWC's customer experience report "Experience is Everything"[36] notes that "human interaction matters now—and 82% of US and 74% of non-US consumers want more of it in the future."

The first thing we can do is become far more nuanced in how we judge our relationship with this "third person in the room," and begin by recognizing the "otherness" of the digital product and the digital dimension.

The Power Of Being Human

The average human brain has 100 billion neurons firing in it at any time. The fastest supercomputer outpaces us in measurements so large many of us don't even know they exist: if you knew what a Petaflop is I would be surprised.[37] That is a thousand trillion "floating point" operations per second.

If we are measuring speed and scale, the human is at a disadvantage. But the history of humanity is that we create extraordinary tools and use them to develop and build something which can't quite be measured: society.

Neuroscience shows that the default position of the healthy human brain at rest is to concern itself with one thing and one thing alone above all other thoughts and tasks: love. The social condition of the human is our defining speed, scale, and strength.

So, when we look at the human in the era of applications, algorithms, robotics, machine learning, and that wonderfully named limitless "cloud," it's important to remember the tension that the human is ground-based, non-flying, limited, and irreplaceable.

From my own research for this chapter, the landscape of work is one, in the main, of freedom alongside complexity. So only 3% say that "all technology does is complicate tasks," with 54% agreeing with the statement that "Technology speeds up how quickly you can do things." That said, 61% felt that work-related time is affected by technology with "pluses and minuses equally spread."

I asked people to comment freely after they had ticked the data boxes and they did. One said this: "Technology is no substitute for leadership, innovation, entrepreneurship, and good management at work. Technology is like office space:

It can divide people or unite them ... don't force people to run around in circles, climb over furniture, and crawl through a maze to get a task done."

Let that be the last word. If your organization is a maze (albeit a cloud-based one); if your office and technology divides instead of unites; if you expect your humans to think in petaflops rather than neurons: think again. Celebrate the resource which is not—with careful conservation, sustainability and management—going to match the digital with a strange, wonderful, analogue power: the power of being human.

FOCUS ON THE FRONTLINE

1. As more and more "hard skills" will be able to be completed by machines, robots and AI, employers must focus on the "soft skills" that make humans irreplaceable and make sure frontline employees are hired and trained for these skills.
2. Embrace mobile technology: Your frontline workforce wants the flexibility that mobile technologies can support. In order to attract and retain them you must "be mobile, enable mobility, and embody its essence."
3. Remember that today's workers are available and "always on" in a way they were not in the past, yet we are often expecting an old fashioned eight-hour day out of them on top of always on connectivity. Look for ways to provide flexibility to your frontline workforce in recognition of this seismic shift in the way we work.
4. There is such thing as too much connectivity and it's resulting in stress and burnout. Look for ways to promote wellness and mindfulness with your frontline workforce and find ways to encourage disconnecting at times.
5. Technology should make the lives of your frontline workforce better—talk to them about if this is how they feel or not. If it's not, look for ways to change the way they use technology in order to better support success.

ENDNOTES

[1] *Ursulakleguin.com.* A Rant About "Technology" (2004). https://conversations.e-flux.com/t/ursula-k-le-guin-a-rant-about-technology/3977

[2] Antonio Regalado, "Who Coined 'Cloud Computing'?" *MIT Technology Review* (October 2011). https://www.technologyreview.com/s/425970/who-coined-cloud-computing/

[3] Statista. Social Media Marketing Usage Rate in the United States from 2013 to 2019. https://www.statista.com/statistics/203513/usage-trands-of-social-media-platforms-in-marketing/

[4] Greg Gardner, "Autonomous Vehicles Face Consumer Attitude Problem: Cox Automotive," *Forbes* (Aug 16, 2018). https://www.forbes.com/sites/greggardner/2018/08/16/autonomous-vehicles-face-consumer-attitude-and-congestion-problems/#463e874e4e1a

[5] Unisys. The New Digital Workplace Divide (2018). https://www.unisys.com/digitalworkplacedivide

[6] LinkedIn. Workplace Learning Report Key Findings: Why 2019 is the Breakout Year for the Talent Developer (2019). https://learning.linkedin.com/resources/workplace-learning-report

[7] Aruba Networks. Are you Ready for #GenMobile? (2014). https://www.arubanetworks.com/pdf/solutions/GenMobile_Report.pdf

[8] Korn Ferry. Global Talent Crunch Survey (2018). https://www.recruitment-international.co.uk/blog/2018/05/skills-shortages-could-impede-global-growth-says-korn-ferry

[9] See Patty McCord's memoir *Powerful: Building a Culture of Freedom and Responsibility* (San Francisco: Silicon Guild, 2017). https://www.amazon.com/Powerful-Building-Culture-Freedom-Responsibility/dp/1939714095

[10] This quote by Mark Zuckerberg is famously used to illustrate the essence of tech disruption. https://www.wired.com/2015/03/mark-zuckerberg-f8-keynote/

[11] James Manyika, Michael Chui, Mehdi Miremadi, Jacques Bughin, Katy George, Paul Willmott, and Martin Dewhurst, *"A Future that Works: Automation, Employment and Productivity,"* McKinsey Global Institute, January 2017. https://www.mckinsey.com/~/media/mckinsey/featured%20insights/Digital%20Disruption/Harnessing%20automation%20for%20a%20future%20that%20works/MGI-A-future-that-works-Executive-summary.ashx

[12] Caitlin Moran, "I've Lost My Political Faith," *The Times* (April 5, 2019). https://www.thetimes.co.uk/article/caitlin-moran-i-ve-lost-my-political-faith-and-it-s-such-a-relief-mjrg8w3nl

[13] Klaus Schwab, *"The Fourth Industrial Revolution: What it Means, How to Respond,"* World Economic Forum, January 2016. https://www.weforum.org/agenda/2016/01/the-fourth-industrial-revolution-what-it-means-and-how-to-respond/

[14] Hannah Arendt, *The Human Condition* (Chicago: University of Chicago Press, 1958 and republished in 1998). https://www.amazon.com/Human-Condition-2nd-Hannah-Arendt/dp/0226025985

[15] MIT has extensively studied the way humans project social qualities on to robots. https://www.media.mit.edu/posts/making-new-robot-friends/

[16] World Economic Forum. The Future of Jobs Report (2018). https://www.weforum.org/reports/the-future-of-jobs-report-2018

Also The RSA. The Four Futures of Work: Coping with Uncertainty in an Age of Radical Technologies Report (2018). https://www.thersa.org/discover/publications-and-articles/reports/the-four-futures-of-work-coping-with-uncertainty-in-an-age-of-radical-technologies

17 ManpowerGroup. Skills Revolution 2.0 (2018) https://www.manpowergroup.com/wps/wcm/connect/59db87a7-16c6-490d-ae70-1bd7a322c240/Robots_Need_Not_Apply.pdf?MOD=AJPERES

18 Frances Cairncross, *The Death of Distance: How the Communications Revolution is Changing Our Lives* (London: Texere Publishing Limited; Boston: Harvard Business School Press, 1997 and updated 2001). https://www.amazon.com/Death-Distance-Communications-Revolution-Changing/dp/157851438X

19 Begun by technology firm Intel Corporation in 2009. https://www.intel.com/content/www/us/en/company-overview/company-overview.html

20 Kronos Workforce Institute Europe. Always on Con Report (2017). https://www.kronos.co.uk/about-us/newsroom/french-and-german-workers-consistently-outperforming-brits-work

21 Aruba Networks. Are you Ready for #GenMobile? (2014). https://www.arubanetworks.com/pdf/solutions/GenMobile_Report.pdf

22 Kronos Workforce Institute Research. The £60bn Question (2016). https://www.kronos.co.uk/resources/work-engaged-ps60bn-question-press-version

23 Editorial Intelligence Research (2019). https://www.editorialintelligence.com/index.html

24 Vanessa K. Bohns, "A Face-to-Face Request Is 34 Times More Successful Than an Email," *Harvard Business Review* (April 11, 2017). https://hbr.org/2017/04/a-face-to-face-request-is-34-times-more-successful-than-an-email

25 The British Academy. Future of the Corporation: Research Summaries (2018). https://www.thebritishacademy.ac.uk/programmes/future-of-the-corporation

26 Health and Safety Executive. Working days lost in Great Britain Data (2017/2018). http://www.hse.gov.uk/statistics/dayslost.htm

27 APA Center for Organizational Excellence. The American Institute of Stress Data (2019). http://www.apaexcellence.org/resources/special-topics/work-stress

28 See Jeffrey Pfeffer, *Dying for a Paycheck: How Modern Management Harms Employee Health and Company Performance—And What We Can Do About It* (New York: Harper Collins, 2018). https://www.amazon.com/Dying-Paycheck-Management-Employee-Performance/dp/0062800922

29 Julia Hobsbawm, "Why Corporate Wellness Programs Fall Short," *Strategy + Business* (September 28, 2018). https://www.strategy-business.com/blog/Why-Corporate-Wellness-Programs-Fall-Short?gko=6dda6

30 Court of Justice of the European Union. Press Release No 61/19 (May 14, 2019). https://curia.europa.eu/jcms/upload/docs/application/pdf/2019-05/cp190061en.pdf

31 Julia Hobsbawm, "Overcoming Digital Distraction: Six Steps to Help You Limit Connectivity and Improve Your Focus and Productivity," *Strategy + Business Blog* (January 23, 2019). https://www.strategy-business.com/blog/Overcoming-Digital-Distraction

32 Harvard Health Publishing. Understanding the Stress Response. (May 1, 2018). https://www.health.harvard.edu/staying-healthy/understanding-the-stress-response

33 Gloria Mark, Daniel Gudith and Ulrich Klocke, "The cost of interrupted work: More Speed and Stress," *ACM Digital Library CHI '08 Proceedings of the SIGCHI Conference on Human Factors in Computing Systems* (April, 2008). https://dl.acm.org/citation.cfm?id=1357072

34 James Manyika, Michael Chui, Mehdi Miremadi, Jacques Bughin, Katy George, Paul Willmott, and Martin Dewhurst, *"A Future that Works: Automation, Employment and Productivity,"* McKinsey Global Institute, January 2017. https://www.mckinsey.com/~/media/mckinsey/featured%20insights/Digital%20Disruption/Harnessing%20automation%20for%20a%20future%20that%20works/MGI-A-future-that-works-Executive-summary.ashx

35 Editorial Intelligence Network Survey (April 2019). https://www.editorialintelligence.com/index.html

36 David Clarke and Ron Kinghorn, "Experience is everything: Here's how to get it right," *PWC Report*, (2018). https://www.pwc.com/us/en/services/consulting/library/consumer-intelligence-series/future-of-customer-experience.html

37 Indiana University. Measure Computer Performance in FLOPS. (2019). https://kb.iu.edu/d/apeq#measure-flops

SECTION THREE

WORK INSPIRED

Your people are the heart of your organization. Build a culture that empowers employees to reach their full potential, work their way, and work smarter. You'll unleash exceptional results for your organization and all of its stakeholders.

Alexandra Levit is the internationally best-selling author of *Humanity Works* and *They Don't Teach Corporate in College*, as well as a globally recognized consultant, speaker, workplace expert, and futurist. She has conducted proprietary research on the future of work, technology adoption, the millennial generation, gender differences and bias, and the skills gap. She is a former syndicated columnist for *The Wall Street Journal* and writer for *The New York Times, Fast Company*, and *Forbes*. In 2017, she became a partner at organizational development firm PeopleResults. She served as a member of Business Roundtable's Springboard Project, which advised the Obama Administration, the US Department of Labor, and the US Department of Defense on current employment issues. She was named an American Management Association Top Leader, as well as *Money Magazine's* Online Career Expert of the Year. Ms. Levit received her BS and the prestigious Emerging Leader Award from Northwestern University. She is a member of the University's Council of 100 and Young Entrepreneur Council and this year received the Thinkers50 Radar Award for the dissemination of forward-thinking business ideas.

CHAPTER TEN

The Future Of Education

Alexandra Levit
Partner, PeopleResults
Author, Speaker, Futurist

My son is 11 years old and attends public school in Oak Park, Illinois, a progressive neighborhood to the west of downtown Chicago. As a member of Generation Z (born 1996 - 2012), my son learns differently than his much-older peers. He completes online math coursework with students at his level from all over the world. In social studies, he participates in a flipped classroom, a new model in which students read about a subject first, and then the teacher facilitates a discussion rather than introducing a lesson.

If something interests him, my son doesn't wait for the topic to find its way onto the official curriculum. He uses software installed on his tablet to take short, massive, open, online courses and complete quizzes to show proficiency. And most importantly, my son recognizes that there's no such thing as being "done" with learning. There is always more information he can consume and new ways he can manipulate data. My son is a proud member of the first generation of learning agile students. But is the business world ready to take advantage of his skills?

In this chapter, we'll explore how traditional schools are evolving to meet the needs of the modern workforce and examine alternative education methods such as microcredentials and certifications that move with the employee. We'll describe how schools and companies are partnering to close skills gaps and improve talent pipelines, and advise how you as a leader can emphasize the increasingly essential notion of learning agility.

This Isn't Your Mother's (Or Even Your) Elementary School

I don't know about you, but my K-12 years were marked by structure. You knew where you were supposed to be and what you were supposed to be doing every minute. You learned "standard" subjects like math, reading, and science. Lessons didn't change from year to year, and you had homework every night, and a test at the end of each unit.

Today's schools are different, although the changes are subtler in some. Generally, education is becoming more personalized and informal. With the help of in-classroom technology, children learn at their own pace and, like my son, select topics of interest to them. The "science fair" model of working on a project solo and displaying your findings / creations to parents, teachers, and peers has extended to other subjects. Many teachers have replaced the rigid form of homework with more free-form instruction to read or talk with your parents and friends about what you're learning. Some school systems, for example the Croton/Harmon district in Westchester, NY, have even abolished grades until high school. One desired outcome is that students push themselves rather than stopping their efforts once they adhere to a predetermined standard.

In the classroom itself, your seating might be far more comfortable. To encourage creativity, some schools have replaced metal chairs and desks with bean bags and rugs. Instead of writing on a white board, you'll show your work on a larger smartboard or a smaller laptop or tablet. Via a variety of software offerings, teachers can review work and respond with feedback in real-time.

Private schools obviously have the most leeway when it comes to driving the future of education. According to a recent *CNN* article by Katie Pisa, Portfolio School in New York City is a vibrant example of a micro-school, which aims to broaden children's creativity, and is based on the philosophy that kids need an interdisciplinary education model. The open floor-plan school says it's using the most current research about education to reinvent everything about school from the curriculum and classroom management to the student's engagement with the outside world. Portfolio mixes technology into learning experiences, encouraging kids to spend time "tinkering."

Pisa also highlighted the Steve Jobs Schools in the Netherlands (not affiliated with the Apple founder), which give elementary students total control over the subjects they study, how they want to learn, and at what pace. Teachers are mentors and coaches, and students are grouped by their strengths rather than their ages. In Singapore, the robot Pepper helps preschool teachers impart social skills, and in the United Kingdom, the Sevenoaks School outside of London uses virtual reality to take students on field trips to other geographies and historical time periods and create their own three-dimensional paintings.

As you might be thinking, the way today's student learns is not necessarily well-suited to a single degree program at the university level. And indeed, skill requirements that will power tomorrow's organizations and careers are so fluid that single degree programs might not even make sense for much longer. This is where the microcredential comes in.

Microcredentials Transform Career-Related Learning

A microcredential is a digital certification indicating competency in a skill. A white paper produced by Digital Promise and the Center for Teacher Quality defined a microcredential as competency-based, self-directed, sharable, personalized, and available on demand. Created in direct response to the needs of educators, students, and organizations, microcredentials involve the demonstration of new expertise, have job-embedded learning and application, and specify learning by doing. Learners advance to higher levels based on their mastery of concepts and skills regardless of their background or how or when they accessed the training.

According to a report by iNACOL and Competency Works, being competency-based means that microcredential training includes explicit, measurable, and transferable learning objectives. It is usually brief (i.e., MUCH faster than a traditional degree program). Assessment is meaningful and positive, and learners receive timely and differentiated support. The designers must consider a few questions, namely: what do you want earners to be able to know or do after completing the microcredential, and what evidence can learners provide that illustrates that they know or can do it?

Microcredentials can be designed and offered in stacks, or combinations, of courses that allow a learner to achieve mastery of a broader concept. For example, Digital Promise offers the following "Learning Differences" stack to educators:

- Module 1: Demonstrate Understanding of Working Memory
- Module 2: Demonstrate Understanding of Executive Function
- Module 3: Demonstrate Understanding of Motivation
- Module 4: Build a Student-Centered Plan to Support Learning Differences

- Module 5: Apply Student-Centered Strategies to Support Learning Differences
- Module 6: Engage Your Peers in Supporting Learning Differences

Given the lightning-fast pace of technology and its integration into the workplace, it's not surprising that "show us what you know right now" microcredentialing is picking up speed as well. On the education side, Digital Promise has partnered with organizations like Bloomboard, the Friday Institute, Relay GSE, and Future Ready Schools to develop microcredentials. The Florida Department of Education and the Arkansas Department of Education are also gearing up for microcredential partnerships, as are school districts like Kettle Moraine in Wisconsin and Dysart United in Arizona.

In the business world, microcredentialing got its start with the rise of massive open online courses (MOOCs). As I shared in my book *Humanity Works: Merging Technologies and People for the Workforce of the Future*, hedge fund manager Salman Khan launched The Khan Academy as a series of YouTube video lectures intended to teach math to his young relatives. Now, the Academy houses thousands of videos on everything from art history to physics, most only a few minutes long. Udacity, Inc. offers nanodegrees, which provide training and certification in technical subjects and skills (e.g., cybersecurity, software engineering, etc.), and take six to 12 months to complete.

An intriguing development involves partnerships between high-profile companies and universities that want to help existing professionals keep up with new and more complex workforce demands. For instance, MIT and Harvard University established the nonprofit edX in 2012 to offer free versions of their online (and in some cases, in-person) coursework. MIT went a step further with its Digital Plus Programs, which provides unique certificates to employees whose organizations sponsor them. Unlike many edX classes, Digital Plus courses are much smaller and cap at around 50 students.

You CAN Take It With You: Degreed And The Growth Of Portable Education

Organizations are catching on that offering access to portable microcredentials and certifications that employees can take with them when they leave the company is a competitive differentiator. Microsoft, for example, not only has a unique badge program that provides proof of competency in given skills but is also working to standardize those badges across the technology field so employees can showcase their expertise anywhere they work in the future.

Many Fortune 500 companies from Airbnb and Mastercard to Tesla and Prudential are using certification services like *Degreed.com* to offer employees portable professional development. In 2012, co-founders David Blake and Eric Sharp started Degreed as an education technology company with the mission to "Jailbreak the Degree." The Degreed Skill Certification is a scientifically-backed process that combines skill evidence, data science, endorsers, and reviews by an expertise panel that recommends a Skill Level Ranking. The result is a professional credential based on an employee's current ability and skills that, according to the co-founders, is 95% accurate in proving skill acquisition in a universal, up-to-date way. Employers can purchase employee seats to gain certification in more than 1,500 skills and connect their people to millions of courses, videos, books, podcasts, and expert interviews. Individuals who aren't affiliated with a company can pay to be certified in one Degreed skill for approximately $100 or can purchase an unlimited certification membership for approximately $400.

How does it work, exactly? An individual asserts their skill by providing three broad statements of behaviors that demonstrate expertise. They then describe their experience with each of these skill behaviors. Finally, they provide two references who have first-hand knowledge of their skill and can vouch for the accuracy of their evidence. After the completed application is reviewed, endorsed, and assessed, skill mastery is ranked objectively on a scale from one to eight. They receive a digital certification and verification link and can share, post, and print their Degreed Skill Certification, and crucially, employees retain access to the Degreed credentials after they leave the company that initially sponsored them.

According to a recent survey of Degreed customers, active users are 50% more likely than non-users to say they're more productive and more effective in their jobs and in growing their careers, and nine in ten Degreed users agree they're able to adapt to shifting market needs faster and more efficiently.

Other Ways Schools And Companies Close Skills Gaps

In addition to expanding the use of the "official" microcredential and skill certification, universities and organizations are using other techniques to close skills gaps.

The first involves creating your own pipeline for the skills you specifically need by partnering with a university. The US Federal Bureau of Investigation (FBI) for instance, needed more cybersecurity professionals. The FBI's recruiters had challenges finding these skills in the general market and didn't want to hire people from outside the US for security reasons. So, the Bureau worked with DeVry's College of Information Sciences to create a curriculum that would target the exact skills the FBI required and send students directly there upon program completion.

Around a decade ago, school-to-employer collaboration expanded beyond the traditional college senior preparing for graduation. Many organizations shifted their recruiting attentions to internship programs for college freshmen and sophomores who could begin training over a summer or two and come in post-graduation as full-time employees who already have many of the essential skills. Still other organizations are starting with even younger candidates.

Especially in the technology space, it's not unusual to see companies in a geographic area developing longstanding relationships with junior high and high schools. Once an organization connects with a student through a bootcamp or other short-term educational program, it can keep in contact with that student—becoming involved with the student's educational decisions throughout the remainder of their K-12 and post-secondary education journeys. In some instances, by the time a student finishes college, they are so loyal to the company that helped them for years that they can't imagine launching their career anywhere else.

Many organizations are also getting creative with respect to how they train and retrain current employees. Some companies build learning portals featuring customized learning, which permit workers to take specialized, bite-sized, video-based courses on demand and access training where and when they can. An automated system keeps track of course completion and communicates with employees, managers, and HR regarding progress. As an example, AT&T's portal features a host of job categories that correspond to necessary competencies and specific learning opportunities. In every employee's dashboard, they can see whether their job is in danger of becoming obsolete, and what coursework they need to take to develop an adjacent skillset or make a career transition that facilitates ongoing competitiveness.

Every year, more organizations experiment with new technology-based learning vehicles such as augmented reality, virtual reality, gamification, and simulation. Augmented reality overlays additional, helpful information like images, diagrams, and links onto a real-world learning environment. Virtual reality projects the learner into a totally new situation—for instance, an office in a foreign country where their avatar can work for a few days or weeks to gain critical experience conducting business in that culture. Gamification applies typical elements of game playing to a work-related task, while simulations take employees through models of disruptive real-world scenarios. In my book *Humanity Works*, I shared *eLearningIndustry.com's* Li Whybrow's story of Lloyds Banking Group in the U.K., which incorporated simulation into its customer service onboarding program.

"When contact center staffers begin their careers with the bank, they spend a long time getting to know the customer call system. Staff must understand the complexity of the regulations and good practice regarding handling sensitive customer data and verification of customers," Whybrow wrote. "This can't be done using live customer data, so Lloyds Banking Group worked with several technology vendors to build a fully simulated clone of the system using synthetic data provided by the bank."

The simulation-driven program uses a walled garden, or an environment that directs the user's navigation within individual areas by facilitating a clear progression. Its strong scripting and storyboarding and rich video content help new associates build empathy with customers and learn to seek appropriate help from internal resources.

All these innovative approaches cement learning and drive action by motivating employees to move through the content completely and with attention. As we move closer to 2030, more sophisticated and immersive renderings of customized curriculums, augmented reality, virtual reality, gamification, and simulation will reinvigorate interest in and usage of eLearning.

The Rise Of Applied Technology Skills

In a recent study I conducted with DeVry University's Career Advisory Board, we asked 500 hiring managers about the skills human candidates will need in a world increasingly run by machines. Here, we discovered the desire for greater applied technical skills, or the ability to leverage technology for the benefit of an organization rather than the ability to deploy specific technologies oneself. 75% of our respondents said employees should understand how to use technology to inform and drive business decisions, while 84% claimed employees who know how to use the right tech tools in their fields are more effective.

Employees with strong applied technology skills don't program or develop new technology themselves, but they understand the software that's available to solve specific business problems, how technology-based systems integrate, and how data from disparate sources can be mined and measured. And according to DeVry's Career Advisory Board, training existing employees in these skills presents a challenge to organizations because many current professionals did not receive this type of instruction via traditional education paths. If you graduated college before 2015, you might not know anything about how technology is used in business unless you received your degree in computer science or an associated field.

It's also not something that can be done overnight—or only once. Because technology is evolving more quickly than in the past, much of applied technology skill acquisition will be spread out over an employee's lifetime. I use social media as an example for why applied technology skill training must be continuous. You might recall that a lot of companies said to themselves 10 years ago: "Wow, we better train everybody on social media and how they should use it." Well, if you did in fact conduct that training in 2009 and haven't revisited it since, you're well behind the curve because the social media world is completely different than it was a decade ago.

Fortunately, many respondents in the CAB survey understood this, and are ensuring that their workforces regularly train and retrain on applied technology skills through the development of internal courses (40%), internal trainings (38%), tuition reimbursement (35%), and external trainings (31%).

How To Foster Learning Agility In Your Team

In case it wasn't clear already, the days of learning a single skillset and being able to lean on it for the rest of your career are behind us. While it's at least partially an employee's responsibility to seek out new skills when one becomes outdated or the market demands a new one, organizations can play a critical role in cultivating a mindset of continuous, self-initiated learning and development—otherwise known as learning agility.

Learning agile people constantly seek new information, even if it conflicts with what they'd previously assumed to be true. They gain insights readily and then apply them to a diverse array of experiences. Unafraid of change, they are willing to take risks and experiment in the service of an end goal that will leave the organization better than they found it. And while status quo-oriented teammates may be threatened by them, learning agile individuals are often unperturbed by political skirmishes.

I'm fond of a survey on learning agile performed a few years ago by the Columbia University Teachers College and consulting firm Green Peak Partners. Their study found that leaders who scored highly on an assessment for learning agility also outperformed less-agile peers in revenue growth and "boss ratings" issued by their Boards. But while some degree of learning agility is innate, there is much organizations can do to encourage it. Here are a few suggestions to that effect:

- **Put learning front and center:** Integrate a variety of learning formats, including online and offline courses, coaching, mentorship, and cross-functional shadowing and experiences into your team's daily operations. Instead of insisting your employees acquire new skills on their own time, or aside from their routine responsibilities, map them to job tasks and performance evaluation. Offer rewards to team members who learn and help others to do the same.
- **Customize roles:** Provide your employees with defined choices for how they might create a work experience, work environment, and work structure that best suits their learning style. Support flexwork and alternative scheduling where you can. For example, if you have an employee who wants to work on conflict resolution and learns well on the job, you might suggest a role that has her regularly interfacing, in-person, with senior executives as opposed to her current arrangement working at home. Leaving role design completely up to the discretion of the individual employee isn't the best approach, as it may create "analysis paralysis"—not to mention team confusion. Also, you should limit the frequency with which employees revisit their roles. Prompt them to think in timeframes of one to three years so they can focus on concrete goals and limit their learning options and activities to a reasonable and effective number. You don't have to accept every role suggestion an employee makes, and if a teammate's plan for a new role is unorthodox, set up a pilot to test the scenario before committing to a permanent arrangement.

- **Reward sideways or lateral moves:** If your reward structure is tied exclusively to promotion up the ladder, you might want to revisit that. In the 21st century work world, employees should be compensated for achieving learning-oriented goals and the developing of cross-functional expertise that will help the organization sustain its overall agility. Make sure your CEO is willing to communicate support for lateral moves, and that your team is aware of opportunities to learn and grow in different parts of the organization. If you can, put your employees' development needs ahead of your desire to keep them in role.
- **Don't fall into the obsolescence trap:** The minute we turn a manual process into an automated one, it's normal to forget the skills we once had to know inside and out. This is probably a mistake. For instance, though we have accounting and email software, we will need to understand basic math and how to construct a coherent sentence. Make sure your employees retain basic knowledge of how things work, even if they don't need to use it every day.
- **Be intrapreneurial:** Intrapreneurship refers to the practice of using entrepreneurial strategies within the context—and leveraging the resources of—an established organization. Intrapreneurship can involve giving employees time to tinker with new products or services, or establishing an innovation committee, but it also requires a mindset shift. Communicate to your employees that it's valuable to be open to new ways of doing things and consider fresh strategies to solve problems. Your team culture should promote reflecting on past experiences and projects and absorbing learnings, examining patterns that tie outcomes together, collecting feedback from a variety of constituents, taking risks and facing failure with grace and equanimity rather than blame.
- **Bolster learning efforts with the right tech:** Even if it's just for your team, consider creating a digital learning portal complete with skills assessments so that you can more easily build synergies between the skills you need and the skills your employees have. Such a system will also help you show proof of job-essential competencies by providing objective evidence that an employee has beginning, intermediate, or advanced proficiency in a given area. If your software is artificially intelligent, it may even point out skills gaps and offer up appropriate training recommendations and additional career paths to explore.

My 11-year-old son and his self-directed, multifaceted approach to learning represent the changing face of human skill acquisition. As long as we have the ability and support to conquer new learning frontiers, we will always have a way to add value to our organizations. Hopefully, you now have a sense of education's evolution, and what you need to do as a leader to ensure that your workforce is in the best position to refresh existing skills and identify and master new and yet-to-be discovered ones.

FOCUS ON THE FRONTLINE

1. Don't forget your frontline employees when it comes to learning and development. Where you can, integrate a variety of learning formats, including online and offline courses, coaching, mentorship, and cross-functional shadowing and experiences into their daily lives.
2. Encourage frontline intrapreneurship! Given the autonomy to tinker with and improve daily operations, your frontline staff may surprise you with incredible ideas on improvement and efficiency.
3. Create a digital learning portal just for your frontline employees. This will help you build synergies between the skills you need and the skills your employees have.
4. Be flexible—and provide your employees with defined choices for how they might create a work experience, work environment, and work structure that best suits their learning style. Support flexwork and alternative scheduling where you can—workforce management software can help with this task if you have a large number of employees.
5. Explore whether it might make sense to partner with a certification service like *Degreed.com* to offer frontline employees portable professional development.

REFERENCES

Pisa, Katie. "Are these the schools of the future?" *CNN*, November 1, 2018. https://www.cnn.com/2017/09/27/health/future-schools/index.html

Brown, Dan. "Research and Educator Micro-credentials." Digital Promise and the Center for Teacher Quality White Paper, February, 2019. https://digitalpromise.org/wp-content/uploads/2019/02/researchandeducatormicrocredentials-v1r2.pdf

iNACOL Staff. "What Is Competency Education?" iNACOL and Competency Works Report, March 11, 2016. https://www.inacol.org/news/what-is-competency-education/

Levit, Alexandria. *Humanity Works: Merging Technologies and People for the Workforce of the Future.* London/New York: Kogan Page Inspire, 2019. https://www.amazon.com/Humanity-Works-Merging-Technologies-Workforce-ebook/dp/B07HQKQSZZ

The Harvard Gazette. *"MIT and Harvard Announce edX."* New and Announcements, May 2, 2012. https://news.harvard.edu/gazette/story/2012/05/mit-and-harvard-announce-edx/

The Degreed Skill Certification. https://degreed.com/skill-certification

US Federal Bureau of Investigation (FBI) and DeVry's College of Information Sciences Curriculum. https://www.devry.edu/online-programs/career-fields/business/criminal-justice-careers.html

DeVry University Career Advisory Board. "Technology Skills Gap Research Reveals Growing Lack of Tech Preparedness for the American Workforce." Technology Skills Gap Survey, March 6, 2017. https://bit.ly/2NoxCbf and https://www.careeradvisoryboard.org/content/dam/dvu/www_careeradvisoryboard_org/exec-summary-screen-shot6.png

Flaum, J.P., and Becky Winkler. "Improve Your Ability to Learn." *Harvard Business Review,* June 8, 2015. https://hbr.org/2015/06/improve-your-ability-to-learn

John Hollon is an award-winning journalist and nationally recognized expert on such topics as leadership, talent management, and smart workforce practices. He's currently Contributing Editor at ERE Media, where he works with the recruiting website *ERE.net*, sourcing website *SourceCon.com*, and *TLNT.com*, the popular talent management website he founded and edited for six years. Mr. Hollon is also a regular contributor at *Fistful of Talent*, a daily blog made up of an all-star team of talent management experts and influencers. Over the course of his career, Mr. Hollon served as Editor-in-Chief of *Workforce Management* and *Workforce.com*, was Editor of *RecruitingDaily.com*, and held editing positions at the *Los Angeles Herald Examiner* and the *Orange County Register*. Mr. Hollon was Executive Editor for Gannett Company at two statewide papers—*Montana's Great Falls Tribune* and *The Honolulu Advertiser*. He also worked in magazine and online publishing as Editorial Director at Fancy Publications, Vice President of Editorial at dotcom favorite *Pets.com*, and as Editor-in-Chief of the *San Diego Business Journal*. Mr. Hollon is an Adjunct Professor at California State University Fullerton. He holds an MBA from Pepperdine University and a BA in Journalism from California State University Long Beach.

CHAPTER ELEVEN

Rethinking Frontline Hiring With An Eye Towards Transferable Skills

John Hollon, MBA
Contributing Editor, ERE Media
Adjunct Professor, California State University Fullerton

It was a move that left a lot of people scratching their heads.

When Angela Ahrendts, Apple's Senior Vice President of Retail and Online Stores, announced she would be leaving in February 2019 after five years on the job, there were lots of questions about who would replace her running Apple's highly successful retail stores operation.

It's a huge and important position.

Apple has 506 retail stores in 24 countries on five continents, including 272 in the US, as well as 35 online stores. And as anyone who has been in an Apple Store knows, they're constantly busy—a critical connection between the company and its loyal and demanding customer base.

One would think that Apple would want someone with deep retail experience to replace Ahrendts, who joined the company back in 2014 and was formerly the CEO of well-known fashion company Burberry, and before that, with Liz Claiborne and Donna Karan.

Well, you might think that—but you would be wrong.

Instead, the company announced that Deirdre O'Brien, Apple's Vice President of People, would run the retail operation AND human resources in her new role as Senior Vice President of Retail and People, where she reports directly to Apple CEO Tim Cook.[1]

The decision to promote the HR chief into a role running the company's retail stores was a head-scratcher to many, but not to Jeff Hyman, longtime CEO, executive recruiter, and author of the book *Recruit Rockstars.*

Here's what he said about Apple promoting Deirdre O'Brien in his daily newsletter:

> "It's a brilliant, unusual, atypical move. Just like Apple is wont to do. Cook is no amateur at spotting talent. And in this case, he could have picked any retail guru for the role. Instead, he picked his head of HR. She's been with the company for 20 years. So, it's a safe bet that what she lacks in retail experience, she more than makes up for in living and breathing Apple's DNA. And that's what the stores are all about. Hiring amazing Apple DNA fanatics who deliver remarkable experience and service every single time. I predict it'll be a home run … "[2]

That's an incredible statement when you consider that O'Brien has never worked in retail yet is now overseeing one of Apple's most critical, customer-facing operations. It also raises an important question: why would a smart CEO like Tim Cook roll the dice on someone with zero experience in retail as his new retail chief?

Jeff Hyman thinks the answer is pretty simple. He says: "The folks on your team who live and breathe your firm's DNA are far more 'portable' than you think to other roles, departments, functions, and geographies. And the more you expand their role—and challenge them—the more likely these Rockstars are to stay."

In other words, it's less about having experience in a specific area, and more about something else you seem to hear a lot about—transferable skills. Tim Cook felt that Deirdre O'Brien had the transferable skills that would help his long-time HR chief to succeed in running Apple's retail operations. Only time will tell if he's right, of course, but it's an important reminder that in the 21st century workplace, transferable skills have become an important factor for both employees AND the many people who manage them.

Just What Are Transferable Skills?

If you asked 10 people for a definition of "transferable skills," you would probably get 10 different answers. That's because everyone seems to have a different perspective on what might actually be a skill that is transferable from one job to another.

Indeed.com, which touts itself as "the Number One Job Site in the World," defined it like this:

> "Transferable skills, also known as 'portable skills,' are qualities that can be transferred from one job to another. You likely already possess many transferable skills employers want, like organization or strong communication. You can strengthen those skills and develop new ones that employers value across industries and jobs.
>
> Transferable skills are any skills you possess that are useful to employers across various jobs and industries. These might include skills like adaptability, organization, teamwork or other qualities employers seek in strong candidates. Transferable skills can be used to position your past experience when applying for a new job—especially if it's in a different industry."[3]

If transfeable skills sound oddly familiar, it's because you probably have heard them described by their more common name—soft skills.

Yes, "transferable" skills are really just another name for what most people refer to as "soft" skills, and there is a growing body of evidence that soft skills are not only extremely important but a critical factor that recruiters and hiring managers need to be looking for.

Fast Company described the challenge like this:

> "Soft skills may seem like a buzzword, but our research shows they actually account for the biggest skills gap today. In fact, 57% of leaders say soft skills are more important than hard skills. Certain soft skills like intellectual curiosity, grit, and adaptability may help compensate for the more traditional experience employers are seeking in candidates. ... Soft skills can impact the bottom line as well. In a study with Shadi Exports in India, researchers from the University of Michigan, Boston College, and Harvard University found that training in communication and problem-solving skills boosted productivity and retention by 12% and led to a 256% return on investment due to improvements in retention."[4]

That all sounds good, but in practice, soft skills aren't always valued as much as many people say they are. Jeff Weber, Senior Vice President of People and Places at educational software company Instructure, recently wrote in *Forbes*:

> "The biggest challenge with soft skills is that they are undervalued in today's economy. ... The term itself is a misnomer, especially when you consider that 'soft' skills like leadership, communication and problem-solving are the bedrock of our collaboration-centric, knowledge worker-driven, digital economy."[5]

Part of the problem is the current focus on hard skills, teachable abilities, or skill sets that are easy to quantify. For example, engineers are in short supply because they have hard-to-find technical skills that they have gathered in the classroom, training, or directly on the job.

Jobs that are currently in high demand and short supply include accounting, nursing, engineering, computer science, and other such professions that require very specific skills that are not easy to acquire.[6]

Soft skills don't get as much respect. Soft skills seem to get downplayed at just about every level, from recruiter to hiring manager to line manager to top-level executive. In fact, far too many high-level managers downplay the need for soft skills despite the growing research showing their importance.

The ability to connect with employees and get the most out of them continues to grow in importance. This is especially true when it comes to the Millennial generation given how they don't respond well to top-down edicts or military style command-and-control management systems.

Given the intense competition to hire people with strong technical skills—like engineers, who aren't known for their people skills—it's no wonder that people with good soft skills are in short supply. That's probably because they haven't been valued all that much.

If there's one thing the Millennials have made clear, it's that the ability to connect with people personally will never go out of style. If you aren't focusing on soft skills in your recruiting and hiring, you better get to it because you'll need them more and more as Millennials and Gen Z become the largest—and most important—part of America's workforce.

In other words, although soft skills, *aka* transferable skills, seem to be pretty important, they seem to be getting swept under the rug as recruiters and hiring managers focus on technical skills and specific job experience in their day-to-day hiring.

Transferable Skills Don't Get Much Respect

If soft, transferable skills are so critically important, particularly when it comes to dealing with Millennials and Gen Z, you would think that recruiters would be jumping on job candidates with a strong track record with these soft skills.

Yes, you would think that—but you might be wrong.

Way back in 2010, Liz Ryan, a former *Fortune* 500 HR Senior Vice President who now writes about talent management for publications such as *Bloomberg, BusinessWeek, LinkedIn,* and *Forbes.com*, wrote an article titled "The Myth Of Transferable Skills" where she took a verbal cleaver to the notion that transferable skills were all that important. In fact, she made the case that "transferable skills are a crock."[7] Here's the crux of her argument:

> "We are taught in book after book, in seminars and podcasts and job search networking events, that people get jobs by trumpeting their Transferable Skills. … (but) there is one big problem with the Transferable Skills dogma. People are not actually ambulatory sets of disembodied, abstract skills. Describing ourselves as packages of skills is about the worst way imaginable to get a hiring manager excited about us."

This take on transferable skills runs against the common wisdom that gets thrown out to applicants in today's job market, because candidates are constantly told to highlight their skills to better attract recruiters and hiring managers. In fact, most online profiles that job seekers fill out specifically ask them to list their most critical and important skills. Many people utilize this online feature to highlight the soft, transferable skills for which they believe hiring managers are looking.

Again, Liz Ryan doesn't agree. She makes the point that a resume listing someone's transferable skills is incredibly "boring," and really doesn't tell us all that much about them. She supports her point by listing the "five big problems" with the focus on transferable skills:

1. **Talk is cheap.** *You say you have Communication Skills … but (no offense) who cares what you say? I'm the hiring manager, and I don't even know you. Why would I trust your assessment of yourself?*
2. **Skills are framed so broadly that they could describe almost anything.** *When you say you have Negotiation Skills, what do you mean? … Does the person who brokered an international peace accord claim the same Negotiation Skills as the person who got the company's coffee vendor to throw a few extra creamers into the order? How would we know?*
3. **Skills are latent.** *When I say I have Writing Skills, I'm saying that I know how to write and could potentially write something at some point. Big deal! Do I know when to write, and what to write, to whom, when? Do I know what sorts of writing work best in different situations? We don't want to tell a hiring manager that we possess potential power, and that it's sitting on the shelf. We*

want to tell him or her that we know when to use every tool in our toolkit, and … when we've pulled those tools down from the shelf and used them to great advantage.

4. **When we list our transferable skills on a resume, we recite them without context.** *What could be incredible Communication Skills in one setting (getting a sales team jazzed up at the annual sales meeting, for example) might be terribly out of place in another setting (calmly negotiating a union contract). Stories, in contrast to skills listings, are loaded with context. … That's when our job-search pitch has power!*
5. **Skills are trite.** *Everyone claims the same ten done-to-death skills (Communication, Negotiation, Teamwork, Organizational, Writing, Leadership, Technical, Administrative, Customer Service, and Process Improvement). We won't make our mark sounding like every other skill-toting job seeker in the pack. We need powerful* stories *to convey our power, battle-tested and concrete, to the person who's reading our resume.*

Although most don't agree with Ryan's perspective on transferable skills, there are many who agree that there has been so much focus on why candidates need to have soft, transferable skills that people tend to forget that having such skills is just part of the hiring equation.

Longtime manager Alison Green made this very point in her *Ask a Manager* blog when answering the question: "Why Don't Managers Appreciate Transferable Skills?" Her response cuts to the heart of the transferable skills debate.[8] She says, in part:

> "Employers have no incentive to take a risk on someone without a track record in what they're looking for when they have plenty of good candidates who do have that track record. … And it's not like it's a question of smart, capable people with no direct experience but transferable skills against not-so-smart-or-capable people with direct experience. There are smart, capable people in both groups, so of course the smart, capable people with direct experience are the most attractive. … (Even if) there are some transferable skills … you're probably going to go with the person with the track record actually doing the work you're hiring for, unless there's something about the other person that really impresses you, enough to trump the experience issue."

In other words, transferable skills are nice to have, but candidates with the specific experience, a strong track record and transferable skills will trump those with just transferable skills no matter how much soft skills seem to be in demand.

Or as Green gently puts it:

> "None of this means that hiring managers never take a chance on people who are less tested. They do ... but surely you can understand why that's more the exception than the rule when employers have plenty of options, right?"

Beyond Transferable: Hiring For The Specific

Way back in the late 1990s, during the great "dot-com boom,"[9] technology companies were desperate for employees. As an article by the Federal Reserve Bank of St. Louis noted, "During that boom, national employment in the tech sector shot up by 36%, while average wages for tech workers doubled. At its peak in 2000, tech employment represented just over 4% of total private jobs."[10]

There are a lot of lessons we can learn from the dot-com boom, but one of the biggest has to be how employers hungry (some might say desperate) for top talent were so willing to consider transferable skills in the job candidates they were targeting. Back then, the economy (especially technology) was booming, and many companies were growing and needed talent. I worked as a vice president at a San Francisco dot-com during that time, and a lot of my time was spent trying to hire people, or, fending off people calling and trying to hire me. In a great many cases, I was pitched jobs that had titles way outside my area of expertise. When I questioned that, I heard over and over that they didn't see that as a particular problem because I had demonstrated the "broad" skills they needed at some point during my career.

Yes, back then recruiters, hiring managers, and other Talent Acquisition professionals were ready and willing to look at someone's transferable skills if it meant they could fill one of the many jobs they needed to hire for. Back then, "transferable" skills were a hot commodity—but if you fast-forward to today, you'll find a little bit different perspective. A recent *Forbes* careers article described it like this:

> "At a recent workshop, one experienced professional asked how to package her skills to show employers that what she could offer was transferable to a new career. People do change careers—i.e., moving from one industry to a different one or moving from one role to another. Therefore, employers will hire candidates without direct experience and with the expectation that whatever skills they do have are transferable. How-

> ever, employers will always prioritize the candidate who has already done a similar job before over a candidate new to an industry or functional area. A career changer has no track record and therefore is a riskier hire."[11]

That's the problem with transferable skills—everybody likes them and feels they're important, but for many employers, they pale in comparison to direct and specific experience. But a growing number of companies (some would say the BEST companies) have embraced the notion that soft, transferable skills, along with a philosophy of hiring "nontraditional" talent, can actually lead to outside-the-box promotions and hiring decisions—like the one Apple made in promoting its HR chief to run the company's retail stores division.

As LinkedIn's Head of Talent Acquisition Brendan Browne wrote in *Fast Company:*[12]

> "Ultimately, as hiring managers continue to embrace the idea of transferable skills, the perception of "nontraditional" talent will shift to be "the right" talent. ... At LinkedIn, we've found success seeking talent outside of Silicon Valley and beyond the tech industry because we want people with different experiences and different points of view on our team. By readjusting the idea of "experience" and being open to nontraditional job candidates and career paths, companies can access a much bigger talent pool at a time when competition is fierce, and certain skills are hard to come by. Whether you seek talent with the drive to upskill, or with skills that are transferable, looking beyond traditional experience can help find the right candidates, often in unexpected places."

That all sounds good in principle (and thank goodness for LinkedIn and other forward thinking organizations for getting outside the box in their hiring practices) but maybe there's another answer for all those companies that are harder to convince.

Making The Case For "Moldable" Skills

Fans of the late, great Theodor "Dr. Seuss" Geisel know that the critical scene in his classic tale, *How the Grinch Stole Christmas*, comes after the Grinch has snuck into Whoville on Christmas Eve and stolen everything from the Whos—their presents, trees, decorations, and even the food for their Christmas dinners. As dawn arrives, the Grinch waits at the top of Mt. Crumpet with all his stolen booty waiting with great anticipation to hear all the Whos "crying boo-hoo." Instead, he hears them singing a beautiful Christmas carol. It's then that he has the revelation: "Maybe Christmas," he thought, "*doesn't* come from a store. Maybe Christmas … perhaps … means a little bit more."

What does the Grinch have to do with the debate about the usefulness of transferable skills? It's this: just like the Grinch finds that Christmas is more than what it looks like on the surface—perhaps those who recruit and hire need to consider that transferable skills are a lot more than what they appear to be and are more than just boring "sets of disembodied, abstract skills," as Ryan puts it.

Somebody needs do to this—and in fact, somebody already has.

Karina Brown, co-founder of GroHappy, a British technology company that "helps motivate and retain great employees by giving them a platform to invest in their own growth," has an interesting perspective on transferable skills that changes the nature of the conversation.

In a blog post on *Medium*, Karina Brown said that the focus today shouldn't be on soft, transferable skills, but rather, on developing "moldable" skills instead.[13]

She writes: "We need a better way of thinking and talking about skills. One that is more realistic and empowering. One that enables us to see how our unique skill-set equips us to grow meaningfully in our current career or, indeed, one that empowers us to follow a different career path that might not be immediately obvious. Let's scrap *transferable*, and get *molding*."

If "molding" sounds like an odd term, it is—but only if you're hung up on the notion of transferable skills. Karina Brown believes that we should take another look at our skills and view them as a blob of putty that "represents the skills that you acquire, build and hone through life." She also believes that the putty that represents our skill set has been shaped and molded for the work environment we're currently in. It's been formed to help us connect with our co-workers, the organization's culture, and to maximize our ability to grow and get promoted in our current job. To her, that's all well and good, but she questions, what happens to that carefully molded putty when we decide to look for a new position somewhere else? How do those molded skills work in a new organization? She writes: "To connect with your new colleagues and show what you bring to the table, chances are you'll need to shape your putty for your new work world." She adds: "How else will they know that, in your case, *'community development specialist'* translates to *'I'm awesome at creating events that people love to come to'?*"

It's a good question, and it cuts to the heart of what's wrong with the notion of transferable skills: they're basic, they're bland, and they're generally one size fits all. The answer to the problem, according to Karina Brown, is that job seekers need to do three things to remold their transferable skills for a different workplace environment. They must:

- **Dig in to better understand** the "work world" they are curious about and possibly working in.
- **De-jargon their skills** so they would be understandable to someone outside their current organization.
- **Go and apply a "so what?" standard to those de-jargoned skills** in these three ways:
  1. *How do my skills make me an interesting and valuable person for this career/industry/role?*
  2. *What do your skills (or perhaps your combination of skills) enable you to do that sets you apart from others?*
  3. *How are your skills relevant to this career/industry/role now and in the future?*

In other words, when we focus on the need for transferable skills, Karina Brown says: "It sounds like you can pick up your box of transferable skills and plonk it down on the doorstep of your dream career without any real effort." That's because, "It narrows our view of what's possible"—and that's probably the best reason for listening to Karina Brown and "shifting the conversation towards *moldable* skills."

When that happens, we'll find out what the Grinch discovered—that the conversation about a candidate's soft, transferable skill set is a lot more than what it looks like on the surface because it will be more focused, and hopefully, more fruitful, too.

In The End, "Transferable" Skills Are Really, Really Important

The job skills that are important and transferable are in the eyes of the beholder.

Apple's Tim Cook felt his HR chief had the right skills to run the company's retail division, and time will tell if he's right about that. It's not the first time a prominent company has promoted or hired someone outside of their traditional area of expertise, and it surely won't be the last.

But it raises a good question: What transferable skills did the company's Vice President of People have that made the Cook decide to add oversight of Apple's retail stores operation to her portfolio? Here's what he said:

> "At Apple, we believe our soul is our people, and Deirdre (O'Brien) understands the qualities and strengths of our team better than anyone. For more than three decades, she has helped keep Apple focused on serving customers and enriching lives. She's an exceptional leader and she's been a vital partner to our retail teams around the world since the very beginning. I am thrilled to work alongside Deirdre in her new role, and I know our 70,000 retail employees will be, too."[14]

Tim Cook wasn't terribly specific, but it seems clear that Deirdre O'Brien's people skills and ability to communicate—both critically important soft, transferable skills—are key factors in her getting tapped to supervise an area she doesn't seem to have a lot of expertise in. Deirdre O'Brien seemed to confirm this about her new job. She said:

> "I have been an incredible believer that the special thing about Apple is its people. And for so many years I built my career here and I've watched so many other people build their careers here and I've seen people join the company from outside and seen people be successful and sometimes not successful. I've always loved the way Apple works. I've always been fascinated by it ..."

You can make a case that Deirdre O'Brien's long and notable career at Apple is proof positive that people skills (yes, one of many transferable skills) are really the key to great employees. This points out something that many recruiters and hiring managers seem to forget: While an employee's technical skills may get their foot in the door, it's their people skills—*aka*, soft or transferable skills— that will open most of the doors to come. It's a person's work ethic, attitude, communication skills, emotional intelligence, and other soft skills that are critical for career success.

Slowly and surely, recruiters and talent acquisition professionals are embracing the notion of transferable skills. Some may still call these soft skills, or moldable skills, but whatever you call them, they are critical to career success in the years to come.

LinkedIn's Brendan Browne probably said it best when he made the case:

"Whether you seek talent with the drive to upskill, or with skills that are transferable, looking beyond traditional experience can help find the right candidates, often in unexpected places."

Yes, it's pretty clear and it's terribly true—being able to harness transferable skills, and finding great talent in hidden places, will be the key to building great teams with top-notch talent moving ahead. And you don't need to be puzzling like the Grinch on Christmas morning to figure that out.

FOCUS ON THE FRONTLINE

1. Don't hire frontline workers based on hard skills alone.
2. Take a chance on a new hire who may not have the specific experience you are looking for but whose soft skills are "moldable."
3. Don't typecast your employees—including those on the frontline—in one role forever. Look for development paths that will leverage their unique skills in the organization.
4. Cultivate employees who "live and breathe your company's DNA" and do everything you can to keep them and help them grow at your organization.
5. Come up with a list of some of the soft skills you think are critical to succeeding at your organization and share that list with recruiters and hiring managers to make sure you are hiring with those skills in mind.

ENDNOTES

1 Juli Clover, "Angela Ahrendts Departing Apple in April, Deirdre O'Brien to Oversee Retail and People," *MacRumors* (February 5, 2019). https://www.macrumors.com/2019/02/05/angela-ahrendts-leaving-apple/

2 Jeff Hyman, "Omg … Apple just did it again," *Jeff Hyman Newsletter* (February 6, 2019). https://www.linkedin.com/in/jeffhyman/

3 Indeed Career Guide, Transferable Skills: Definitions and Examples. https://www.indeed.com/career-advice/resumes-cover-letters/transferable-skills

4 Brendon Browne, "Linkedin's Top Recruiter Says Experience Doesn't Matter if You Don't have These Skills," *Fast Company* (December 12, 2018). https://www.fastcompany.com/90278549/how-to-hire-for-potential-why-transferable-skills-outrank-experience

5 Jeff Webb, "'Soft' Is An Understatement: The Importance Of Transferable Skills," *Forbes* (April 26, 2019). https://www.forbes.com/sites/forbeshumanresourcescouncil/2019/04/26/soft-is-an-understatement-the-importance-of-transferable-skills/#16c6b6225ea9

6 Alison Doyle, "Hard Skills vs. Soft Skills: What's the Difference?" *The Balance Careers* (February 04, 2019). https://www.thebalancecareers.com/hard-skills-vs-soft-skills-2063780

7 Liz Ryan, "The Myth of Transferable Skills," *Glassdoor* (April 21, 2010). https://www.glassdoor.com/blog/myth-transferable-skills/

8 Alison Green, "Why Don't Managers Appreciate Transferable Skills?" *Ask a Manager* (April 4, 2013). https://www.askamanager.org/2013/04/why-dont-managers-appreciate-transferable-skills.html

9 Techopedia, Dot-Com Boom Definition. https://www.techopedia.com/definition/26175/dot-com-boom

10 Federal Reserve Bank of St. Louis, "Tech Employment Returns to Dot-Com Heights," *Forbes* (August 15, 2017). https://www.stlouisfed.org/on-the-economy/2017/august/tech-employment-returns-heights

11 Caroline Ceniza-Levine, "How To Show Employers You Have Transferable Skills To Successfully Change Careers," *Forbes* (March 9, 2019). https://www.forbes.com/sites/carolinecenizalevine/2019/03/09/how-to-show-employers-you-have-transferable-skills-to-successfully-change-careers/#55e158375540

12 Brendon Browne, "Linkedin's Top Recruiter Says Experience Doesn't Matter if You Don't have These Skills," *Fast Company* (December 12, 2018). https://www.fastcompany.com/90278549/how-to-hire-for-potential-why-transferable-skills-outrank-experience

13 Karina Brown, "The 'Transferable Skills' Myth," *Medium* (June 1, 2016). https://medium.com/@karinagrohappy/the-transferable-skills-myth-aa215f1158d1

14 Buster Hein, "Apple Names New Retail Boss as Angela Ahrendts Exits Company," *Cult of Mac Blog* (February 5, 2019). https://www.cultofmac.com/605054/apple-names-new-retail-boss-as-angela-ahrendts-exits-company/

Mark Wales is a global workforce management industry advisor, writer, and speaker. He has deep experience working with global organizations, including Starbucks, Ralph Lauren, Williams-Sonoma, The Gap, Levi Strauss, Selfridges, Tesco, IBM, and Price Waterhouse. He brings a holistic approach to workforce management that targets key performance improvements across divisions and geographies. Working at strategic, tactical, and operational levels to build sustainable capabilities with internal and external partners, he focuses on building effective ecosystems for change. His recent focus has been on developing a next generation model for workforce management that drives company performance through impacting the customer experience by investing in the employee experience. He is an Executive Council member for the Milgard School of Business, University of Washington Tacoma, Board Member for Workplace21, Board Trustee for the Washington State Historical Society, a member of the Retail Analytics Council, and holds an MBA from University of Stirling, and a BA from University of Nottingham.

CHAPTER TWELVE

Why Your Organization Needs A Burning Water Plan

Mark Wales, MBA
Global Industry Advisor, Thought Leader—Workforce Management

The California Camp Fire was in the news for several weeks in 2018, garnering a significant amount of attention for its' scale and ferocity. We all heard of the tragic plight of the homeowners who fled the fires, and those that resolutely remained to safeguard their properties and pets. We also heard of the impact the fire had on the air that we breathe, extending for several hundred miles. Companies and local government were issuing face masks and issuing advisory warnings to stay indoors if you could.

While much of the news focused—understandably—on the immediate disaster and the responses to deal with it, another story was happening as well. The fire had a significant impact on workers, their jobs, their futures, and their quality of work-life balance.

Many of the themes and ideas in this book focus on how to create the right environment to do well by your employees, which then benefits both the employee and the organization through employee engagement and increased business performance. However, what happens when things are seemingly outside your control as we often find in a disaster situation? Your policies and practices may work for a normal situation but what should you do in a disaster? It is time we ask the hard questions of ourselves and our organizations to truly understand what support we should give our employees.

An Increasing Problem

Disasters are no longer one-off events that companies can treat as special charitable cases. Rather, disasters are becoming an unrelenting occurrence every year. The effects of climate change, political stalemates, and global terrorism, have all combined to make disasters frequent enough to be deemed regular events.

If we review the list of declared disasters by the Federal Emergency Management Agency (FEMA) in the United States in the last six years, we start to truly see the growing scale of events that impact employees and employers. Here is a high-level summary of declared FEMA disasters:

- **2019**—Fires, storms, earthquakes, tornadoes and flooding in New Mexico, Alabama, Washington, Kansas, Alaska, North Carolina, Mississippi, Texas, Minnesota (as of April 25, 2019)
- **2018**—Hurricanes, storms, flooding, tornadoes, typhoons, earthquakes in Texas, Mississippi, Minnesota, North Carolina, Virginia, Connecticut, Alaska, Arizona, Pennsylvania, California, Alabama, Montana, Wisconsin, Georgia, Florida, Hawaii, Wyoming, South Carolina, Iowa, Oregon, Nebraska, Washington, South Dakota, Utah, Michigan, Idaho, Massachusetts, Colorado, Maryland, Nevada, New Hampshire, New Mexico, Maine, Kentucky, Ohio, American Samoa, Guam, and Mariana Islands
- **2017**—Hurricanes Maria, Irma and Harvey creating humanitarian crises in Texas, Florida, South Carolina, Louisiana, Alabama, Georgia, and Puerto Rico
- **2016**—Hurricane Matthew, blizzards, wildfires and floods in Tennessee, Florida, Georgia, Carolinas, West Virginia, Southeast through Mid-Atlantic to Northeast
- **2015**—Floods and wildfires in Carolinas, Utah, Washington, Texas, Kansas, and Oklahoma
- **2014** —Snow storms, tornados, mudflows, cold wave & wildfires in New York, Great Lakes, Nebraska, Louisiana, Oklahoma, Illinois, Florida, North Carolina, Washington, Eastern US, and California

Currently this means that, in the United States, we experience a federally declared disaster every five days.

And the FEMA list does not even include all major events that disrupt people's ability to work. For example, the government furlough of 2018/19 led to 350,000 employees across the country being impacted. This situation generated examples of the "one off" charitable responses, including food drives to support government employees who were not being paid. What has not been made clear was the impact on all the employees and contractors supporting government functions, the local businesses servicing government employees, or the tourism related businesses affected by the closure of park and recreational facilities. While most of the direct employees eventually received back pay, those in supporting roles did not.

The impacts of all of these disasters are far wider and deeper than most of us realize: lost family members, inability to insure or rebuild homes, emotional stress and disruption to both parents and children, air and water quality, and the economic impacts on working life.

If we review the Camp Fire in California, we start to see the scale of the impact. During this disaster there were:

- 20,000 structures damaged or destroyed
- 52,000 people displaced
- 6,000 fire fighters onsite at the peak
- Significant numbers of other first responders and support
- Unquantified numbers of service industry workers at hotels, motels, restaurants, coffee shops, supermarkets and various other businesses, who increased their working hours to help
- Unquantified scale of cleanup and rebuilding that is ongoing

Disasters And Risk Management: A Burning Water Policy

With disasters more frequent and costly, organizations must start proactively planning for them. This is what we typically call "risk management." Risk management is practiced by most larger companies and organizations when it comes to areas like information technology, financial accounting, physical assets (such as buildings), and general risks to the continued operation of the supply chain or business model. What is less recognized or valued are the risks to employees and their families. As this book illustrates, for most companies and organizations, success is heavily dependent upon creating the right environment for employee engagement and retention. Now is the time for employees, and even their families, to be added to the list of critical organizational risks that require disaster plans and board-level oversight.

So, what is a Burning Water Policy? Why do companies need one?

The term "burning water" comes from eyewitnesses to many of these natural disasters. When involved in such an incident, your world is turned upside down, and when you step out into the street you may see burning water. While this occurrence has a logical explanation due to fractured gas and water mains, it is a visceral image left in the minds of many victims. It is their way of remembering that things were very different and the unexpected was happening. Instead of naming this an employee disaster recovery plan (EDRP), which has no emotional connection, you need to instill in your colleagues that this plan is about how to help real people in desperately abnormal circumstances, with very personal and urgent needs. And these needs will exist long after the initial disaster has been dealt with. The long-term disruption and impact will continue to be felt for months or even years after, and this gives your organization the opportunity to create real value for your employees to show them you care about them and their well-being above all else.

Most companies have disaster plans for their buildings, their data centers and systems, and their supply chains, but how many have put the same energy, thought, planning and preparation, into perhaps their biggest asset, their people? And how many have thought that step further and realized that their employees are not just individuals but members of families, with responsibilities and commitments that have a direct impact on how they perform at work. In this book many of the chapters deal with the latest thinking on how to best manage your policies and practices to get the best out of your workforce while supporting both business performance and ethical practices. The question now is how do you do that in abnormal circumstances and how far should you go?

Creating A Burning Water Policy

While your company's business model and principles will shape any response, I strongly recommend that companies take time to consider the options and develop a playbook that can be referenced in the event of each disaster. Here is a list of questions to get your organization started in creating that playbook that will help speed the response and maintain a level of consistency and effectiveness for both employees, their families, and the organization:

- What is the established policy? Where is the documented disaster plan and does it fully cover this situation?
- Who makes the call if decisions are required? Timing of assistance or level of assistance?
- Who is needed to execute any actions? Are operations, logistics, HR and

payroll teams required to provide special or out-of-hours services on top of their normal duties?

- What is required? How to communicate with employees who are displaced or required to work extra hours, especially with the possibility to be without power or cell service? How to pay employees if banking facilities and credit card machines are down? Are employees expected to reach out to you or you reach out to employees?

Below is an illustration of how this thinking can be employed at an organization:

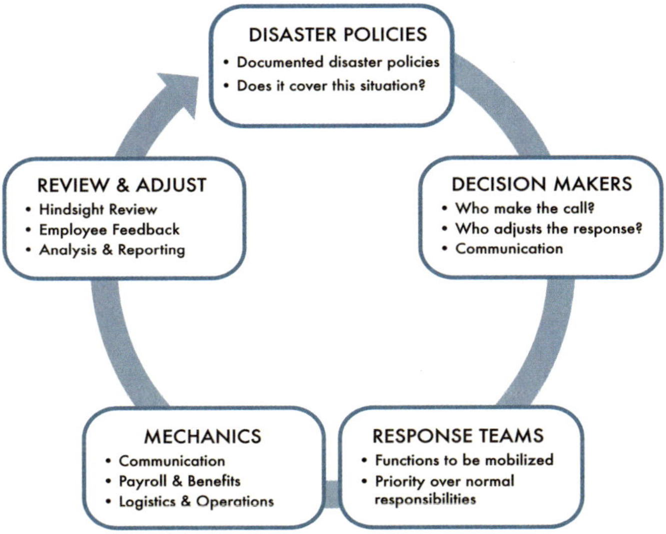

I recommend that after each disaster the Burning Water Policy be assessed and any adjustments made based on the learnings from the latest situation. No response will ever be perfect and there should be significant learnings from each situation. These could be based on the type of disaster, the location, and any changes in expectations due to the needs of the business or the employees.

One significant area to consider is that not all services or benefits will have the same value for each employee. Those employees without dependents may have more flexibility in terms of location of work or type of shifts, whereas an employee with dependents may have differing needs based on care or educational needs. As companies become more aware of what individual factors motivate an employee in their normal work life, the same is also true in abnormal circumstances such as a disaster. Therefore, the ability for an employee to personalize their situation could be a significant benefit and maximize the value to the employee and ultimately the organization.

Phases Of Response To Consider

It is helpful to break down the areas to consider into three different groups or phases. The first being the critical "immediate response" to deal with the immediate disaster situation. Next is a secondary phase of "expanded response" over a more prolonged period. Finally, there is a third "deep response" phase that incorporates risk management and risk mitigation into the DNA of your business model. This final stage can be modeled on the way organizations have increased the awareness and corporate response to sustainability and incorporated greener practices into their business model.

Immediate policies and practices covering the initial disaster period can all be thought through and documented. You may wish to add a scale based on the size and severity of the disaster to help determine which of these will be used based on the severity of the situation. On the next page is a table that can be used to kick start thinking for an organization.

While the immediate response is critical and needs to be fast, efficient, and well organized, you also need to be prepared for the extended response. After the initial furor has died down, the need for support can stretch from months to years. Therefore, a second part of the Burning Water Plan should cover the policies and practices that follow the immediate response.

On page 166 is a table that can be used to kick start planning around your extended responses.

Finally, any Burning Water plan would not be complete without taking a harder and deeper look into how to architect your policies and practices to better support your investment in your employees. This last section deals with far-reaching changes, including formalizing your employees as part of risk management planning process, incorporating opportunities to reduce risk for your employees, and how to use your care for your employees as a recruitment and retention strategy.

On page 167 is a table that can help kick start planning for more far reaching policies and practices.

Policies & Practices: Immediate Responses		
Categories	**Questions to consider**	**Factors to keep in mind**
Communication	• How do you reach employees? • How do they contact you? • What is the frequency of contact? • How do you track and monitor effectiveness of each communication?	• Do not assume employees have access to email. • Do not assume cell phone service is available.
Payment	• Who will you be paying? • What will you be paying? • How will they be paid? • What off-cycle payroll runs will be made? • What priority versus normal payroll processing?	• Do not assume normal bank or ATM access is available. • Do not assume time and attendance data will be available.
Hardship Support	• Will you pay for scheduled shifts not worked? • Will you pay additional allowances? • What other hardship funds may be available from employee funds or company donations? • What assistance will you give for applying for federal or state benefits?	• Do not assume that employees know which benefits to claim or have access to make claims. • Do not assume employees have access to their records.
Employment	• How long will your employees not be able to work? • Will you offer work in other locations? • If this means working across states, how will you manage payroll and labor law requirements?	• Do the abnormal circumstances warrant changing standard practices?
Community	• What do you share with all employees? • What sharing of well wishes, support or offers of help and items will you support?	• Employees will use social media. Do you want this outside the company?
Giving	• What will you request in terms of money, time and resources to support affected employees?	• How frequently are you asking your employees?
Recognition	• How and when will you recognize and celebrate employees who step up to support their colleagues? • How will you recognize local employees who put in extra shifts and services to support victims, first responders and media presence?	• If you recognize frontline frontline volunteers, then don't forget to recognize the backroom technicians and operators who put in extra effort.

Policies & Practices: Extended Responses		
Categories	**Questions to consider**	**Factors to keep in mind**
Transition	• When do you declare the initial response over and transition to the extended response phase? • What criteria do you use? • Do all areas of the immediate response transition at the same time. • How do you communicate this to employees?	• Affected employee's situations and needs will vary significantly based on the degree they were affected. • You will probably have to have both immediate and extended responses active at the same time.
Cleanup & Rebuild	• How long before locations will be operational? • How long before employees can safely move home?	• Think about physical logistics, availability of basic services and safety of the environment.
Impact to cost of living	• Is a cost of living adjustment warranted for employees? • Is there a need for temporary accommodation while employee housing is renovated or rebuilt? • Are employees facing increased travel to and from work because of being displaced, loss of personal transportation, or disruption to public transport?	• Do not assume that certain essential items such as car and home insuance have not increased. • Do not assume that costs have not risen for items such as drinkable water, gas and other products.
Increased complexity of life management	• What flexibility will be allowed to help employees meet the challenges in re-establishing normal life for the families? • How much stability can you give in schedules to help manage more complex life situations? • What flexibility for lateness, unplanned absenteeism, and time off for dependent support time will you grant above the normal policies?	• The complexity of reestablishing their lives may affect the availablity to work or require more special circumstances.

Overall, it seems that the growing number and increased frequency of disasters, means that it is beneficial for companies to take the time and effort to plan upfront what their responses will be. If you have ever managed through any form of corporate level disaster, then you will understand the level of confusion, missed opportunities, and sheer effort that goes into the immediate response. As teams rush back to catch up with their normal day-to-day responsibilities, the opportunity is lost to have detailed plans prepared. As organizations better understand the value of creating the right policies and practices for normal times, there will be a movement to deal with the abnormal times. Hopefully the ideas in this chapter will provide some inspiration and materials that can be used within your organization for planning the immediate responses, the extended responses, and the deeper responses to the growing trend of disasters.

Policies & Practices: Deep Responses

Categories	Questions to consider	Factors to keep in mind
Formal Risk Management	• Who will own the employee-focused disaster recovery plan? • Who will manage funding for the plan and continued upkeep? • Who will oversee the plan? • Will it be incorporated into the annual report? • Who will research best practices and evolving trends on an ongoing basis?	• It may take time to educate and bring onboard the various functions in an organization to understand the value of this approach.
Risk Mitigation	• Who will ensure plans for business growth, relocation and renovation include a review of latest risk of disasters? • Who will develop policies to mitigate risk to employees?	• Again, this requires education of and involvement from multiple functions.
Ongoing Employee Fund	• Does it make sense to create an employee contribution fund that is deducted from pay on a regular basis? • Will there be company matches?	• Beware the danger of charitable fatigue with the increasing frequency of disasters.
Recruitment and Retention	• How can you make prospects and current employees aware of your principled approach to disasters that affect your employees?	• The shift towards sustainable business practices shows the value of this approach to both customers and employees.
Changing Policies	• Can we learn from how we respond in a disaster and apply those behaviors and practices in normal times?	• Many processes are designed to minimize abuse of company policies and therefore you miss the opportunity to benefit most employees. Sometimes relaxing policies can work.

FOCUS ON THE FRONTLINE

1. Don't stick your head in the sand when it comes to disaster planning: as disasters become more frequent, It critical that your organization plan for them.
2. Business continuity planning goes well beyond getting your properties and systems back up and running—you need to plan for the long tail of human impacts of disasters.
3. Get to know your frontline employees and managers: understanding their lives, family obligations, technology preferences, living situation, etc. will help you connect with them during normal and abnormal times.
4. Use the tables provided in this chapter to start discussions within your organizations about how best to serve your employees in a disaster.
5. Talk about the work you are doing with current and prospective employees—people appreciate knowing their employer cares about them.

REFERENCES

Declared US Disasters List, Federal Emergency Management Agency (FEMA). https://www.fema.gov/disasters/year

Brusentsev, Vera, and Wayne Vroman. "Disasters in the United States: Frequency, Costs, and Compensation." The W.E. Upjohn Institute for Employment Research, 2017. https://research.upjohn.org/up_press/242/

Irfan, Umair. "Why the Wildfire in Northern California was so Severe." *Vox*, November 16, 2018. https://www.vox.com/energy-and-environment/2018/11/13/18092580/paradise-california-wildfire-2018

Wootson, Cleve R. "The deadliest, most destructive wildfire in California's history has finally been contained." *Washington Post*, November 26, 2018. https://www.washingtonpost.com/nation/2018/11/25/camp-fire-deadliest-wildfire-californias-history-has-been-contained/?utm_term=.6e1a53bd08fc

Martin Armstrong is Vice President of Payroll Shared Services for Charter Communications, the second largest US cable provider. He is also the Accounting and Finance Area Chair for the University of Phoenix, where he was named the 2018 Distinguished Faculty of the Year. Over the course of his career he has achieved extensive training and expertise in performance metrics, mergers and acquisitions, process improvement methodologies, strategic tax planning, and change management, and has held executive roles with Time Warner Cable and Caesars Entertainment. The author of over 45 published articles, he is a retired Navy Supply Corps Officer, and former Vice President, Board Advisor, and current member of the APA. An active member of SHRM, NATP, ASQ, and AOM, he authored the Institute of Management and Administration seminar book entitled *Leading and Managing Payroll*. He holds an MBA from the University of Maryland University, a DBA from Argosy University, and is a Certified Payroll Professional.

CHAPTER THIRTEEN

What Frontline Leadership Needs Now

Martin Armstrong, MBA, DBA, CPP
Vice President, Payroll Shared Services for Charter Communication

Think you're having a bad day? Think again. Imagine being a frontline leader who recently transitioned from an individual contributor to a people leader, and is expected to manage employee productivity, solve operational problems, and deliver a superior customer experience—all with little to zero training.

A recent survey found that although frontline leaders make up or influence 80% of the workforce, these leaders receive only 20% to 30% of a typical company's leadership development efforts.

In a February 2019 article entitled "What Are the Greatest Challenges Frontline Leaders Face," Development Dimension International (DDI) executives Mark Busine and Evan Sinar, PhD reported that 60% of frontline leaders say they have never received any training or preparation for their new leadership role; two-thirds of frontline leaders felt unprepared for the role, and 87% of first-time leaders feel frustrated, anxious, and uncertain about their role.

The ineffectiveness of frontline leaders is costly, particularly for the frontline employees who they manage. Woohoo Inc., a group of leading international experts who consult on the topic of "happiness at work," reported the following top five factors that contribute to employees having a bad day:

- A lack of help and support from my boss (40%)
- Negative co-workers (39%)
- Lack of praise or recognition for the work I do (37%)
- Uncertainty about the workplace's vision or strategy (37%)
- Busy-ness or high workload (36%)

According to a survey conducted by the Global Leadership Forecast in 2018, as well as DDI's assessment data from more than 13,700 frontline leaders, on average, people are 40 years old when they first go through leadership development courses—four years after the average age of 36 when they first become leaders.

Needless to say, companies can do better in equipping their frontline leaders with the tools to successfully meet the challenges they face when managing frontline employees and executing an organization's strategy.

In order for frontline leaders to execute a company's strategy and grow the capability of frontline employees, employers should focus their frontline leadership development efforts on three critical areas: Strategic Thinking, Communication, and Execution.

Strategic Thinking

In this era where social media is woven into the culture fabric of organizations, where we have five generations from Traditionalists to Gen Z working side by side in the workplace, where humans talk to a "Chat Bot," and where Robotic Process Automation (RPA) and Artificial Intelligence (AI) are part of our operational strategy, today's frontline leader needs to define what is strategically needed now for their organization and redefine what will be strategically needed in the foreseeable future.

To determine what's needed now and in the future, frontline leaders need to begin their action plans by exercising the art of strategic thinking—a defined process to think and make decisions required to develop and execute a plan.

In a 2012 *Inc. Magazine* article, Paul Schoemaker outlines "6 Habits of True Strategic Thinkers":

1. **Anticipate**
    - Look for game changing information at the periphery of their industry
    - Search beyond the current boundaries of their companies
    - Build wide external networks to help scan the horizon better
2. **Think Critically**
    - Reframe problems to get to the bottom of things
    - Challenge current beliefs and mindsets
    - Uncover hypocrisy, manipulation, and bias in organizational decisions

3. **Interpret**
   - Seek patterns in multiple sources of data (encourage others to the same)
   - Question prevailing assumptions
   - Test multiple hypotheses simultaneously
4. **Decide**
   - Carefully frame the decision to get to the crux of the matter
   - Balance speed, rigor, quality, and agility (leave perfection to higher powers)
   - Take a stand even with incomplete information and amid diverse views
5. **Align**
   - Understand what drives other people's agendas (including what remains hidden)
   - Bring tough issues to the surface (even when its uncomfortable)
   - Assess risk tolerance—follow through to build the necessary support
6. **Learn**
   - Encourage and exemplify honest, rigorous debriefs to extract lessons
   - Shift course quickly if you realize you're off track
   - Celebrate both successes and (well intentioned) failures that provide insight

While the profile of today's frontline workforce may require the traditional use of exhibiting empathy, demonstrating good listening skills, exercising effective verbal and written communication, and being responsive, the needs for tomorrow's profile, such as root cause analysis, analytical thinking, technology acumen, and problem solving skill sets are quite different than the status quo.

The question becomes, what should frontline leaders strategically think about to shift their behaviors and mental attitudes to achieve what's needed now and in the future?

Reskilling The Workforce

One strategy to prepare for this mind shift is to upskill and reskill the frontline workforce. As technology continues to play an increasingly important role in daily frontline operations (i.e., systems, processes, and people), frontline leadership will need to embrace technology to creatively solve problems—their willingness and flexibility to embrace technology will be the key to reskilling themselves and frontline employees.

Synchrony Financial, a bank and provider of cobranded credit card programs, is deploying artificial intelligence in myriad ways: it's using machine learning to detect fraudulent transactions, robotic process automation to handle mundane operations tasks, and a virtual assistant named Sydney to answer basic questions by text chat.

According to Deirdre Allen, Senior Vice President of Operations for Synchrony Financial, Synchrony has taken critical steps to not only redefine the next generation profile of their frontline employees to meet future needs, they are also reskilling their frontline workforce to embrace the Artificial Intelligence (AI) that virtual assistant "Sydney" needs to answer customer inquiries.

Because AI learns from human decisions to make fast judgements when interacting with other humans, Sydney's learning capacity depends on data shared by Synchrony's frontline employees to accurately provide answers to basic questions via its Chat Bot interaction with customers.

Frontline employees are often asked by frontline leadership, "What was Sydney's deflection rate today?" Sydney's deflection rate refers to questions that Sydney can't answer (and thus transferred to a "human" customer associate to address); this gives frontline employees the opportunity to help train, and ultimately reduce, Sydney's deflection rate.

This type of employee collaboration enables frontline leadership to build their technological acumen and, at the same time, reskill their frontline workforce to be more accepting (as opposed to being intimidated) of innovative advances like Robotic Process Automation (RPA), and Machine Learning (ML), and AI.

Refining the frontline employee profile for the future requires frontline leadership to diligently practice the art of strategic thinking, to consistently assess what's needed now, and to integrate a systems thinking approach to reinforce reskilling efforts on a consistent basis.

Communication

"Talk is easy. Everybody talks. The question is, how can you make your words really count?" This quote by internationally respected leadership expert John Maxwell speaks to how challenging it is to know if frontline leaders are connecting when they are communicating.

Understanding Communication cites communication as a "process by which information is exchanged and understood by two or more people, usually with the intent to motivate or influence behavior." Simply put, communication is a basic component to human relationships.

To be effective in communicating within our human relationship networks, frontline leaders should use communication to accomplish the following objectives:

1. **Inform**—Develop relationships by actively sharing information with stakeholders.
2. **Motivate**—Frontline employees need encouragement, acknowledgement, and appreciation.
3. **Persuade**—Practice being a good listener, have an open mind, and stick to the facts.
4. **Elicit**—Consider ideas, suggestions, and concerns from others who do the work.
5. **Explore**—What are the potential pitfalls and additional opportunities that need to be evaluated?

What do people really hear? Dr. Albert Mehrabian, currently a Professor Emeritus of Psychology at UCLA, is best known for his research on the relative importance of verbal and nonverbal messages. His findings on conflicting messages of feelings and attitudes led him to develop a communication model known as the "7% - 38% - 55% Rule."

Mehrabian demonstrated that only 7% of what we communicate consists of words, 38% consists of one's tone (such as voice, intonation, and volume), and 55% of communication consists of body language. Who would have thought that 93% of communication is non-verbal?

Non-verbal communication includes facial expressions, body gestures, eye contact, voice, posture, and even your dress attire. I once had a mentor who suggested that "you should be able to determine who is in charge when you walk into the room by the dress attire of the leader." Non-verbal communication speaks volumes to how you are perceived (charisma), and the level of influence that you project.

Whether communicating in a quick huddle meeting, presenting new information to team members, or speaking in front of an audience, frontline leaders should know that their non-verbal communication reflects their excitement and enthusiasm in relation to what they are saying and how people react to the message.

How important is your message? What is the sense of urgency that you are trying to project? What do you want frontline employees to think, feel, or do? John Maxwell's mentor Howard Hendrick says that three essential components comprise all communication:

1. Intellectual (what we know)
2. Emotional (what we feel)
3. Volitional (what we do)

When any of these components are unsuccessful, the communicator does not connect.

Mastering the art of communication is essential for growing your personal and professional relationships. In 2010, Maxwell authored an influential book *Everyone Communicates, Few Connect: What the Most Effective People Do Differently.* In this book, Maxwell suggests five principles of connecting, and five practices to becoming a communicator who connects.

Principles behind connecting:

1. It increases influence in every situation.
2. It is all about focusing on others.
3. It requires communicating beyond using words.
4. It demands energy.
5. It involves skill more than natural talent.

Practices to become a connector:

1. Find common ground.
2. Make communication simple.
3. Create an enjoyable experience.
4. Inspire the audience.
5. Be authentic by living what one communicates.

Ros Jay, author of the book *The Seven Deadly Skills of Communicating,* presents evidence that productivity, motivation, and loyalty can be achieved from frontline employees if, and only if, they know what is happening around them—this is particularly important when internal changes impact customers and other external stakeholders.

Ros Jay also offers three important communication rules that I have diligently followed for the past 10 years:

1. Tell them as much as you can.
2. Tell them as soon as you can.
3. Never lie to your staff.

Frontline leaders would be wise to adapt the following seven core skills of good communication that Jay argues will lead to a productive and motivated frontline workforce within an organization:

1. **Develop a Corporate Personality**— Resembles your organizational culture and helps to establish cross functional relationships.
2. **Written Communication**—Memos, letters, e-mail, fax, writing with a shared meaning, and writing for effectiveness are used to present a situation, explain complexity, offer a resolution, and resolve with action.
3. **Verbal and Non-Verbal Communication**—Presentations, tone, body language, listening, and department meetings are used to inform, discuss, and decide.
4. **Communicating with Senior Management**—Peak with brevity, transparency, urgency, use business case metrics, provide options, identify risks, and recommend a course of action to be taken.
5. **Communicating with the Team**—When communicating with your team, use meeting agendas, exercise diversity and inclusion, separate facts from opinions, solicit ideas and feedback, set a clear direction, utilize empathy, and show fairness.
6. **Communicating with the Individual**—Communicate on an individual level for performance appraisal, employee motivation, reward, and discipline, don't force a decision, show respect, and be firm.
7. **Communicating Under Pressure**—Keep everyone informed, deliver consistent messaging, encourage questions and ideas, practice collaborative decision making, be available and supportive, and keep a sense of humor.

Communication is a balancing act. In the same manner that words can nurture and resolve misunderstandings, they can also strain relationships and destroy trust. And even the best communication cannot solve all interpersonal problems as workplace relationships can be demanding.

Frontline workforces are diverse (i.e., gender, age, ethnicity, race, status, sexual orientation, and generational gaps) and thus require the highest level of communication commitment that frontline leadership needs to incorporate *now* to achieve operational excellence through teamwork and collaboration.

Execution

Earlier, we discussed how strategic thinking is critical to the process of strategic assessment and action planning, and how frontline leadership should use communication to skillfully share essential information, establish effective relationships, and build trust. At this point, we have positioned frontline leadership to now make things happen, that is, to execute.

Execution is about carrying out, or putting into effect, an order or a course of action (i.e., the execution of a plan). Military officers execute orders given to them by senior ranking officers such as generals and admirals, a quarterback executes plays on a football field that are communicated by a head coach, and in a similar fashion, a frontline leader executes an organizations' strategic plan that is disseminated from the top down by company leadership.

From the standpoint of a frontline leader, execution involves perfecting a specific set of behaviors and techniques that over time will become habit forming, which will generate into what every frontline leader should aspire to achieve operational excellence (i.e., the system is working)!

In 2002, world-renowned business advisor and author Ram Charan, and former Honeywell CEO Larry Bossidy, coauthored the book Execution, *The Discipline of Getting Things Done.* The book spent more than 150 weeks on the *New York Times* best-seller list. I was so captivated by the book's insights that I made this book required reading for a number of management courses that I've taught over the years. (The majority of the book's core principles are still very relevant today.)

The book appropriately addresses a gap whereby leaders fall victim to the promises they've made and the results that were delivered. How can the best made plans fall flat on their face? Have leaders made a process so difficult and too complex that customer facing employees can't consistently execute? Are the right people in the right jobs? Have we misidentified the problem?

These questions are commonly asked when reflecting on the aftermath of when leaders fail to deliver on promises made that didn't come to fruition. Charan and Bossidy explain that "the gap nobody knows is the gap between what a leader wants to achieve and the ability of the organization to achieve it."

To shorten this gap, frontline leaders must understand that execution is a discipline that encompasses three core processes:

1. **The People Process**—Who has the best skill set for this job and are we providing the appropriate level of training for the person to be successful?
2. **The Strategy Process**—Have we set and communicated to stakeholders what we are planning on doing and how we will do it?
3. **The Operations Process**—Have we reviewed the working components of our operations to ensure that they are working seamlessly with one another and transparent to our customers?

For frontline leadership to be successful in execution, it is imperative that they deeply understand what's needed to develop frontline employees in a high-performing culture, determine and implement a strategy that will address gaps that are barriers to success, and effectively manage the operations process that will determine a customer's overall superior customer experience.

The true test of execution is measured by delivering results. Quite frankly, the information in this chapter will mean nothing if you do not have the ability to execute. In a results-oriented society, the legacy of frontline leaders will be told through their decision-making skill sets and their response to change. To this end, employers should focus their execution efforts for frontline leadership development on three critical execution areas: decision-making, change management, and focusing on delivering results.

Decision-Making Techniques

Decision-making is part of leadership life and having a disciplined decision-making strategy or framework will help leaders make sound decisions without regret. However, as a frontline leader, you are likely to make decisions based on your experiences, which may not be timely based on stand-up comedian Steven Wright's saying, "Experience is something you don't get until just after you need it."

The good news is that you can train your brain to think differently about decision-making by adopting the use of a mental model. What are mental models and what's in it for frontline leadership?

A mental model is an overarching term for any sort of concept, framework, or worldview that helps your mind explain how something works. Michael Karnjanaprakorn, author of "16 Mental Models for Founders and Leaders," describes mental models as "your mind's toolbox for making decisions—the more tools you have, the more equipped you are to make good decisions."

Frontline leadership should seek to expand their mental model toolboxes as the quality of decision-making is proportional to the models known to leaders and their situational usefulness.

Try these mental models to help you make decisions and/or solve problems derived from Karnjanaprakorn. Note the method you choose will change depending on the situation you're addressing:

1. **10/10/10 Rule**—Helps with taking the emotions out of making long term decisions. Ask yourself, how would I feel about it 10 minutes from now, 10 months from now, or 10 years from now?
2. **Inversion Mental Model**—Rather than thinking about your desired outcome, consider the outcome you'd like to avoid and ensure not to do any of the things you wish to avoid.
3. **Rule of Three**—Whenever you are trying to persuade a senior person to do something, always present three reasons (not two, not four, but exactly three).
4. **Directly Responsible Individual** (**DRI**) —A management principle that was championed by Apple, whereby one person is responsible for something; this clarifies ownership and accountability.
5. **Listen, Decide, Communicate**—You first listen, then decide, then you communicate it, in this specific order, and in close proximity to one another; this helps with active listening and communication.

Other decision-making techniques, and their situational usefulness, include the following tools:

1. **5 Whys**—Originally developed by Toyota founder Sakichi Toyoda in the 1930s, when a problem occurs, the "5 Whys Technique" works by repeatedly asking the question "why" five times to determine the root cause of a problem.
2. **Pareto Analysis**—Uses the Pareto principle, which states 80% of problems may be caused by as few as 20% of causes; use this technique to prioritize problem-solving work.
3. **Plus/Minus /Interesting** (**PMI**)—Weighs the pros and cons of a decision to determine if the choice will improve the situation.

4. **Force Field Analysis**—Created by social psychologist Kurt Lewin in the 1940s, this technique measures the pressures for and against change, using a specialized method of weighing pros and cons to arrive at a decision.
5. **Cost Benefit Analysis (CBA)**—A quantitative comparison by adding up the value of the benefits of a course of action and subtracting the costs associated with it.

Paul Parcon, author of the book *Develop Your Decision Making Skills,* provides guidance on common decision-making mistakes that frontline leaders should watch out for: (1) relying too much on "expert" information—humans have biases too; (2) overestimating the value of information received by others—keep opinions in perspective; (3) underestimating the value of information received by others we don't align; (4) only hearing what you want to hear or seeing what you want to see; (5) not listening to intuition.

Making decisions is a leadership competency that demonstrates your willingness to take decisive actions in management situations. It also illustrates that you are action-oriented and speaks to your ability not to become overwhelmed or paralyzed when faced with making decisions that can only be made by you as a frontline leader. What do frontline employees need most from you? Support, guidance, and decision-making!

Change Management

People are creatures of habit. They sit in the same seat at church and order the same meal at their favorite restaurant—all because people like predictability and hate the fear of the unknown.

Peter Senge, a MIT based author, researcher, and educator is known for his findings that suggest "people don't resist change; they resist being changed." Perhaps this explains why, despite all of the academic research, white papers written, and experienced change leaders, that nearly 70% of all change initiatives fail. If change was easy, everyone would do it!

This overall change failure rate is substantiated by a recent Bain and Company survey[1] of 250 large companies who executed major changes. Based on past studies, their results are typical:

- 12% achieved or exceeded expectations
- 38% failed to deliver, producing less than 50% of the expected results

- 50% settled for dilution of value and mediocre performance

By way of definition, change is a complex process, characterized by intended and unintended consequences that have the potential to disrupt the life of an organization.[2] In the workplace, there are many changes that impact frontline leadership and their employees:

- Marketplace changes
- Competitors
- Product Changes
- Technology & ERP Systems
- Mergers & Acquisitions
- Re-Organizations
- Leadership
- Efficiencies

Frontline employees are responsible for managing the human side of change. When frontline employees face some sort of change, there are three types of transition stages that they experience:

1. Ending—letting go of the old
2. Neutral Zone—between the ending and new beginning
3. New Beginning—new status quo

During these stages, there are a broad series of reactions to the transition, ranging from denial, anger, and fear, to hope, energy, and excitement. During the life cycle of the change, it is the frontline leader's responsibility to communicate the reasons for change, provide clear direction on how change will be achieved, and create excitement and enthusiasm regarding what change will look like after it is achieved.

It should come to no surprise that not all stakeholders will be excited about the impacts of change and thus will inherit resistance to various change events. In 2011, I successfully defended a dissertation where I examined employee readiness for change. As a result, I researched why employees resist change—and therefore offer to frontline leadership the following 14 reasons why change is resisted:[3]

Reason	Explanation
Dislike of change	People simply do not want to change.
Discomfort with uncertainty	Dislike of ambiguity, fear of the unknown
Perceived negative effect on interests	Impact on status, rewards, security
Attachment to the culture	Change conflicts with organizational identity; values or beliefs and norms of organization.
Perceived breach of psychological contract	Related to trust and loyalty—The organization is not honoring "its side of the bargain."
Lack of conviction that change	Different levels have different perceptions of whether a change initiative is a necessary change initiative: "It ain't broke. Why are we trying to fix it?"
Lack of clarity as to what is expected	Different levels have different perceptions of the intent of a change initiative, or what exactly is expected of organizational members to support the change initiative.
Belief that the specific change being proposed is inappropriate	Different levels have different perceptions of whether a change initiative is the right or necessary change initiative.
Belief that the timing is wrong	Conditions are not right for change *now*—The organization is still trying to cope with a previous change, morale is low, it could impact customers, etc.
Excessive change	Too much simultaneous change equals change fatigue, low morale, even the convergence of different change initiatives could create bigger problems than they are designed to fix due to negative Interactions.
Cumulative effects of other changes in one's life	Related to both organizational and personal changes in an organizational member's life
Perceived clash with ethics	Members resist because the change initiative is perceived to clash with their own ethical principles, or they perceive the change clashes with the ethical principles of the organization.
Reaction to the experience of previous changes	Negative past experiences result in cynicism and a "this too shall pass" attitude.
Disagreement with the way the change is being handled	The change initiative is not necessarily disputed, rather, how it is being implemented. To an extent, this gets at the credibility of the change leader.

An important development in academic research (see diagram below) is the "recognition that employees can be committed to many different work-related motivations."[4]

In an effort to obtain positive change outcomes, historically, research on organizational change had nearly overlooked the importance of employee change readiness, as the focus of most academic research has been on organizational capability and organizational readiness.[5]

However, with respect to an employee's commitment to organizational change, the following actions all influence an employee's commitment to change:

1. Fit of the organizational change with a strategic vision
2. Quality of relationship with an employee's manager
3. Job motivation
4. Autonomy within an employee's job role

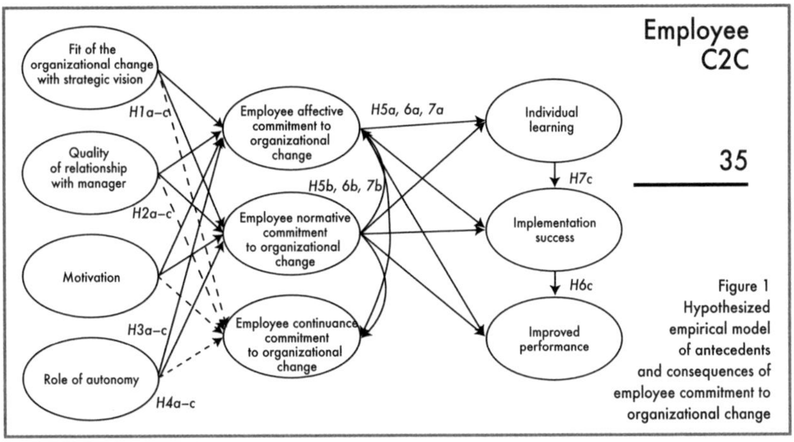

Figure 1
Hypothesized empirical model of antecedents and consequences of employee commitment to organizational change

Above diagram is from "Want to, Need to, Ought to: Employee Commitment to Organizational Change" published February 15, 2008 in *Journal of Organizational Change Management*.

Given the nearly 70% organizational change failure rate, coupled with 14 reasons why employees resist change, it may appear to frontline leadership that achieving successful change is as likely as winning the lottery.

However, additional research uncovered six employee readiness drivers that when present, increase an employee's readiness for change (see chart page 185). We also explain the meaning these drivers have for the employee during the change process. That is, what questions do employees ask as they experience the change, with the answers determining the employees' change readiness:

Readiness Drivers	**Definition**	**Question it looks to answer**
Self-efficacy	Confidence in individual and group's ability to make change succeed	Can we do this? Will this work?
Principal Support	Key organizational leaders support this particular change	Is management consistent? Do organizational leaders believe in this change?
Need for change	A gap between the current state and ideal state	Why a change?
Appropriateness of the change	The correct reaction to fix the identified gap	Why this change?
Personal valence	Clarifies the intrinsic and extrinsic benefits of the change	What's in it for me?
Understanding of the change	Informs the individual of the specific change requirement	What is the change?

Above chart is from "Expanding Our Understanding of the Change Message" published March 1, 2004 in *Human Resource Development Review*.

Change is achieved at the individual employee level. As such, it is the responsibility of frontline leadership to drive change through actions that promote readiness for change environments. The likelihood that organizational change initiatives are successful can be influenced if the frontline workforce possess the aforementioned readiness factors.

When it comes to change at the frontline leadership level, leaders must be vigilant towards their personal attitudes about efforts to change as the first step toward getting somewhere is to decide that you are not going to stay where you are.

Bringing It All Together—Focusing On Delivering Results

It takes a certain mindset to be a frontline leader—and 100% of the time, that mindset needs to be "Mission Focused" versus "You Focused." When you are Mission Focused, you are dedicated to executing the company's strategy, growing the capability of frontline employees, and everything else that we discussed thus far—there are no days off for the frontline leader!

Being Mission Focused is the opposite of being You Focused. Adopting a You Focused mentality is when you allow distractions to hinder you from achieving your overall mission. For example, during my tenure as a Naval Officer, I was recalled to active duty to serve in Afghanistan for 18 months.

During this period, our mission was to train the Afghanistan National Army to defend themselves against the Taliban. Each and every day, no efforts were spent on activities that did not relate to our designated mission. Did we have You Focused distractions during this time? You bet!

Examples of You Focused distractions were family related issues from back home such as missed child births, funerals, graduations, marital issues, and various Red Cross notifications—all served as distractions from concentrating on our Mission Focused obligations.

Frontline leadership experience the same type of distractions such as employee performance issues, technology issues that impede on employee productivity and customer service levels, unconscious biases, and personality conflicts with others for which you discount their suggestions, ideas, and contributions to the extent that your thinking is now You Focused as opposed to Mission Focused.

Note to self: your problems are never bigger than the purpose of the mission. Expert motivational speaker Les Brown once suggested that some people are so negative that the only time they develop is when they walk into a dark room. Don't let this be you as your frontline workforce is counting on 100% of your leadership!

Being a frontline leader who is expected to deliver results with little to zero training is tough, especially when you consider that they only receive 20% to 30% of a typical company's leadership development efforts. Despite this herculean task of succeeding as a leader, being a Mission Focused frontline leader is a humbling experience for those that are privileged enough to impact the lives of others.

Strategic thinking, communication, and execution—this is what frontline leadership needs now.

FOCUS ON THE FRONTLINE

1. Leadership training for frontline managers is critical, yet 60% say they haven't received any! Make sure you aren't overlooking these folks at your organization.
2. Don't underestimate the value of strategic thinking for frontline managers—make them aware of the habits that strategic thinkers possess and encourage them to develop these six habits.
3. Focus training for frontline managers on communication and connecting—this can go a long way towards positively impacting both their team and business outcomes.
4. Make sure your frontline leaders know the specific goals of the organization so they can help align the frontline workforce with these goals.
5. Most people—including those on your frontline—are resistant to change. Don't forget that if your expectations are going to change, you must do the change management work to ensure success.

ENDNOTES

1 Alan Bird, Torsten Lichtenau and David Michels, "The What, Who and How of Delivering Results," Bain & Company. (February 9, 2016). https://www.bain.com/insights/what-who-and-how-of-delivering-results/

2 Steven H. Appelbaum, Jonathan Berke, Joe Taylor and Jose Alberto Vazquez, "The role of leadership during large scale organizational transitions: Lessons from six empirical studies," *Journal of American Academy of Business, Cambridge*, 13(1), 16-21. (March, 2008). http://www.jaabc.com/jaabcv13n1preview.html

3 Ian Palmer, Richard Dunford, Gib Akin, *Managing Organizational Change: A Multiple Perspectives Approach* (Boston: McGraw-Hill Irwin, 2006). https://www.amazon.com/Managing-Organizational-Change-Multiple-Perspectives/dp/B002RMIZJW

4 Janet Turner Parish, Susan Cadwallader and Paul Busch, "Want to, Need to, Ought to: Employee Commitment to Organizational Change," *Journal of Organizational Change Management*, 21(1): 32-52. (February 15, 2008). https://www.deepdyve.com/lp/emerald-publishing/want-to-need-to-ought-to-employee-commitment-to-organizational-change-dMQMtygWbW

5 Lester Coch and John R. P. French, "Overcoming Resistance to Change," Human Relations, 1, 512-532. (November 1, 1948). https://journals.sagepub.com/doi/abs/10.1177/001872674800100408; Kurt Lewin, Field Theory in Social Science, (New York: Harper & Row, 1951). https://trove.nla.gov.au/work/14289400?q&sort=holdings+desc&_=1563318423419&versionId=21752338; Andrew M. Pettigrew, "Context and Action in Transforming the Firm," *Journal of Management Studies*, 24(6), 649-670.

(November, 1987). https://bit.ly/2L0Z385; Jeffrey Pfeffer and Gerald Salancik, The External Control of Organizations: A Resource Dependence Perspective (New York: Harper & Row, 1978). https://www.gsb.stanford.edu/faculty-research/books/external-control-organizations-resource-dependence-perspective

REFERENCES

Busine, Mark and Evan Sinar, PhD. "What Are the Greatest Challenges Frontline Leaders Face." *Development Dimension International Blog*, February 2019. https://www.ddiworld.com/blog/tmi/february-2019/frontline-leader-challenges

Global Leadership Forecast 2018. https://www.ddiworld.com/glf2018

Schoemaker, Paul. "6 Habits of True Strategic Thinkers." *Inc. Magazine*, March 2012. https://www.inc.com/paul-schoemaker/6-habits-of-strategic-thinkers.html

Synchrony. "Synchrony Study: AI Emerging as Imperative for Nation's Retailers." *Cision PR Newswire*, Mar 04, 2019. https://www.prnewswire.com/news-releases/new-synchrony-study-ai-emerging-as-imperative-for-nations-retailers-300805793.html

John Maxwell. https://www.johnmaxwell.com/

Course Hero. https://www.coursehero.com/file/p3venkv/1-Communication-is-defined-as-the-process-by-which-information-is-exchanged-and/

Understanding Communication. https://courses.lumenlearning.com/boundless-management/chapter/understanding-communication/

Dr. Albert Mehrabian. https://en.wikipedia.org/wiki/Albert_Mehrabian

Howard Hendrick. https://www.christianbook.com/iron-sharpens-building-character-mentoring-relationship/howard-hendricks/9780802456311/pd/56316

Maxwell, John. *Everyone Communicates, Few Connect: What the Most Effective People Do Differently.* Nashville: Thomas Nelson, 2010. https://www.amazon.com/Everyone-Communicates-Few-Connect-Differently-ebook/dp/B003BWL0TE

Jay, Ros. *The Seven Deadly Skills of Communicating.* London: International Business Press, 1999. https://www.amazon.com/Seven-Deadly-Skills-Communicating/dp/1861523734

Bossidy, Larry, and Ram Charan. *Execution, The Discipline of Getting Things Done.* New York: Crown Business, 2002. https://www.amazon.com/Execution-Discipline-Getting-Things-Done/dp/0609610570

Clear, James. "Mental Models: Learn How to Think Better and Gain a Mental Edge." James Clear, 2019. https://jamesclear.com/mental-models

Karnjanaprakorn, Michael. "16 Mental Models for Founders and Leaders." *Medium*, May 23, 2017. https://medium.com/personal-growth/16-mental-models-for-founders-and-leaders-25c3724a5208

Parcon, Paul. *Develop Your Decision Making Skills.* Darya Ganj New Delhi: Lotus Books, 2007. https://www.amazon.com/Develop-Your-Decision-Making-Skills/dp/8183820948

Peter Senge. https://executive.mit.edu/faculty/profile/30-peter-senge

Les Brown. https://lesbrown.com/

Raciel Sosa is the Chief Executive Officer of Leadex Solutions, a leadership development firm based in Mexico City focused on building and enhancing leadership capabilities, developing healthy work environments, and enabling high performance teams. He has over 20 years of experience working with teams in human resources and organizational development, including at Great Place to Work® Institute Mexico and Latin America, Hewlett Packard, Lucent Technologies, and Alcatel Lucent. A highly respected coach, certified consultant, and sought-after speaker on leadership, high-performance teams, and the universal qualities that make a workplace in any region of the world healthy, Mr. Sosa has ongoing desire to help create winning corporate cultures and develop leaders who will innovate for years to come. He has delivered keynotes at many cross industry global conferences including in Spain, Rome, London, Argentina, Chile, Uruguay, Colombia, Venezuela, Perú, Panamá, El Salvador, Guatemala, and Mexico. He holds a BA from the Instituto Tecnológico Autónomo de México.

CHAPTER FOURTEEN

Frontline Leadership Development

Raciel Sosa
Chief Executive Officer, Leadex Solutions

The most important documented economic eras in the history of mankind are the hunting and gathering era, the agricultural era, the industrial era, and the digital information era. Each one of these has been accompanied by different tools and paradigms, as well as by different leadership models.

The end of the 20th century clearly marked the beginning of the digital era and, even though the era's tools were already available (e.g., computers, cell phones, tablets, etc.), the paradigms and leadership models have not yet been meaningfully updated.

At the beginning of the 21st century, leaders had been educated by the Traditionalist and Baby Boomer Generations. The leadership style was hierarchical, authoritarian, and based on control with punitive consequences to guarantee changes in behavior. Leadership during the 20th century was characterized by exercising control to ensure consistent quality through very well-defined processes, as well as by the repetitive scheduling of tasks that generated consistent results.

Today's Digital Age presents new challenges. Technology allows us to have immediate access to necessary information and facilitates connectivity between all human beings—at a speed that was unimaginable in the 20th century. We are entering the era of largely free content and many of the economic models that enjoyed success in the 20th century are declining. The leadership style of the 20th century is also facing decline.

Organizations are unable to retain new talent for the long-term. Millennials have a new way of viewing life that is incomprehensible for Baby Boomers and Gen Xers. There's a "Tower of Babel" in the organizational world that, coupled with startup companies with exponential results, is placing large corporations at risk and in danger of extinction. Leaders do not understand how to communicate with these new protocols. Concepts such as the balance between personal life and work seem utopian and impractical to them, and they accuse the new generations of being egocentric, unproductive, and disoriented. Consequently, Millennials judge Baby Boomers and Gen Xers as being retrograde and insensitive.

Fortunately, there is new research that casts light and provides guidance on how we must evolve as leaders. Respect, trust, and admiration play a fundamental role. Happiness in the work environment today is an evolving, but mandatory matter. The balance between personal life and work must be anchored in specific practices, not just talked about in platitudes.

Leadership in the 21st century is in crisis and must be re-thought. I believe there are six behaviors leaders in the 21st century must learn, execute, and master to become efficient and effective in today's labor environment that is not well-known—and is therefore, challenging.

1. **Release Your Own Potential**

   Personal leadership is not based on a single experience. It does not start and end with the writing of a personal mission statement. Rather, it is a process that consists of keeping in mind our own personal vision, mission, and values—and organizing our lives to be consistent with the things that matter most to us.

   Whether in the personal or professional aspect, if the only vision we have of ourselves comes from the social mirror (of the current social paradigm and of the opinions, perceptions, and paradigms of the people around us), the concept that we have of ourselves will be similar to the image reflected in the distorting mirrors of amusement parks.

   Our basic nature is to act, not to be acted upon, which allows us to choose our own responses to particular circumstances and empowers us to create contexts that favor us.

   No one can grow and learn on our behalf; existence does not acknowledge representatives. Let's take the initiative!

   To take the initiative does not mean to be insistent or aggressive, but rather to recognize our responsibility in making things happen. We are responsible for acting. The difference between those taking initiative and those who don't is like the difference between day and night. Specifically, if we prove to be aware and sensitive to the needs of others, always staying alert, we will take the initiative by taking responsibility for our actions.

All human beings have more potential than what we show and execute daily. In this sense, each moment is an opportunity to identify, liberate, and expand our talent and become more autonomous, productive, and happy. The three basic premises for self-realization as individuals, and to free our potential are:

- **Execution**—The ability to identify what you do best; and do so proactively, is based on the human privilege of self-consciousness. The two additional human privileges that allow us to expand our productivity and to exercise personal leadership in our lives are our imagination and our moral consciousness. Through imagination, we can visualize potential worlds that lie in our interior. Through moral consciousness, we can come in contact with universal laws or principles, with our own particular talents and specific forms of contribution, and with our personal guidelines with which we can develop ourselves more effectively. Together with self-consciousness, these two human characteristics will allow us to write our own script.

  No matter what we are doing, we must do it with discipline, performing activities we do not like equally as well as the ones we enjoy, in order to dedicate our life to those key things that are important for us. Even if it sounds contradictory, discipline generates freedom.
- **Vision**—Our dreams free our potential. Whenever we commit ourselves to our dreams, everything around us will conspire to make them come true, which in turn will help us achieve the results that we want. Our emotions define our conduct and determine our results.
- **Collaboration**—Let's have fun, and let's work as a team and choose positive attitude. Let's always love what we do so that one day we can do what we love.

In the 21st century, those individuals who want to lead must have mastered the competency of directing their own activities and attitude, which will generate respect and admiration, and positively impact the behavior of others.

2. Capacity To Lead The Way

Currently, most organizations are suffering from a shortage of leaders as a result of not investing the necessary time and resources to develop them—even though developing leaders represents a company investment, generating excellent results in the short, medium, and long term.

Research shows that leadership is a change agent that can take the company to "the next level," having an exponential affect. Organizations focused on forming and developing leaders are betting on the strongest link to "move" the organization. A good leader makes things happen and achieves the desired business results by answering four questions:

- What do I want to achieve; where do I want to take the organization?
- Why do I want to achieve this? (This will inspire the entire team.)
- How am I going to achieve this? (This requires developing a method and a strategy to achieve the objective.)
- How am I going to measure results?

3. Effective Communications For The Achievement Of Results

A communication style oriented to results is about sharing something that generates a mutual benefit. According to the authors of *Crucial Conversations: Tools for Talking When the Stakes are High*, effective communication protects us as well as those around us. They advocate for grounding conversations, especially difficult ones, on the achievement of a mutual purpose. When leaders and workers are working toward a common objective, mutual trust is more readily achieved.

Currently, there are very convincing statistics that bosses and employees are often failing to achieve that trust. The 2018 Great Place to Work Institute results for Mexico indicated that 60% of respondents felt their managers did not clearly communicate their expectations. If we want our team to achieve the expected results, we must always keep them informed, expressing our expectations and conveying what is expected of them, so that they do not have to guess. This is the first aspect that a team leader must consider.

What a work team expects from its leader:
Members of a work team expect closeness with their leader, and the way to make this happen is, of course, through communication. They expect their leader to be available to them—to be someone who cares and is occupied with their well-being, who understands what is happening, who supports them from the point of view of development of competencies, and who recognizes them. But for all this to happen, there must be communication, which is the tool that is needed to transmit expectations, the goals that must be achieved to delegate adequately, to perform development plans, to provide feedback, and to recognize individual achievements, among other aspects.

Effective and assertive communications in every area of the company are directly linked to positive results for the entire organization. The steps to producing positive results in an organization include clearly establishing the objective, the empowerment, the development process, the feedback, and the recognition.

What a leader must do to establish effective communication results:

- **Select the right battles**—The first problem we find is that there are leaders who speak but do not choose properly where "it would be worthwhile to be" and, therefore, should adequately "filter" their battles.
- **Have the right reasons for communicating**—Reasons are intentions. Leaders should always communicate with the right intention. If the intention is to punish or to blame, obviously the employees will perceive it that way. If the intention to communicate is to nurture and grow employees, to support them, or to seek the truth, the whole process is modified and that is what ultimately achieves the desired results.
- **Learn to put facts first and emotions last**—People tend to mix what we think and what we feel with what really is. Faced with this, an assertive leader knows how to start from facts in order to justify that effective communication.

Constant feedback to the work team is something that must be especially cared for, because that is what allows us to improve, to grow, to develop, to be constantly exceeding our own limits, and to exceed organizational expectations. Feedback is based on effective communications and when it is lacking, stagnation occurs.

The benefits of establishing effective results-oriented communications in the organization are many, but it is important to note that because of them, collaborators experience a better work environment and therefore, employees are happier and will project their positive experience toward the customer.

Even though it is true that in the 20th century, minimal information was communicated to employees under premises of "don't give them more information that what they need to know," or "it is better if this remains between us," current leaders have to change this attitude because the more information they share with their collaborators, the easier they will be able to access "the complete picture" of the company. In turn this opens the possibility of being able to innovate, create, and better understand the direction of the company and how and where to apply their efforts.

Likewise, given that we are in a very rapidly changing world, there is a human demand to use communications more because of the proximity required by daily activities; more communications are also required to innovate and be closer to the customers. We must learn to use all the tools of electronic communications that are available, and we should not demonize them, but rather use them appropriately for the company's benefit. Today, we can be in constant communication and that is something good. Let's use everything that is available to us to encourage effective communications.

4. Developing Other Leaders

Leaders should have the capability to empower individuals on their teams to become leaders themselves. One of the greatest challenges that leaders face is that the competence of leadership not only requires academic preparation, but also practical training. It is a bit like learning how to ride a bicycle. Human beings acquire the competency of riding a bicycle with minimum knowledge, but with a very important dose of practice. With this simple analogy, I want to demonstrate that training within the company is very important in order to create organizational leaders.

Steps that a leader must follow to develop his collaborators in the competency of leadership:

- **Diagnosis**—It is essential to understand the current situation of the collaborator and to determine all the experience that he has in the art of leading a work team. This should encompass the employee's childhood experiences through adulthood. Let's remember that leadership is a skill that is learned through practice and that it considers all aspects of human life.
- **Establish a development plan**—Providing a roadmap to the individual to get where they need to be is critical. The development plan must include elements such as reading, videos, practices, mentoring by a manager, assignment of projects, etc. It is extremely important for employees to understand that their own development is a responsibility largely their own.

5. Establishing Recognition Environments

There must be a consistent and adequate recognition system that favors interpersonal relations within an organization. Unfortunately, recognition is not a generalized practice. A large portion of managers do not understand the impact that recognition has on long-term relationships. Most individuals confuse recognition with reward. By definition, reward is always accompanied with the organizational authorization and with an economic amount that may be granted in cash or in kind.

However, recognition must comply with these characteristics also:

- **Generous**—It must be granted with the best intentions and with the purpose of strengthening interpersonal relationships and to genuinely celebrate the success or the efforts of a collaborator
- **Personalized**—This implies that the recognition is totally aligned with the concerns, interests, and personal and specific needs of each collaborator; this implies a deep knowledge of the individual that is being recognized.
- **Unexpected**—Those recognitions that are granted spontaneously and surprisingly have a strong repercussion on the emotional state of the individual and, unfortunately, it is a resource of which very few leaders take advantage.
- **Low-cost**—Since this is not a reward, the recognition is something that implies a very low market cost, but since it is unexpected, it has a high value on the attitude of the person recognized.
- **Timely**—If an individual generates good results or has attributes that the organization values, these must be recognized over a short period of time in relation to the moment in which the conduct or the positive result occurred.

6. Collaboration

For a work team to be successful, a common objective must exist where all the members have one single vision of what must be achieved, and the roles must be well-defined.

Under a win-win vision, the members of a work team achieve cohesion, obtaining a mutual benefit and a long-term relationship. In this context, trust plays a relevant role, since trust is precisely the element that joins a person with another. That is, if there is no mutual trust, there is no possibility of creating a healthy and real linkage, since trust is fundamental to achieve cohesion. Without trust there is no cohesion and without cohesion there is no team.

The core of trust is reliability—to our fellow co-workers and to our customers. To generate an environment of trust between the collaborators on a work team, the following must exist:

- **Intent**—There must be a positive intent of all the members of the team; intent is the first incentive to build trust. If we feel that someone has negative intentions against us, the first thing we will do is to withdraw our trust and close all communications channels in order to protect ourselves.

- **Mutual respect**—An environment of mutual respect must be created. If we damage the environment of respect, we can ruin the entire relationship. Respect is like air: no one perceives it, but when it is missing, it is the only thing you notice. Lack of respect directly damages the trust of a work team.
- **Mutual purpose**—We must clearly state a common purpose and make sure that all collaborators understand the measurement parameters in terms of quality, quantity, time, and cost.

To generate trust and teamwork, we must establish common values, such as honesty, learning how to manage conflicts, and promoting dialogue. If we don't discuss the things that are bothering us, we are not working as a team. Silence is, at times, a poorly understood tolerance and finally becomes a pressure cooker. It is all about creating an environment of trust, which is what really sustains teamwork.

Trust is not something that is established by decree. It is a human process. Therefore, it needs to be gained, nurtured, and fed so that over time it may gain a strong foothold within the team. There must be a concerted effort over time among all team members to build trust. Of note too, trust is not something that once achieved, goes on by itself. Trust has the same behavior as a fluid: it must be contained. If a container has holes in it, fluids will drain.

It is important to note that the sole fact of coexisting with another human being generates wear on trust. That is, if you work with another person, the sole fact that you are different and generate individual expectations, gradually generates wear on trust. That's why it is important to perform daily activities to continue nurturing trust. It is what some authors call a "deposit of trust"—actions that nurture the relationship with the other person. To maintain a good level of trust, we must be making deposits of trust consistently by keeping our word, maintaining an environment of mutual respect (with our co-workers), and creating an environment that translates into behaviors that maintain over time a high level of trust. This is a continuous process.

For the company to be successful, we must be aware of the importance of trust, how to plant it, how to build it and how to maintain it, particularly in a multigenerational environment such as the one we currently live in. Previously, control was enough to keep a team together. Today, new generations are looking for new elements to work with each other in a cohesive environment—and to achieve this, trust is a basic element. It also facilitates the resolution of conflicts within the company, since everyone works in a context of dialogue and problem solving.

When one works in an environment of trust, synergy and teamwork are strengthened and the benefits are greater for all. There cannot be a healthy work relationship if there is not a mutual benefit.

The Challenges Of The 21st Century Leader

I believe the 21st century leader has two very important challenges ahead:

- **To learn to interact with heterogeneous, multigenerational groups.** This is one of the elements that is currently very important in the work environment. The generations that are working today are different and the way to approach them must be different as well. Today, we work with people that are very different from us in many ways. The leader of the future must learn how to work with this diversity of individuals.
- **Create and promote environments of innovation.** An individual who only does his or her job and nothing else is no longer enough. The work environment today requires individuals who think, create, propose, and challenge. This creates an environment where everyone can come up with ideas—and this generates the creation of an environment of innovation. Given this scenario, leaders must find a way or method that will allow them to capitalize on knowledge because, obviously, not all ideas are good. It is important to know how to identify and promote those that are truly worthwhile.

Change is the constant of the 21st century. The competencies that were useful during the 20th century are mostly obsolete today. Reimagining 21st century Leadership is not a luxury, but rather a must-have for organizational survival.

FOCUS ON THE FRONTLINE

1. You may be thinking of your frontline leaders simply as managers, but not as true leaders. It's time to re-think this because your frontline managers can be some of your most strategic and effective leaders if you give them the chance.
2. Invest the time and money to build leaders within your organization—it will pay off in the long run.
3. Give your leaders the opportunity to take coursework to improve their communication, if needed. Clear communication is a critical aspect of good leadership.
4. Empower your frontline leaders to identify and foster leaders they see on their team.
5. Don't underestimate the power of recognition. Building a culture of recognition creates trust and goodwill amongst your frontline employees.

REFERENCES

Patterson, Kerry, Joseph Grenny, Ron McMillan, and Al Swizler. *Crucial Conversations: Tools for Talking When the Stakes are High.* New York: McGraw-Hill, 2002. https://www.amazon.com/Crucial-Conversations-Tools-Talking-Stakes/dp/0071401946

Great Place to Work® Institute Survey Report. (2018). https://www.greatplacetowork.com/resources/reports

Christian Kromme is an award-winning futurist keynote speaker, innovative technology entrepreneur, TEDx speaker, and best-selling author. Central to all of his work is the connection between people and technology. In 2002, he founded Artificial Industry, an agency providing disruptive ideas and incubator solutions to global brands including Randstad, Oracle, Philips, Toyota, Auping, Adidas, Bjorn Borg, Endemol, Rabobank, Corio, EyeWorks, and ABP. Today he focuses on giving lectures, keynotes, presentations, and workshops to entrepreneurs, business leaders, and policymakers around the globe on exponential technologies, disruptive innovation, and the radical impact of disruptive technologies on humans and organizations. He is the author of the best seller *Humanification—Go Digital, Stay Human,* which focuses on the parallels between biology and technology and on turning a perceived threat into a new opportunity. Mr. Kromme attended HU University of Applied Sciences Utrecht, the Mind Academy Institute, Studie for Applied Biophoton Sciences, Deltion College, and The Resonance Academy.

CHAPTER FIFTEEN

The Humanification Of Work

Christian Kromme
Technology Entrepreneur, Futurist, Speaker, Author

What happened to our world?

Generations before us lived in a world that changed slowly. Their reality was no bigger than the distance their feet could walk, and their eyes could see. The changes that impacted their lives happened within their line of sight and happened over generations. Our world used to be a relatively slow, stable, and predictable place. But not anymore.

We now live in a world that's changing at breakneck speed. We are interconnected by a giant global nervous system called the Internet; when something happens on one side of the world, we know about it on the other side of the world within seconds.

Change is happening exponentially fast, it no longer takes generations to affect our lives. Massive global shifts don't take generations (or even decades) anymore but can be witnessed in years, months, weeks, and even days.

We are living in a new era of radical change and global disruption. It's both exciting and scary. In the next decade, artificial intelligence, robots and new technologies are likely to take over many of our jobs. We are going to be forced to rethink what it really means to be a human being, about how we work, what we do, and the future of ourselves and our planet.

We Don't Live In A Time of Change, But In A Change Of Times

Today the world is going digital at warp speed. Exponential technology is giving birth to an entirely new type of economy: Robotics, Artificial Intelligence (AI), 3D Printing, Augmented Reality, Internet of Things (IoT), and Blockchain are already impacting our world more than many people realize.

As these advances move from the margins to become the hub of businesses, our lives, and our jobs, the impact is triggering seismic shifts for us all. Our personal lives are also likely to totally transform in ways that we haven't even considered yet.

Technology is moving ever closer to our physical being too, it's even getting under our skin! In Sweden more than 3,000 people have chips implanted into their hands; they can enter a building or book a train ticket using just their chip. That's taking wearable technology further than people thought would be acceptable just a decade ago. It's not just man-made tech that's impacting us either, we are now biohacking our way to longer lives and even finding ways to hack happiness.

It's been suggested by many futurists and scientists that that by 2030, we will live until we are 150! Biohacking will allow us to access parts of ourselves that monks have had to meditate for decades to reach, and exponential advances to our minds and body connection, advanced treatments for disease, and our ability to read and alter our DNA, have the potential to transform our time on this planet.

What Will Be The Impact On Our World?

Despite all the technological advances and possibilities at our disposal, our world is still divided.

The rich are still getting richer and the poor are getting even poorer. A self-interested elite with precious little shared purpose are behind many decisions that affect millions of people. Governments don't seem to represent their civilians anymore, banks can't be trusted, healthcare systems are making us sick instead of healing us, and our kids are being educated for a world that on longer exists.

We are seeing a backlash: children and teenagers are having more political impact than many of our politicians. Greta Thunberg is moving more people to take action on climate change than the US president. Malala Yousafzai is having a massive influence on the treatment of girls across the world. We all have the potential to make an impact in a way that wasn't possible 20 years ago.

But sadly, the smartest people in the world are often not being hired to make our world a better place; they are being hired by the highest bidder. Wealthy tech giants focused on product marketing or getting our data to drive future AI applications have very deep pockets. They can afford to hire the brightest people to find ways to enter every crevice of our lives and build our dependence on their apps, and persuade us to click and spend money we don't have, on products we don't need, to impress people we don't care about.

Of course, some companies are trying to change the world by working out how we can reduce our energy burden, live more sustainably, and save our planet—and they are attracting some bright young talent—but their pockets often aren't as deep.

So, we live in a technologically advanced society that's supposed to be more connected than ever, but has disconnected us from our fellow humans on a massive scale. Social media fuels mistrust, adds social pressure for perfection, is increasing our anxiety, and meddles with our political systems. We are growing evermore disconnected from ourselves and the ones we love.

So, what can we do about it?

The Tipping Point

Imagine a world where human beings are at the center of everything once again. Where we live in a human-centred society that's united, aligned with nature and driven by purposeful eco-systems. Where governments are once again in service of the people who voted for them, where healthcare systems keep us healthy, and where children are educated to listen to their heart and design a meaningful life.

A world where people are deeply connected with each other and united for shared goals. A world where you can be your true and authentic self, and where learning and working are an integral part of living a purposeful and meaningful life.

Humanity has arrived at a critical tipping point in the evolution of our species. We are about to enter an era of transformation beyond the scale of our current imagination. A transformation from a divided world, driven by *EGO-systems* (driven by power and money), and instead towards a world driven by *ECO-systems* (driven by compassion, dignity, and equality).

But how do we escape from the current system? The one that has enslaved millions to work for money and forget about true purpose? Well, one thing we should NOT do is to fight the old system. Instead, we need to build new systems that make the old system obsolete. Although you might think it's a huge gap to bridge between today's world and this imaginary future, what if that gap was not as big as you thought it was?

To transform our current organizations towards more *purpose-full* organizations, we need a radical plan—a roadmap that moves us to a more sustainable and meaningful future. But how do we design that roadmap? Who (or what) has the experience and intelligence to do something *that* big?

Well, the answer is all around us. Nature.

Nature has hundreds of millions of years of experience. Nature knows how to adapt to an ever changing environment. Nature can show us a roadmap towards a sustainable and purposeful future. All we have to do is to follow the clues that she gives us. It's time to align ourselves with nature and the natural waves that already exist.

Nature Had Already Solved The Adaptability Challenge

The changes we see around us are affecting every industry, every job, and every level of society. With the world currently so unstable and unpredictable, how can we plan for the future?

Well, a few years ago I made a remarkable discovery. One that completely changed my perspective on our world, technology, organizations, and our future, and it turns out that nature is at the heart of the solution.

For a moment, think of how the human body works. It's a highly advanced society/community of trillions of cells. Remarkably, these vast numbers of cells work together in harmony. As human beings, we balance inputs and outputs, energy, rest, harmony and different needs without any conscious thought. Nature has solved that for us. We just live.

Our body is a society of cells, a highly intelligent society built from trillions of living cells that solve problems in the same way and in the same order as we whole human beings do. The only difference is that living cells use biological systems to build organisms, and humans use technological systems to build organizations.

I discovered that cells and humans follow the same universal pattern, a pattern of seven disruptive waves.

Each wave solves problems—but at the same time it creates the next set of problems! These seven waves may sound a bit weird at first, but it helps when you realize that these waves are part of a pattern that started long before people. They started with the first single cell organisms that inhabited the earth.

The biology behind much of our technology starts to really make sense when you start to spot the connections.

1. **INTERACTION: The Multi-cellular Life Revolution**—The first biological wave helped single cell organisms to meet their basic needs. Cells started to develop some kind of communication and started to work together and form multicellular culture and communities. These became organisms that were, in effect, using bio-technology to increase their survival rate. These single cells started to work together and form bigger structured communities like coral reefs (shelter) to gather and filter food more efficiently (agriculture) from the ocean tides.
2. **INFRASTRUCTURE: The Organ/Tissue Revolution**—The second biological wave helped the cell communities (organisms) to meet their needs of safety and comfort. It helped the organisms to form a digestive system (industry) that processed food more efficiently and distributed nutrition (energy) through a vascular system (infrastructure). In this way organisms could distribute energy more efficiently throughout the organism, which enabled it to thrive and grow even faster (health).
3. **INFORMATION: The Nervous System Revolution**—The third biological wave helped the fast-growing cell communities (organisms) to meet their love and connection needs. The cell communities have grown rapidly, and distances became bigger between separate parts of the cell community (organism). Cell communities start to form nerve networks that re-connect the outer parts of the community real-time so that they can work together even more efficiently (connection). Cell communities also start to develop senses that helped the community to create a better awareness of their surroundings.
4. **INSTINCT: The Reptile Brain Revolution**—The fourth biological wave helped the cell communities (organism) to meet the needs of self-esteem and autonomy. Cell communities (organisms) start to develop automated routines that helped them to automate internal processes and also helped them to hunt more efficiently. Cell communities developed an operating system (reptile brain) that was like a software layer upon all the biological hardware.
5. **IMITATION: The Limbic Brain Revolution**—The fifth biological wave helped the cell communities (organisms) to meet their cognitive

needs. Cell communities developed a mammal brain technology that provided memory (knowledge) which helped organisms to remember specific environments, situations and behaviors, it also gave the organism social skills (self-awareness and expression) that enabled them to share and copy successful behaviors from other mammals.

6. **INTELLIGENCE: The Neocortex Brain Revolution**—The sixth biological wave helped cell communities to meet their aesthetic needs. Technology like the neocortex brain helped them to learn and adapt in real-time, to learn faster, and solve more complex problems, it also gave rise to the first tools and drawings (beauty and form), it helped to walk upright (balance), and it enabled the development of basic communication (self-reflection).
7. **IMAGINATION: The Prefrontal Cortex Revolution**—The seventh biological wave helped cell communities to meet their needs of self-actualisation and transcendence. Technology like the prefrontal cortex enabled cell communities (organisms, including we humans) to improve themselves and develop advanced language and share concepts and ideas (personal growth and self-knowledge), it helped us to develop agriculture and civilization (morality and place others need above self), and it helped us to do things that gave us satisfaction (fulfilment and purpose).

Each new biological wave pushed these cell communities to the next level of complexity. New biological systems enabled organisms to process more information and become more adaptable so they could dramatically increase their survival rate. The invention of advanced communication skills enabled human beings to collaborate on a larger scale and the seven-wave process starts all over again. Living cells (the building blocks of organisms) created new building blocks, these new building blocks are homo-sapiens (building blocks of organizations) and have sparked a new phase of evolution.

What Will Be The Impact On Technology?

Let's take a short walk through the seven waves that enable the evolution of organizations. When you understand the seven-wave pattern, you will be able to see the evolutionary pattern that shapes our organizations and the technological world we live in today.

1. **INTERACTION: The Agricultural Revolution**—The technological Wave 1.0 delivered technology that met our basic physiological and biological human needs. Technology like agriculture (food), buildings

and towns (shelter/sleep), irrigation (water), fire and tools (warmth), laws and government (homeostatis), and many more.

2. **INFRASTRUCTURE: The Industrial Revolution**—The technological Wave 2.0 delivered technology that met our needs for safety and comfort. Infrastructure technologies provided us with a stable environment to build nations, we were able to have employment (industrial infrastructure), reliable transportation systems (transport infrastructure), constant energy flow (pipeline and cable infrastructure for oil and electricity), pharmaceuticals (healthcare infrastructure), etc.
3. **INFORMATION: The Telecom Revolution**—The technological Wave 3.0 delivered us technology that met our needs to connect with each other. Telecommunication technology enabled real- time communication between family, and our loved ones (meeting our love needs), and let us build and maintain relations over long distances (meeting our connection needs).
4. **INSTINCT: The Automation Revolution**—Technological Wave 4.0 delivered us new technology that meets our need for autonomy. Software technology like operating systems and applications automated all kinds of processes and routines for us. Software gave our technology almost instinctive behavior that was "programmed in" and made our technology much easier to manage.
5. **IMITATION: The Social Media Revolution**—Technological Wave 5.0 delivered new technology that met our cognitive needs. Technology such as search engines (our need for knowledge), social networks (our need for self-awareness and self-expression), and task specific communities (our need for meaning).
6. **INTELLIGENCE: The AI Revolution**—Technological Wave 6.0 holds the promise to deliver new technology that will help us to meet our aesthetic needs. Technology like cloud based neural networks that are able to learn and create almost perfect algorithms (to enhance beauty and form), robots that learn to walk and move like people (balance), and even create advanced virtual agents who can help us with all kinds of processes (self-reflection).
7. **IMAGINATION: The Creative Revolution**—Technological Wave 7.0 holds the promise to deliver new holographic and virtual 3D spatial technology that will meet our need of self-actualization and transcendence. I think it's likely that we will see the advent of digital personal coaches (who will help us achieve faster personal growth, self-knowledge,

and transcendence), hive minds and decision making platforms (that will help us with tough morality questions and give us a mechanism to place the needs of the many above the needs of self), and we will see more co-creation platforms (to help us reach fulfilment and help us serve our purpose).

The evolutionary parallels between biological organisms and technological organizations are no coincidence. Complementary research from Arthur M. Young (the inventor of the Bell Helicopter) shows us that these seven waves are repeating on every level of evolution since the beginning of time and space.

We see these seven waves repeating themselves consistently in all the building blocks of our universe. We see them in the evolution of organizations, organisms, living cells, molecules, atoms, subatomic particles, and light. Seven waves of building blocks, and seven waves per building block. If we place these seven waves of building blocks in a matrix together with their seven evolutionary waves per building block, some very interesting patterns start to emerge. Patterns about our past—and patterns about our future.

I believe that more and more human needs can, and will be, fulfilled by the use of technology. Each technological wave helps us to meet our needs, and in turn pushes the focus of humanity to an ever-higher level of consciousness.

What Will The Impact Be On Organizations?

Each new technological wave has enabled humans to build organizations that are more complex. We are able to manage 10 times more people than the people in previous generations of organizations could. This is how organizations have evolved and become more adaptive, and as a result they increase their survival rate. But what will be the impact on organizations and society over the next decades?

Once again, the answers can be found in nature. A flock of birds is a great example of how nature creates advanced organizations. How do thousands of birds fly as a flock in a perfect synchronicity as if they are one singe organism with no CEO bird or management birds? Nature knows things that we don't. These swirling flocks are highly advanced autonomous systems, they aren't just fascinating to watch; they have secrets that can help us solve our most challenging problems.

The Max Plank Institute in Germany is researching this behavior. Scientists have discovered that flocks are 99% more effective in problem solving and avoiding danger than an individual bird. It turns out that each individual bird takes seven other birds in physical proximity into account and follows three simple yet elegant rules:

Rule 1: Move in the same direction as other birds.

Rule 2: Move with the same speed as other birds.

Rule 3: Don't collide with other birds.

If the birds (or fish, bees, etc.) obey these three rules, the flock/shoal/swarm moves and behaves elegantly as if it was one single organism.

As communication technology gets exponentially faster it will enable human beings to do the same—to behave elegantly and as one.

In the agricultural revolution (Wave 1), human beings were dependent on local word of mouth communication only, but when new technological waves arrived, we added documents, fax, telephone, video-calls, e-mails, and created ERP and CRM systems that automated all the basic information flows within our organizations.

These telecom tools allowed us to manage people on a more global scale. Today we use the internet, smartphones, social media, sharing platforms, big data, analytics, and many more tools to manage the information flow within our global organizations and workforces.

The AI Revolution

The next technological wave will change the DNA of organizations dramatically. In the next wave (Wave 6), we will see advanced AI in the Cloud that will enable organizations to learn and adapt in real-time and manage tens of millions of people located all over the world. Companies like Uber are already algorithm driven organizations, and in 2019 were able to manage approximately 3.5 million drivers all over the world. The next wave will enable even more complex organizations. Perhaps we will see platform organizations able to manage 40,000,000 people in real-time all over the world.

Many people are afraid of AI, they even think it may be our last invention. Well, I don't think that will happen any time soon. If we look at nature again, the

Era	Technological Waves	Communication Technology (approx.)	Complexity Organizations	Examples
10,000 BC	1) Agricultural Revolution	Word of mouth, symbols	400	Small Villages
1750 AC	2) Industrial Revolution	Paper documents, technical drawings/ blueprints	4,000	First Factories (Henry Ford)
1850 AC	3) Telecom Revolution	Telegraph, telephone, fax, microphone, camera, radio, TV	40,000	Bell Company
1950 AC	4) Automation Revolution	Computers, operating systems, drivers, software	400,000	IBM
2000 AC	5) Social Media Revolution	Internet, big data, analytics, social media platforms	4,000,000	Uber
2018 AC	6) AI Revolution	AI (self-learning systems), neural networks, IOT	40,000,000	?
2027 AC	7) AR Revolution	Holographic technology (Augmented Reality, 3D Spatial Web)	400,000,000	?

Each new technological wave pushed organizations to a higher level of complexity.

Neocortex brain (our biological AI in the cloud) helped organisms to increase their rate of survival dramatically, AI in the cloud will do exactly the same for human beings and organizations. AI will help us to learn and adapt in real-time and collaborate on a much higher level.

I believe that in the next decade we will see the advent of swarm organizations. AI powered organizations that behave like a flock of birds. This new breed or organizations will be highly adaptive and prove tough competition for traditional organizations. AI will empower people and coordinate massive numbers of people. Future organizations will be comparative to an orchestra; an orchestra with many passionate people who are specialists playing their instrument. AI will be like the conductor, orchestrating all the individuals with their specialities and passions into a single harmonious symphony.

The AR Revolution

The seventh technological wave will enable completely new types of organizations that will use things like holographic technology like Augmented Reality (AR), Mixed Reality, Virtual Reality, and the Spatial (3D) Web. Time and space becomes less relevant as we create very powerful global and holistic organizations.

People all over the world will be able to work together as if they were a finely tuned part of one single organism. AI will help us to speak and understand any language, AR will help us to collaborate with people on the other side of the world and it will feel like they are in the same room, and advanced 3D visualizations and simulations will help us to collaborate much more efficiently. Wave 7 will potentially create platform organizations with as many as 400 million people working together in harmony like one organism. Just imagine the power of an organization like that, 400 million purposeful people working together on meaningful projects to make our world a better place.

What Will Be The Impact On The Workforce And Individual Workers?

All that technological progress doesn't deliver unless we push ourselves to evolve our consciousness, thinking, and behavior to keep up. What's the use in all that change if we don't do something useful with it?

If we don't develop our consciousness and thinking as fast as the technology, we will become empty vessels with very little to contribute. There's no doubt that many of our jobs are going to be automated by smart technology in the very near future. That means we are all going to be challenged to answer serious questions about our purpose and usefulness. As our own technology makes us progressively more redundant and gives us more free time, we are going to be forced to answer these challenging questions: Who are we, and why are we here? What does it mean to be human? How do I lead my life and what does useful work look like?

Skill Versus Will

We are still educating people for a world that no longer exists. Our entire educational system and economy has, for the last 100 years, been focused on people learning the skills required to perform largely repetitive and routine tasks. (See more about this in Alexandra Levit's chapter in this book.) We have been teaching people how to follow procedures to produce consistent results. Most of us are trained for a life of "hard skills" that are easily measured. Learning and performing these easily quantifiable hard skills is (and has been) a good thing. That model has helped millions of people to generate economic value, become part of the system, secure a home, buy food, look after their families, and enjoy their leisure time.

But things are changing rapidly. Technology will soon augment or replace many of those hard skills we have been educated to rely on to produce value. Even professional roles that were once considered immune to the march of the robots will be affected. Some of them are already feeling the effects and people don't know what to do about it.

We are going to have to find a way to stay relevant as human beings. In the more uncertain times that are coming, I believe a strong will is going to be more important that a strong skill.

Hard skills can be replaced, a strong sense of purpose and powerful motivation is uniquely human, and these are the qualities that are going to become ever more valuable. Being purpose driven and to do work you really care about will perhaps be the biggest asset of future workers.

So How Do We Stay Ahead Of The Machines?

Some experts estimate that between 78% and 86% of the jobs in our current economy are based on hard skills. The harsh reality is that the human body is actually not very well equipped to perform them for long periods of time without significant strain. The most valuable skills that take people years to learn also involve us making a lot of (expensive) mistakes during the learning process. Those skills aren't easily interchangeable either, making us somewhat inflexible.

Everything that can be digitized will be—and that's going to lead to a dramatic decrease in value. Future technology will be cheap, efficient, and extremely fast at automating repetitive and routine tasks. Those tasks then become a commodity. It makes perfect sense that businesses are going to expect more and more routine tasks to be done by AI or by robots, and I'm expecting that to happen within a decade.

But There Is Good News For Team Human!

Technology is going to automate many tasks that aren't worth our human attention. We know that skills that can be digitized and automated are going to become a commodity, but the flip side of that means what can't be digitized and automated will increase in value.

As technology automates many hard skills, businesses will become financially motivated to focus on the development of "soft skills" instead. That will be the big differentiator when everything else has reached maximum efficiency. The truly human qualities such as emotion, ethics, empathy, and creativity are much more difficult to automate. That's why they will increase so considerably in value.

Human Skills Are Not Valued As They Should Be

From the moment we set foot in the world, humans are naturally equipped with those valuable soft skills. We are gifted with imagination, creativity, emotions, empathy, and compassion. Currently these skills aren't always valued in economic terms. If they were, Mother Terresa would have been a billionaire, but despite her considerable influence she was never fiscally comparable to Jeff Bezos or Mark Zuckerberg.

Our children are taught to draw between the lines, sit on their chair, stop dreaming, and keep their mouth closed. Skills like compassion, intuition, empathy, emotion, ethics, and curiosity are not the primary focus in schools (which is hardly surprising as they aren't financially valued in our current economy).

Technology Behaves Like A Mirror

I have been researching disruptive technologies for years now, and it has become more and more apparent to me that it will not be technology alone that answers our really big questions.

Each new wave of disruptive technology is serving more of our human needs and is solving more practical problems, but at the same time it's also creating new issues of a much higher level; issues that are ever harder to resolve.

Ironically, I believe that as we get more technologically advanced, we will become less focussed on the technology itself and more focused on the human beings benefiting from it.

I see technology acting like a mirror, one that reflects our inner world. The more powerful the technology, the clearer and more reflective the image in the mirror becomes. In the end, we will see our true selves looking back at us through our technology.

So, if technology behaves like an amplifier and mirrors our inner world (as I believe it does), it becomes more and more important that there is something positive inside ourselves to amplify and reflect. It becomes critical for us to have a strong sense of purpose, be intrinsically motivated, and have a strong set of soft skills to connect with other people so we can all have meaningful impact in our world while living our purpose.

People without a strong sense of purpose, who are only able to perform hard skills, are likely to be the first to have their jobs automated. If you do machine-like work, machines will outperform you very soon. In the future, doing purposeful and meaningful work will not be a luxury; it will become an urgent necessity.

The Humanification Of Work

So, what will the future of work look like? Well, when machines can do the work with chips, humans can do the work with their hearts.

I believe that the way human beings can differentiate themselves from machines (and therefore stay ahead of them) is to develop our inner human and build on our soft skills.

I believe that disruptive technologies will rapidly destroy jobs that aren't worth our attention but will also create a new generation of jobs that are much more focused on our human qualities. The future of work, in my opinion, will be about knowing your true self and using advanced technology to connect with other people. To use meaningful technology to express and project your true self and your unique value into the world.

Being who you really are and living that to the full is the way to create true happiness in the long term. So, when machines have automated many of our deficiency needs, we will focus on our growth needs, and our work will become a reflection of that.

It's time to begin the purpose revolution.

FOCUS ON THE FRONTLINE

1. Employees whose jobs rely on presence should be encouraged to view their roles in the most human terms possible. Check-out people are already being replaced by self-service, but a machine is less likely to replace that knowledgeable person on the storeroom floor who can listen to a customer request and help them find exactly what they are looking for.
2. Implement programming and training that will give your frontline employees the soft skills they need to remain viable even after a machine has replaced their hard skills—work with your employees to determine what those skills are.
3. Think of the technology your company produces or uses as a mirror that reflects the core being of your employees and culture. Think purposefully about what you want that reflection out into the world to be and design accordingly.
4. Traits like compassion, intuition, empathy, emotion, ethics, and curiosity should be just as important in your workforce as the harder skills—hire for and reward them!
5. If your organization isn't thinking about and testing out AI and AR strategies, now is the time to start—even on a very small scale.

REFERENCES

Arthur M. Young. http://www.arthuryoung.com/about.html

The Max Plank Institutes. https://www.mpg.de/11741001/research_page

Robotics. https://en.wikipedia.org/wiki/Robotics

Artificial Intelligence (AI). https://en.wikipedia.org/wiki/Artificial_intelligence

3D Printing. https://en.wikipedia.org/wiki/3D_printing

Augmented Reality. https://en.wikipedia.org/wiki/Augmented_reality

Internet of Things (IoT). https://en.wikipedia.org/wiki/Internet_of_things

Blockchain. https://en.wikipedia.org/wiki/Blockchain

David Almeda is Chief People Officer at Kronos Incorporated. He drives the company's global human capital management strategy in support of continued growth, innovation, and profitability. Prior to joining Kronos, Mr. Almeda spent 16 years in various senior human resources functions at Staples, a $25 billion retailer with more than 90,000 employees worldwide. Prior to joining Staples, Mr. Almeda held a management position with The Hertz Corporation, a $4.5 billion division of Ford Motor Co. He is an active member of SHRM, serves on the Board of NEHRA, and advises to the Executive Program in Work-based Learning Leadership at the University of Pennsylvania / Wharton. A sought-after human capital management thought leader, speaker and writer, he has presented at or been published by organizations such as The Conference Board, Harvard Business School, and *CMO Magazine*. Mr. Almeda holds an MA and an EdD from the University of Pennsylvania / Wharton / Graduate School of Education.

CHAPTER SIXTEEN

The Revolution Will Be Codified: Defining, Measuring, And Scaling Great Management

David Almeda, MA, EdD
Chief People Officer, Kronos Incorporated
Writer, Speaker, Thought Leader

> "I believe very strongly that the single largest component of a business that adds to shareholder value is great management, and the single largest destroyer of shareholder value is bad management. I think managing and leading people is a privilege. And I don't think we always understand the impact that we have as managers on the people on our teams. I talk to our managers all the time about this. Do you really understand the impact you have? And if you really understand the impact, then how do your actions reflect that you understand that?"[1]
>
> – Aron Ain, *The New York Times,* 2016

The quote above from the Chief Executive Officer of the company I work for, Kronos Incorporated, epitomizes the unique position I have found myself in as the company's Chief People Officer over the last decade. Unlike many of my counterparts at organizations around the world, I've never had to make the case to my Chief Executive Officer for *why* having great managers at Kronos is important—it's a core belief he shares. Because of this, my focus has been on how we best achieve our goals in this space.

It's easy to say that great managers are important, but it's much more difficult to make manager effectiveness and improvement a consistent area of focus every day. Frankly, the competing priorities of a complex business make it challenging to have a consistent focus on anything for too long, but that's just what we've done at Kronos over the past several years. The following chapter will give you some insight into how we've done this and what differences it has made to our company as a whole.

The Landscape

Founded in 1977, Kronos Incorporated is a $1.4 billion global software firm (at the time of this writing). The company's initial product was the first microprocessor-based time clock and since then, we've become a leading developer of sophisticated cloud workforce management and human capital management solutions. Kronos' customers include some of the world's largest and most respected brands—35,000 organizations across 100 countries with more than 40 million people using a Kronos solution each day.

The company has more than 5,500 employees, "Kronites" as we call ourselves, around the world.

When I was hired in 2010, I was tasked with the goal of what I refer to as "culture codification," a fancy way to say, "let's take the great stuff that is happening here at Kronos and find a way to institutionalize it so that every employee around the world—no matter where they work, who they work for or how long they have worked for the company—has the same great experience."

In 2013, we highlighted the strategic importance of employees by defining and branding our corporate culture, calling it WorkInspired. Kronos agreed to provide an inspiring workplace and in exchange, we asked our employees to perform their work in an inspired way.

We immediately saw results: In 2010, 61% of Kronites felt engaged, and by 2013, that number jumped to 73%.

Our next big step was in 2015, when we launched "Courage to Lead," a series of trainings for aspiring and current managers where we guided them to be bold yet humble, to challenge and support their colleagues, to disrupt existing practices, and perhaps most importantly to engage and connect with people.

With this innovative training in place, we felt we were moving in the right direction and our employee engagement scores reflected this by reaching their highest point ever in 2014. But starting that year, we saw those scores begin to plateau (at ~84%). Additionally, pockets of the organization—typically the ones that were underperforming—had lower engagement scores and higher turnover compared with the rest of the global organization.

We knew that developing and scaling great managers would take the business to the next level, but we were lacking a strong manager measurement and accountability program.

So, we set out to create one with a focus on discovering the traits and behaviors that make an effective manager, and perhaps even more importantly, how we could replicate winning behaviors to make sure everyone across the company had a great manager.

We started with three goals in mind. We wanted to (1) define what great leadership looked like at Kronos; (2) figure out a way to accurately measure the leadership qualities of individual leaders; and (3) actively help our leaders to get better.

Defining Great Leadership At Kronos

Broadly speaking, most people agree on what it means to be a good leader: having open communication with your employees, caring about their lives, providing them with the tools they need to succeed, etc. But rather than being concerned with what, generally speaking, good leaders do—we were interested in finding out what *specifically* good leaders at *Kronos* do.

To do this, we started by analyzing the data we already had. This included existing performance reviews and leadership goal ratings, award nominations, and those engagement surveys I mentioned earlier. By looking through these varying data points, we were able to establish which leaders were meeting or exceeding their leadership goals annually, which leaders were most highly rated by their own managers, and which leaders had been nominated by others for leadership awards.

We made it our mission to find out what traits these leaders exhibited and what actions they took to achieve this level of success. We held targeted focus groups with the goal of moving from just recognizing high-level competencies to uncovering actual observable and measurable leader behaviors.

One of the ways we did this was by targeting the employees of especially strong and weak leaders and speaking with both groups to understand the differences in how they described their managers. Time and again, we found the same issues popping up—two sides of the same coin. For example, employees of strong managers talked about being empowered, while employees of poor managers talked about being micromanaged. We also talked directly with our highest scoring managers to find out how they did what they did.

In addition to taking a deep dive into our own internal data, we also conducted external benchmarking. Recognizing that we didn't know everything or have the corner on the market for good ideas, we reached out to companies with corporate cultures that we admired and who we knew based on our own research had taken an evidence-based approach to shaping important aspects of their cultures. In meeting with the HR leaders at these various organizations, we weren't looking for the answers to the equation, rather we were looking for the basis for the equation and the equation itself.

Ultimately, our research confirmed our thinking that this would be a "one size fits one" program, not a "one size fits all" program. The true value of these benchmarking exercises came in exchanging ideas with people who were as passionate about the topic of corporate culture and leadership development as we were, and in expanding our thinking. After our research was done, we synthesized all the external and internal data to design a program that would fit our culture and support our overall business and talent objectives.

Based on our analysis, research, and benchmarking, we found that great managers at Kronos:

- **Communicate openly and honestly**—The best managers share information with employees and provide ongoing feedback. They also help employees find a connection between the work they do each day and the larger corporate strategy while setting clear performance goals.
- **Develop and encourage employees**—Great managers have career conversations with their employees—regardless of what stage of their career those employees are in. Great managers also actively look for opportunities for their employees to grow and develop their skills.
- **Empower and enable**—Effective managers encourage decision-making and risk-taking by their employees. They make sure their employees have the tools they need and then give them the autonomy to work independently and the confidence to not be afraid of failure. Employees need to feel fully supported without being micromanaged.
- **Support the WHOLE PERSON**—Employees want to feel like their managers respect their work-life balance and care about who they are both in and out of the office.

Measurement

Now that we had established specific and tangible guidelines around what constituted great leadership at Kronos, we needed to figure out the best method for measuring our managers' mastery of these areas. We already had a leadership goal for each employee that was rated by their direct manager, but we realized the best and most objective data about management practices would need to come not from the manager's manager, but from the managers' direct reports themselves.

While our bi-annual employee engagement surveys asked Kronites how happy they were with compensation, communications, training, etc., we failed to ask them enough specifics about their relationship with their manager. To remedy this, we incorporated the following 19 manager effectiveness questions into our bi-annual employee engagement surveys with employees responding on a five-point scale ranging from "strongly agree" to "strongly disagree":

My Manager—Communicate

1. My manager is available when I need him/her.
2. My manager makes an effort to get the opinions and thinking of the people in our work group.
3. My manager regularly shares relevant information from his/her manager and functional leadership.
4. My manager ensures I understand the business strategy and how my work influences it.
5. My manager provides ongoing feedback and helps me improve my performance.
6. My manager communicates clear performance goals for me.
7. My manager helps me understand my compensation and conveys the rationale for pay decisions.
8. Within the last six months, my manager had a productive discussion with me/our team about his/her plans to address the feedback from the Manager Effectiveness Index.

My Manager—Develop

9. My manager challenges our work group to meet higher standards of performance.
10. My manager actively looks for opportunities for me to grow and improve my skills.
11. My manager has had a meaningful discussion with me about my career development in the past six months.
12. My manager has ongoing, meaningful discussions with me about my professional development.

My Manager—Empower

13. My manager empowers me to make decisions that enable me to do my job effectively.
14. My manager helps me navigate barriers and roadblocks that prevent me from working effectively.
15. My manager encourages our work group to take appropriate risks to improve business results.

My Manager—Support

16. My manager does what he / she can to ensure I have the flexibility to balance my work and personal life.
17. My manager truly cares about me as an employee.
18. My manager shows appreciation when I do a good job.
19. My manager provides the right amount of direction.

The addition of these questions meant that our surveys became much more specific, including citing the names of the individual managers within the question text, so that we could measure individual managers, not just "general management at Kronos." We carefully crafted the questions to be pointed but not threatening, and we communicated comprehensively beforehand about what we were looking to achieve and why. A meaningful number of these communications came directly from our Chief Executive Officer who, as I mentioned at the outset of this chapter, was an enthusiastic executive sponsor for the program—as well as a recipient of ratings by his own direct reports who were filling out the same survey as all other employees.

The individual management questions were averaged into one comprehensive "Manager Effectiveness Index"[2] or MEI (see example on page 225). Every manager with at least three responses received a report with their specific scores from their direct reports. The report also included an internal benchmark to let them know what quartile they fell into among all managers at Kronos.

Reaction

Anytime you introduce something new—and particularly a new form of performance measurement—to employees, you need to anticipate some trepidation from the measured. We went out of our way to communicate, communicate, and

Overall Manager Effectiveness

* Significance Testing Has Been Applied To This Column
■ Total Company Roll-Up July 2017 Significantly Above This Group(s)
■ Total Company Roll-Up July 2017 Significantly Below This Group(s)

Item Or Category	Total Company Roll-Up July 2017 (n = 4,552)	Total Company Roll-Up Jan 2017* (n = 4,552)	Total Kronos July 2017* (n = 4,552)	Total Company DR July 2017 (n = 8)	Total Company DR Jan 2017 (n = 7)	Total Company DR July 2017 Quartile (n = 8)
Overall Manager Effectiveness	87%	86%	87%	99%	99%	1st
My Manager—Communicate	86%	85%	86%	98%	98%	1st
My Manager—Develop	82%	83%	82%	100%	100%	1st
My Manager—Empower	89%	87%	89%	100%	100%	1st
My Manager — Support	90%	89%	90%	100%	100%	1st

■ Favorable ■ Neutral ■ Unfavorable

MS MANAGER	QUARTILE
Overall Manager Effectiveness	**2nd**
Communication	**1st**
Empowerment	**3rd**
Development	**2nd**
Support	**2nd**

Data from Kronos Manager Effective Index (MEI).

communicate some more about the point of MEI: that we were focused on creating a great employee experience for everyone and on helping managers improve. Our goal was not to weed out weak people, but to help everyone be the best they could be. To keep in this spirit of development rather than punishment, the first round of the MEI was shared only with the manager not up through the chain.

So, how did our managers react when their very first MEI arrived in their inbox? Here are a few real-life examples:

Dory, Director of Interaction Design at Kronos

"I have to admit, my first thought was 'oh no … I'm going to get fired!'"

(So much for all of our communicating!)

Prior to reading that first MEI, Dory had felt pretty good about his skills as a manager and his excellent team of contributors. He considered himself to have a very open communication style and held weekly or sometimes even bi-weekly one-on-one meetings with all of his direct reports. He was on-board with MEI and excited to get his results. He felt quite comfortable that they would be good and had no fear about receiving his first report.

That all changed when he saw his first round of results: both team employee engagement and his personal MEI scores were around 67%, placing him in the 4th (bottom) quartile.

Dory immediately went to his direct supervisor who suggested they meet with HR to go through the numbers and better understand both the scores themselves and the "why" behind them.

One of the areas that came as a surprise to Dory was that his team scored him poorly on "my manager is available when I need him/her." Given his open communication policy, frequent group texts, and regularly scheduled one-to-one meetings, he did not expect that. Other areas where he scored low included "my manager provides career growth and development" and "my manager empowers me to do my work."

HR's advice was for Dory to let his guard down and talk openly and honestly with his team about each area where he had been rated poorly by them. By doing this, Dory gained invaluable insight and was able to come up with some fairly simple behavior changes that made a huge difference.

For example, Dory had the habit of not immediately accepting calendar invites, rather he would tentatively accept all invites and then look at his calendar for the following week on Fridays or over the weekend and solidify what meetings he could attend and which he needed to decline. He had no idea this caused concern amongst his team and made him seem unavailable. Once he learned this, he changed that particular practice. Small fix, big impact.

Dory also set aside two hours every week for "drop in time"—almost like a college professor holding office hours, where team members could come by with issues or questions that may have cropped up. Whether or not team members take advantage of this time, simply blocking it off each week creates the perception of availability and team members really appreciated the change.

Beyond these little changes, Dory has also made some big ones: he has learned to trust his team more, to let them own big projects, and to encourage them to try new things and not be afraid to fail. He realized he wasn't always communicating with them transparently about the reasons why certain decisions were made—sometimes he didn't even know himself. He takes the time now to find out and to communicate the full reasoning to the team. He also has more frequent conversations with his team about their career paths and has brought HR in more to provide specifics.

Finally, Dory also asked his team to write a "manifesto" and present it back to him. The manifesto includes the purpose of the team, how they work together, and perhaps most importantly, what the team expects from Dory as a manager.

Dory's round two MEI scores, taken one year later, were 95%(!), but he's not resting on his laurels. The MEI process has taught him that that 5% could become a bigger issue next year, and he is staying laser focused on how he can be a better manager and help his team be the strongest they can be. His team continues to update and add to the manifesto yearly and communicate openly about their questions and needs.

Chris, Executive at Kronos

Chris is an executive at Kronos who has been with the company for more than ten years and had, at the time of his first MEI, eight direct reports, all of whom were seasoned managers themselves.

Chris felt that he had good relationships with all of his direct reports. They met regularly to go over what they were working on and he would provide insight where applicable. Given that all his direct reports were very senior people themselves and strong experts in their fields, he gave them all a lot of autonomy and often viewed them almost more as peers.

Chris said he was "interested and anxious" to get his MEI scores the first time.

His overall MEI was 90%—an extremely strong first showing. But Chris wasn't satisfied.

"I'm a grade grubber," he noted. "My first thought was, 'I'll get 100% next time'!"

Chris worked with HR to go through the numbers and the one area where he fell short was when it came to the question, "Has your manager had a meaningful discussion about your career in last six months?"

"I absolutely FLUNKED that question," said Chris.

Given that his team was made up of such senior people—the company's General Counsel, Chief Information Officer, Head of Procurement, and others—it had never occurred to Chris that these folks would want or need to discuss their career path.

MEI made him realize that this was a mistake.

Chris shared the results with his team and in each of their next one-on-one meetings, he asked them about their career plans. The discussions were fascinating. One employee told him of his plan to retire in three years and the steps he was taking to groom his replacement, one had a detailed 10-year plan in mind, another thanked him for his interest but said she didn't feel the need for any guidance in that department.

"I learned more than I ever would have imagined," says Chris. "I didn't realize what I had been missing by not having these conversations."

Overall, Chris believes strongly that MEI helps him better manage his people as individuals the way they want and the way they need.

"The MEI survey really showed me my blind spots," he says now.

When his results came back a year later, Chris scored 100% on the career development question. His overall score remained roughly the same as some areas were slightly up and some down, but he feels the important thing is that the lines of communication are now open in a way they hadn't been previously.

"I really think MEI creates a virtuous cycle of trust, transparency, and communication," says Chris.

Susan, Senior Manager

Susan is a senior manager who has been with Kronos for more than 20 years. She oversees a department with more than 1,000 employees and had, at the time of her first MEI, six direct reports who all managed teams of their own.

Susan's very first MEI scores were in the low 90th percentile.

"My first reaction was, 'That's pretty good'!" said Susan. "But when I dug in, some line item behaviors of mine were in the low 80s, so I knew I had work to do. The question for me was, 'How do I go from numbers on a page to get the full story from my team and make the necessary changes?'"

Susan started by sitting down with her HR representative and together they decided that Susan would feel most comfortable having her HR person interview her team members to get more detail and report back. (This is a good example of that "one size fits one" mentality I mentioned earlier in the chapter—each manager needs to make MEI their own.)

When Susan had more detail, she met directly with her team and talked about what she had heard, what she was planning to do differently, and what everyone thought of the plan. Amongst the things she learned from the feedback received was that she needed to talk with her team more about professional development, and also to calibrate her level of involvement more individually—some team members wanted more and some wanted less.

"One of the real revelations for me was that in my own career, I have had lots of exposure to various groups and functions within the company, but many of my reports and our team members have not. I learned I need to find ways to remove silos and connect my team to others to gain insight across different business units."

Susan's hard work and introspection paid off, her MEI scores the following year were 100%.

"I think perhaps the most beneficial part of MEI for me was that it created a foundation for dialogue with my staff that hadn't previously been there. All of my direct reports now proactively offer feedback—that is huge and contributes to a team that is constantly improving."

As you can see from the experiences of Dory, Chris, and Susan, the MEI really does provide insight into those blind-spots we all have. The way we look at it, as long as we have managers who want to get better, we will work with them. It's when a manager doesn't care that we may need to talk with them about if Kronos is the right place for them. And our managers now realize that sometimes small tweaks in behavior can make a huge difference. Some things don't need a week-long training program, they just need a manager to have better self-awareness.

One of the really interesting things we've seen is that the very act of admitting weakness and being willing to have a conversation with an employee where a manger shows vulnerability in fact leads to a stronger manager-employee relationship.

Three years into this MEI journey, the MEI process is now baked into our culture. Twice a year, every year, armed with their MEI results, all managers debrief with their teams—either as a group or individually—to drive ongoing, open discussions about their high and low scoring areas. Using employee feedback, managers work with HR and their own managers to build personal development plans, targeted to their specific development opportunities, while leveraging MEI specific training programs. Group, online, and personal trainings are continuously being created and updated, and are provided to help managers improve in a variety of areas from communication skills to effective delegation.

Results

So, beyond the anecdotal reactions I've shared, what difference has MEI made? Well, in the first 12 months, we saw:

- 6% increase in MEI scores
- 3% increase in engagement scores
- 2% increase in retention indicator (self-reported intent to stay with Kronos)
- 1% decrease in voluntary turnover

Of managers who scored in the bottom quartile in July 2016 (our first survey data point), nearly half improved and moved out of the bottom quartile a year later. Less than a third remain in the bottom quartile and are actively engaged in coaching. Less than that—18%—left the company. Of course, reasons for leaving the company vary across the board, and are not solely linked to the MEI program.

We also learned that low MEI scores do not always equal a "bad manager." They may have inherited a difficult situation where, for example, poor team performance had gone unaddressed. With clarity provided by MEI, managers can take concrete action. As a general rule, low MEI scores only become urgent after at least three measurement periods.

The MEI process surfaced another interesting insight: not everyone wants to be a manager. Some people in management roles did not aspire to manage people and, with the program as a backdrop, were comfortable having this conversation. This contributed to the 6% of managers in the original bottom quartile (July '16) who have since moved into non-managerial roles.

We also uncovered several key insights after completing validation analysis with a third party, specifically comparing MEI data, engagement data, and turnover data. Our data shows:

1. Overall MEI rating is a strong predicter of employee engagement—accounting for a full half of the variability in engagement scores

between teams. This validated the criticality of the people manager role in overall employee engagement. For example, moving a manager's average MEI score from "neutral" to "favorable" resulted in a 13% increase in engagement, on average.

2. There's a correlation between the MEI scores of next-level managers to those of direct-report managers, suggesting a modest "ripple effect" of manager effectiveness through the leadership chain. Stated another way, great managers model behaviors that directly impact how their people manage their own teams. While this mentor-type impact often happens organically, the MEI program amplifies this effect by triggering open, honest, and very pointed conversations about leadership style.
3. Manager effectiveness has a direct impact on retention. In the chart below ("MEI Results by Quartile"), you'll see MEI scores broken out by the four quartiles. Notice the retention indicator for the bottom quartile (78%). We saw the largest rise for MEI scores of those managers in the bottom quartile from 2016 to 2017 (up seven points), which in turn improved the retention indicator by five points.

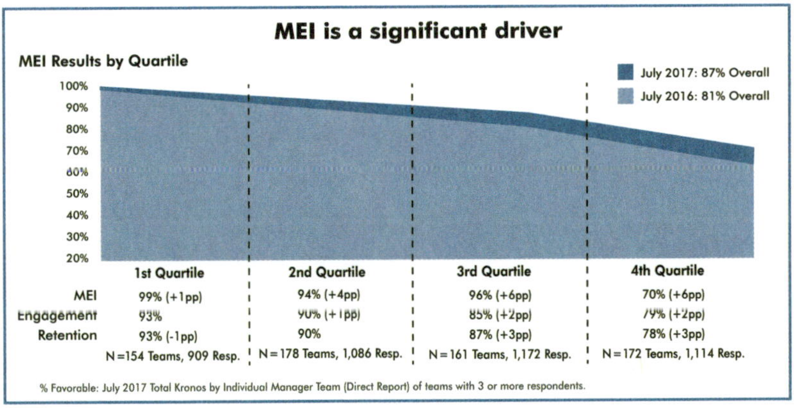

Data from a Kronos Manager Effective Index (MEI) Results by Quartile.

Conclusion

When reflecting upon our MEI journey, a few things come to mind as having been integral to the success of the program.

First, a high-trust culture is a pre-requisite. Prior to launching MEI, we had worked hard to create a corporate culture that stressed respect and collaboration. From the beginning with MEI, we kept the focus on development and all communications were designed to be positive, enlightening, and non-threatening. We made it clear to all employees that this was a way to help managers get better, not to boot them out the door if they scored low.

Second, we had early and active involvement with all levels of leadership. Our Chief Executive Officer and executive team engaged from the beginning with many of the frequent, open, and honest communications around MEI coming directly from this group. This wasn't some ancillary program that HR was creating and pushing in a vacuum—this was a company-wide mindset change given the highest priority and tied directly to our company goals and strategy.

Finally, we believe the magic really was in our commitment to taking an evidence-based, data-driven approach and marrying that with great communication and compassionate support. Our evidence-based approach, driven by employee data, gave all our managers insight into their performance that they couldn't ignore. We coupled this with communication from the highest levels of the organization, support from HR to understand the meaning behind the numbers and our continued focus on development and improvement to make MEI a positive program for our company.

Every manager-employee relationship is a personal one, and every MEI journey is unique. Our goal moving forward is to continue to hardwire the MEI into all aspects of our recruiting, retention, and development programs and to keep managers talking openly with their teams about how best to achieve success together.

One of the numbers that astounds me is that in 2012, we had 32,000 people apply for jobs at Kronos. In 2017, that number rose to 70,000! Couple that with the fact that the company has increased revenues every year since 2009 and you know we're doing something—or hopefully many things—right. By making manager effectiveness and improvement a consistent area of focus and a critical aspect of our culture, we've improved our organization overall and become a place that Kronites around the globe are prouder than ever to work for.

FOCUS ON THE FRONTLINE

1. Frontline managers matter just as much as managers at every level of an organization. Make sure you tell them—and show—them this.
2. All employees—regardless of their role or tenure—deserve a great manager.
3. Give your frontline employees the chance to provide feedback on their managers—they know them better than anyone else.
4. Frontline employees may not have the time (or feel they have the time) at work to take a survey or provide feedback. Carve out time in their day for them to do so.
5. Holding managers accountable for improving their people management skills demonstrates that doing so is critical, not a nice-to-have behavior.

ENDNOTES

1 Adam Bryant, "Aron Ain of Kronos: The Incalculable Value of a Good Boss," *New York Time* (Sept. 9, 2016). https://www.nytimes.com/2016/09/11/business/aron-ain-of-kronos-the-incalculable-value-of-a-good-boss.html

2 The Workforce Institute at Kronos Podcast, "What is Your Manager Effectiveness Index?" (February 28, 2019). https://workforceinstitute.org/whats-your-manager-effectiveness-index/

ACKNOWLEDGMENTS

In this, our fourth book since 2010, we tackle the big topic of the future of work. Arguably a topic that we could have written about 100 years ago—or 100 years from now—the convergence of blinding technological changes and societal upheaval hasn't been this dramatic since the Industrial Revolution.

Luckily, we are blessed to have an intrepid band of gifted contributors willing to share their insights about the world of work with you. They all have challenging day jobs and I appreciate their willingness to carve out the extra time to contribute to this book.

My Workforce Institute "Dream Team" at Kronos—Lisa DeStefano, Domenic Locapo, Jess Myers, Nicola Paira, and Jenna Slattery—all support our efforts throughout the year. Their contributions were significant in shaping the content of this book.

Members of our Creative team designed the cover of this book, artfully capturing its essential focus on the importance of investing in people. Rick Hall, Maradith Markham-Burns, Lacey Roach, and Ken Volk collaborated with us to create our eye-popping cover.

Laura Souza has been my partner on all four of these books. They wouldn't exist, and certainly wouldn't be as good, without her creativity, persistence, and skillful editing. And our publishing partner Mady Gorrell Teigen has yet again guided us through this process with diplomacy and aplomb.

Our leadership at Kronos has supported the Workforce Institute since its founding in 2007. Aron Ain, Michele Glorie, Jim Kizielewicz, and Chris Todd have all contributed to this effort over the years and we're thrilled to have Chris' Foreword to kick off this book.

And finally, thanks to my husband Dennis who is there for all the ups and downs. Your patience is astounding.

Joyce O'Donnell Maroney, MBA
Executive Director, The Workforce Institute at Kronos Incorporated

NOTES